Tiger
S.T.A.T.S.

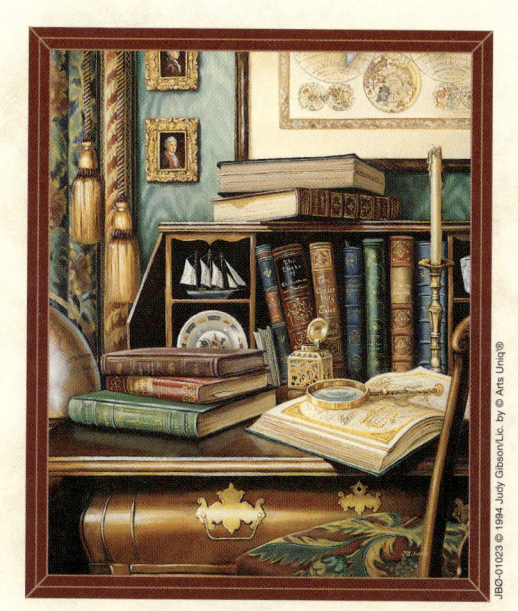

FROM THE LIBRARY OF

To the fans of Detroit Tigers baseball. None have been more loyal than the advertisers in this book whose love for the great game of baseball and confidence in the author have helped make my books possible.

Tiger S.T.A.T.S.

Statistics, Trivia, Alumni, Trades, and Stories

by
Fred T. Smith

Momentum Books Ltd.
Ann Arbor, Michigan

Copyright © 1991 by Fred T. Smith

All rights reserved. No part of this book may be used or reproduced in any manner without prior written permission of the publisher, except in the case of brief quotations embodied in critical articles and reviews.

Manufactured in the United States of America

Cover design by Don Ross

Momentum Books Ltd.
210 Collingwood, Suite 106
Ann Arbor, MI 48103
USA

ISBN 0-9618726-6-7

CONTENTS

A Word From the Publisher	vii
The Early Days of Detroit Baseball	1
Statistics	3
Trivia	235
Alumni	259
Trades	277
Stories	303
Acknowledgements	315
List of Advertisers	316
About the Author	319

A WORD FROM THE PUBLISHER

Different fans have different preferences. Some like a tight, well-pitched duel. Others favor a home run derby. But there is one thing all fans agree on: the all-around player, like Al Kaline, Willie Mays or Mickey Mantle, who can do it all, is rare indeed.

Just as rare is the fan who has seen nearly all of it, read about the rest and knows how to put it down on paper so others can enjoy it. And that accurately describes Fred Smith, the all-around master of the statistics, stories, trivia and traditions that make up the history of the Detroit Tigers.

Fred contracted a terminal case of Tigermania back in the days when Harry Heilmann was racking up batting championships every odd year. That was in the Twenties and Fred has never recovered.

Fred's affliction is balm for the Tiger fan because it has driven him to produce six books previous to his current masterpiece, **Tiger S.T.A.T.S.** Each Smith volume has been snapped up by the thousands by fans. And after each book, the reaction has been the same: "We want more!"

More is certainly what **Tiger S.T.A.T.S.** is. More information on more Tiger subjects than ever before. More fascinating trivia. More up-to-date information on the whereabouts and the doings of great and favorite Tigers from yesterday and from decades ago. More statistics on more players and more categories, records and lists. More intriguing inside stories and little-known facts. In short, more of everything Tiger fans have come to expect from their favorite expert on their favorite baseball team.

Which is no less than a fan should expect from a master at his game.

Bill Haney
January 1991

EARLY DAYS OF DETROIT BASEBALL

When Detroit came into major league baseball in 1881, the old National League was in its sixth year. Cincinnati had been a charter member and Detroit,which at that time was not much larger than the present day city of Saginaw, took over the Cincinnati franchise. Detroit was at that time.

The new team was called the Detroits and they played their home games at Recreation Park, located at Brady and Brush Street.

In 1887, the Detroits won their first championship, and challenged the St. Louis Browns to a World Championship of 15 games. The Browns had won the American Association League pennant that year.

It was a traveling World Series and each game was played in a different city. With Detroit leading the series 7-2, two games were played on October 21. The first was played in Washington and St. Louis won it. The second game was played that afternoon in Baltimore. When Detroit won, they claimed the championship eight games to three. Still, the remaining four games were played as scheduled in other cities. Each player on the victorious Detroit team was given $100 for his efforts.

In Detroit's last season in the National League, in 1888, they finished fifth. Then the club was broken up and the players were sold to various teams. Detroit then became a minor league city in the International League, winning pennants in 1889 and 1890.

In 1894 the Western League was being organized and Detroit became a member. The league name was changed to the American League and in 1901 expanded to the present major league status. The games were played in what was then outside the city limits at Helen and Lafayette Blvd. In early days, Sunday games were played at Burns Park in Springwells Township, on Dix Avenue at Waterman and Vernor.

In their first game in the American League, Detroit was behind 13-4 when they came to bat in the ninth inning. They scored 10 runs to win the game.

When the Western League blossomed into the American League, the Detroit team had moved from Helen and Lafayette to Michigan and Trumbull. The field became known as Bennett Park. In 1912, the name was changed to Navin Field in 1912, then in 1938 to Briggs Stadium, and in 1961 to Tiger Stadium .

The Tigers won pennants in 1907, 1908 and 1909, but could never win the World Series. They had the great Ty Cobb, Sam Crawford, Bobby Veach, Harry Heilmann, Donie Bush, Wild Bill Donovan, and George Mullin, but did not win a pennant again until 1934. But the following year marked a milestone in the history of the franchise - Detroit won their first World Championship. It was to be their first of five championships in their next five appearances in the fall classic.

STATISTICS

Here are the accounts of every Detroit Tigers season from 1934 through 1990, complete with final league standings, individual Tiger batting and pitching records, and details of league playoff and World Series games.

1934

FINAL STANDINGS

	W	L	PCT
DETROIT	101	53	.656
New York	94	60	.610
Cleveland	85	69	.552
Boston	76	76	.500
Philadelphia	68	82	.453
St. Louis	67	85	.441
Washington	66	86	.413
Chicago	53	99	.349

Manager: Mickey Cochrane

The 1934 season highlighted the renaissance of the Detroit Tigers after floundering in the American League's second division for six successive years.

Frank Navin, president of the Detroit Tigers, dismissed manager Stanley "Bucky" Harris in the closing days of the 1933 season—following five years of disappointment with the manager.

Navin launched a search for a new field boss following the conclusion of the Washington-New York Giants World Series.

The famed Babe Ruth lingered in the twilight of his career with the New York Yankees. The Yanks' management would have been in accord to release Ruth as Navin was ready to offer the Detroit managerial job to the slugging outfielder. Navin invited Ruth to Detroit for discussions about the job. However, Ruth declined the travel offer. He was scheduled to be in San Francisco to board a Honolulu-bound ship for a series of exhibition games in Hawaii.

"I'll call you when I return," said Ruth.

"I can't wait," answered Navin.

The Tigers' owner then phoned a long-time friend, H.G. Salsinger, sports editor of the Detroit News, asking his views, opinions and outlook about several potential managerial candidates. Salsinger recommended Mickey Cochrane, the fiery catcher of the Philadelphia Athletics. Navin immediately contacted Connie Mack, owner and manager of the A's, deliberating ways and means to obtain Cochrane. The Philadelphia ball club had not completely recovered from the Depression's economic doldrums and needed money.

Connie Mack offered Navin the contracts of Cochrane and southpaw hurler Lefty Grove for $200,000. But Navin was not interested in Grove—he wanted Cochrane. Besides $200,000 was a king-sized amount for Navin's budget.

Finally, Mack set a $100,000 price for Cochrane's contract.

The $100,000 appraisal was too high for Navin's pocketbook. He contacted Walter O. Briggs Sr., the Detroit Tiger's co-owner. Navin told him about the desire to obtain Cochrane for the Tigers as playing-manager, but, that Mack wanted an unbelievable price of $100,000.

"Forget the costs," said Briggs. "Get Cochrane, I'll pay for the contract." Thus, the Tigers procured Cochrane's contract for a $100,000 Briggs' check and rookie catcher John Pasek.

The 30-year-old Cochrane was named Detroit's manager. A short while later, the Tigers engineered a player deal with the Washington Senators by sending 26-year-old outfielder Jonathan Stone for Goose Goslin, a 33-year-old veteran.

The Detroit Tigers changed spring training sites, shifting from San Antonio, Texas, to Lakeland, Florida.

The Tigers were rated a long-shot choice for the 1934 pennant as manager Cochrane directed the spring sessions at Lakeland's Henley Field.

Detroit grabbed an early season lead, being in first place after two weeks of play, but no one took the Tigers seriously after a so-so month of May. However, Cochrane turned the team around in June.

Cochrane handled the young pitching staff with amazing success and exercised good judgement in molding the team to a pennant contender in a two-team race with Joe McCarthy's New York Yankees. The Tigers moved into first place in August and maintained the winning place.

Defending champion Washington Senators, beleaguered with injuries, fell out of contention quickly.

Under the leadership and inspirational guidance of manager Cochrane, the Tigers won 101 games to capture their first American League pennant in 25 years.

Detroit hitters compiled an even .300 team batting mark, tops in the league. They led the circuit in six categories: runs, hits, total bases, doubles, stolen bases and runs batted in.

Second baseman Charlie Gehringer hit .356, earning runner-up honors to New York's Lou Gehrig, who won the batting crown with a .363 figure.

First baseman Hank Greenberg batted .339 and led the league in doubles with 63, while manager Cochrane posted .320, third baseman Marvin Owen came through with .317, outfielder Jo-Jo White finished with .313 and Goose Goslin ended up with .305 along the pennant route.

Lynwood "Schoolboy" Rowe made good use of that bat to add power to the Tigers' lineup. He led the American League pitchers with a .303 average on 33 hits in 109 times at bat.

Rowe was the pitching sensation of the league. After a slow start, he grabbed the American League spotlight by winning 16 consecutive games between June 15 and late August.

On August 25, Rowe singled in the ninth inning driving in the go-ahead run against Washington to insure his 16th straight victory—that tied Joe Wood, Walter Johnson and Lefty Grove for the league record.

Four days later, before the largest crowd of the season in Philadelphia, Rowe suffered the same fate that halted Johnson and Wood in 1912, and Grove in 1931 in their bids for Victory No. 17 in a row. The A's defeated Rowe and the Tigers, 13-5.

Rowe topped the Tigers' pitching staff with a 24-8 season won-loss record on a 3.45 e.r.a. Tommy Bridges finished with a 22-11 mark and 3.67 e.r.a., while veteran Fred Marberry posted a 15-5, Eldon Auker, 15-7, and Alvin "General" Crowder, picked up on waivers from Washington in mid-season, won five out of six games for the Tigers.

Detroit tied Washington for the league's fielding honors on a .974 mark. The Tigers' infield formed a durable quartet with second baseman Charlie Gehringer, third baseman Marvin Owen and shortstop Billy Rogell playing in every contest of the 154-game schedule while first baseman Hank Greenberg missed only one game and that to observe Yom Kippur. The Tigers' infield participated in the league's only two triple plays. Schoolboy Rowe headed the league's pitchers defensively, handling 55 chances flawlessly.

Three Detroit Tigers were named to the American League's 20-player squad for the second annual All-Star Game at New York's Polo Grounds.

Gehringer, playing the complete game, had two singles in three trips to the plate and three walks, one intentional. Cochrane caught four innings and grounded out in one time at bat as the American Leaguers defeated the National League, 9-7.

Pitcher Tommy Bridges did not see action in the mid-summer event.

On July 13, in Detroit, Babe Ruth slammed his 700th career home run off Tommy Bridges—a dramatic two run smash clearing the right field wall. The ball rolled several hundred feet down the street leading to Navin field, giving the Yankees a 4-2 victory.

Playing manager Mickey Cochrane edged teammate Charlie Gehringer for the 1934 American League Most Valuable Player Award in a close vote by the Baseball Writers Association of America Committee. A two-point margin 67 to 65, gave Cochrane his second MVP award. He was named MVP in 1928 as a member of the Philadelphia Athletics.

Babe Ruth finally attained a managerial role. However, it came in postseason activity. He directed a team of American Leaguers in a 23-game exhibition schedule in Hawaii, Japan, China and the Philippines in late October and November.

Charlie Gehringer was the lone Detroit Tigers member on the 14-player Far East touring squad.

BATTING RECORDS

	B	G	AB	R	H	HR	SB	AVE	RBI
Gehringer, Charles	L	154	601	134	214	11	11	.356	127
Greenberg, Henry	R	153	593	118	201	26	9	.339	139
Cochrane, Gordon	L	129	437	74	140	2	8	.320	76
Owen, Marvin	R	154	565	79	179	8	3	.317	96
White, Joyner	L	115	384	97	120	0	28	.313	44
Goslin, Leon	L	151	614	106	187	13	5	.305	100
Walker, Gerald	R	98	347	54	104	6	20	.300	39
Rogell, William	B	154	592	114	175	3	13	.296	100
Hayworth, Raymond	R	54	167	20	49	0	0	.293	27
Fox Ervin	R	128	516	101	147	2	25	.285	45
Schuble, Henry	R	11	15	2	4	0	0	.267	0
Doljack, Frank	R	56	120	15	28	1	2	.233	19
Clifton, Herman "Flea"	R	16	16	3	1	0	0	.063	0

Less than 10 games: Rudy York, Frank Reiber and Ralph "Cy" Perkins.

PITCHING RECORDS

	T	G	IP	W	L	PCT	ERA
Auker, Eldon	R	43	205	15	7	.682	3.42
Rowe, Schoolboy	R	46	266	24	8	.750	3.45
Bridges, Tommy	R	36	275	22	11	.667	3.67
Hogsett, Chief	L	26	50	3	2	.600	4.32
Fischer, Carl	L	20	95	6	4	.600	4.36
Marberry, Fred	R	38	156	15	5	.750	4.56
Sorrell, Vic	R	28	130	6	9	.400	4.78
Hamlin, Luke	R	20	75	2	3	.400	5.40
Crowder, Alvin (29 Wash., 9 Det.)	R	38	167	9	11	.450	5.77

Less than 45 innings: Clarence Phillips, Vic Frasier and Stephen Larkin.

Statistics 9

1934 WORLD SERIES

Home Team	Date	Winning Team	Winning Pitcher	Losing Pitcher	Score
Detroit	October 3	St. Louis	J. Dean	Crowder	8-3
Detroit	October 4	Detroit	Rowe	Walker	3-2 (12 inn.)
St. Louis	October 5	St. Louis	P. Dean	Bridges	4-1
St. Louis	October 6	Detroit	Auker	Walker	10-4
St. Louis	October 7	Detroit	Bridges	J. Dean	3-1
Detroit	October 8	St. Louis	P. Dean	Rowe	4-3
Detroit	October 9	St. Louis	J. Dean	Auker	11-0

The Detroit Tigers World Series opponent was not decided until the final day of the National League season.

Manager Frank Frisch's St. Louis Cardinals edged Bill Terry's New York Giants by a two-game margin as the Cards finished with four victories over Cincinnati while the Giants collapsed with four losses in a row, a pair of games each to Philadelphia and Brooklyn.

The Dean brothers' pitching featured the St. Louis Cardinals route to the pennant. Jerome H. "Dizzy" Dean won 30 games and lost 7, becoming the first pitcher to post 30 victories since Grover Cleveland Alexander turned in the same amount for the Philadelphia Phillies in 1917. Rookie Paul dean registered an impressive 19-11 mark with the brothers accounting for 31 percent of the Cardinals' team victories.

Tigers' manager Mickey Cochrane surprised the home town fans by starting veteran pitcher General Crowder in the Series opener at Navin Field, opposing Dizzy Dean.

The flamboyant Dean scattered eight Tigers' safeties and the cards won easily, 8-3, aided by Detroit's five errors.

Next afternoon, the Tigers evened the Series with Schoolboy Rowe coming through with a superb pitching performance in an exciting, 12-inning 3-2 victory.

Rowe bounced back after he allowed two early runs. He limited the Cards to only one hit in the final nine frames.

After one out in the 12th, Charlie Gehringer and Hank Greenberg drew walks off southpaw reliefer Bill Walker. Then, Goose Goslin delivered the game-winning run with a single.

Paul, the younger of the Dean brothers, thrilled the St. Louis fans with a 4-1 triumph as the Cardinals moved ahead in the Series in the third game. Tommy Bridges, the Tigers' starter, hurled four innings and was tagged for all the runs.

Detroit squared the Series, taking advantage of five St. Louis errors and coupled with Eldon Auker's pitching, the Tigers won handily, 10-4 in the fourth game.

In the Cardinals' fourth inning, Virgil Davis, batting for pitcher Dazzy Vance, singled to left. Manager Frisch shocked everyone by calling Dizzy Dean to run for Davis.

Pepper Martin bounced a grounder to second baseman Gehringer, whose toss to shortstop Rogell forced Dean. Trying for the double play, Rogell's throw hit Dean on the head with the ball and knocked out the pinch-runner. He was carried off the field by his St. Louis teammates but he recovered and was able to pitch the next day.

Tommy Bridges supplied the pitching in clutch situations to out-hurl Dean and give Detroit a lead in the Series via a 3-1 decision.

The Series shifted back to Detroit's Navin Field with Schoolboy Rowe named to pitch the clincher against Paul Dean.

Young "Daffy" Dean not only outpitched Rowe, but singled in the winning run in the seventh inning. The Cardinals once again evened the Series, this time on a 4-3 squeaker.

The Series finale matched Dizzy Dean and Eldon Auker. The Tigers' underhand right-hander was chased in the third inning.

Manager Cochrane went to the bullpen, calling in Rowe, southpaw Elon "Chief" Hogsett and Tommy Bridges, in the same inning, all in vain. When the dust settled, the Cards had scored seven times to the dismay of the Tigers' fans.

In the Cardinals' sixth inning, Ducky Medwick tripled, sliding hard into third baseman Marvin Owen, resulting in a temporary flareup between the two players. When the inning ended, Medwick trotted to his left field position. He was greeted with a barrage of fruit, vegetables, lunch cartons and other available missiles from the left-bleacher fans.

After several attempts by the umpires and players, pleading for the stormy session to subside, Baseball Commissioner Judge Landis removed Medwick from the game. He explained the dismissal action, "A precaution for Medwick's safety."

The Cardinals went on to win the deciding game via a one-sided 11-0 triumph. It was St. Louis' third World Series crown—all three going seven games.

Dizzy Dean's prediction that the Dean brothers would win all four games became a reality.

The Series hitting honors were shared by Tigers' Charlie Gehringer and Cardinals' Ducky Medwick. Both players registered identical batting averages of .379 on 11 hits in 29 times at bat.

⚾ ⚾ ⚾

The infield of the 1934 American League champion Tigers drove in an incredible 462 runs among them. Leading the way was first baseman Hank Greenberg with 139 rbi, followed by second baseman Charlie Gehringer (127), shortstop Billy Rogell (100), and third baseman Marvin Owen (96).

Statistics ———————————————————————————— 11

WORLD SERIES INDIVIDUAL AVERAGES

	G	AB	R	H	HR	SB	PCT	RBI
White	7	23	6	3	0	1	.130	0
Doljack	2	2	0	0	0	0	.000	0
Cochrane	7	28	2	6	0	0	.214	1
Hayworth	1	0	0	0	0	0	.000	0
Gehringer	7	29	5	11	1	1	.379	2
Greenberg	7	28	4	9	1	1	.321	7
Goslin	7	29	2	7	0	0	.241	2
Rogell	7	29	3	8	0	0	.276	4
Owen	7	29	0	2	0	1	.069	1
Fox	7	28	1	8	0	0	.286	2
Hogsett	3	3	0	0	0	0	.000	0
Crowder	2	1	0	0	0	0	.000	0
Rowe	3	7	0	0	0	0	.000	0
Bridges	3	7	0	1	0	0	.143	0
Marberry	2	0	0	0	0	0	.000	0
Auker	2	4	0	0	0	0	.000	0
Walker, G.	3	3	0	1	0	0	.333	1

PITCHING RECORDS

	G	IP	W	L	PCT	R	H	BB	SO
Auker	2	11⅓	1	1	.500	8	16	5	2
Rowe	3	21⅓	1	1	.500	8	19	0	12
Bridges	3	17⅓	1	1	.500	9	21	1	12
Crowder	2	6	0	1	.000	4	6	1	2
Marberry	2	1⅔	0	0	.000	4	5	1	0
Hogsett	3	7⅓	0	0	.000	1	6	3	3

At The Designated Hatter, we know that every fan is unique.

Sports enthusiasts of all kinds will find merchandise for all 26 major league baseball teams and selected basketball, football, hockey, and college teams.

We know you're one-of-a-kind. We wouldn't have it any other way.

No matter what your style, we have something just for you. Stop by, or give us a call at 313/961-3550.

The Designated Hatter, Ltd.
1740 Michigan Avenue
Detroit, Michigan 48216
313/961-3550
just one block west of Tiger Stadium

1935
FINAL STANDINGS

	W	L	PCT
DETROIT	93	58	.616
New York	89	60	.597
Cleveland	82	71	.536
Boston	78	75	.510
Chicago	74	78	.487
Washington	67	86	.438
St. Louis	65	87	.428
Philadelphia	58	91	.389

Manager: Mickey Cochrane

The Detroit Tigers' sluggish start in the 1935 season brought criticism from many sports fans, but manager Mickey Cochrane never gave up the confidence he displayed during spring training at Lakeland, Florida.

Cochrane told the sportswriters, "We'll win the pennant by five games." They reminded him of the prediction when the Tigers dropped into last place in late April.

However, Cochrane never doubted his team's chances and never gave up, constantly demonstrating managerial leadership as the team moved slowly up in the standings. It was July 26 before the Tigers took over the top spot. They maintained the pennant fever until they clinched the title with a twin-bill victory over the St. Louis Browns before a joyous hometown crowd at Navin Field.

The Tigers won the American League pennant on a three-game margin over Joe McCarthy's New York Yankees; Cochrane missed his spring prediction by two games.

Once again, a combination of hitting, fielding and pitching proved to be a winner for the Tigers.

Charlie Gehringer led the Tigers in hitting with .330—good enough for fifth best in the American League. Washington second baseman Buddy Myer won the AL crown with a .349 average. Hank Greenberg tied Philadelphia Athletics' Jimmie Foxx for the home run title with 36. He also took the American League runs batted in honors with an amazing 170 total; that was 51 more than runner-up Lou Gehrig. Greenberg batted .328 and also led the league in total bases with 389.

Outfielder Pete Fox posted a .321, manager Cochrane hit .319, Gerald "Gee" Walker batted .301 and the veteran Goose Goslin hit .292 giving the Tigers the club batting title for the second straight year, this time on a .290 average.

Tommy Bridges won 21 games and lost 10, Schoolboy Rowe showed a 19-13 record, underhand delivery specialist Eldon Auker won 18 and lost 7, and veteran General Crowder came through with a 16-10 record, while newcomer southpaw Joe Sullivan posted a 6-6 mark, including several early season crucial wins.

Bridges had the league's longest winning streak, a nine-game string between April 29 and June 13. He paced the circuit in strikeouts with 163 victims while Rowe was second with 140 Ks.

Schoolboy Rowe continued his batting prowess. In fact, he improved from the previous season, getting one additional hit in the same number of times at bat, 109, for a respectable .312 average.

Charlie Gehringer's 504 consecutive games played streak ended. It ran from June 25, 1932 to August 11, 1935.

Pete Fox hit safely in 29 consecutive games, longest of the season in the American League.

The Detroit Tigers' strong defense continued in gaining top fielding honors of the league on a .978 figure. Gehringer led the second basemen with a .985 mark, while shortstop Bill Rogell topped the shortstops on a .971. Auker's flawless handling of 49 fielding chances earned him top fielding performance of the season for pitchers.

Five Detroit Tigers were named to the American League squad for the third annual All-Star Game. The team was managed by Mickey Cochrane. Charlie Gehringer played second base and collected two hits in three tries. Del Baker served as coach, while pitchers Tommy Bridges and Schoolboy Rowe did not see action. The American League All-Stars made it three in a row on a 4-1 victory before 69,812 fans at Cleveland's Municipal Stadium.

First baseman Hank Greenberg was voted the league's Most Valuable Player by the Baseball Writers Association of America.

Tommy Bridges

It started out to be a normal Friday afternoon at Navin Field. The Washington Senators were in town and neither the Tigers nor Senators were going anywhere in the pennant race. Tommy Bridges started on the mound for the Tigers and Lloyd Brown was in the box for Washington. In the first three innings, nobody reached first base for either team. The only hard-hit ball for either side was a fly-out to right by Brown in the third inning. The Tigers got to Brown in the fourth, and by the time the ninth inning came around, had scored 13 times.

Bridges, in the meantime, had retired the first 24 batters. He retired the first two in the ninth with Howard Maple swinging weakly at a curve ball. Walter Johnson, manager of Washington, selected Dave harris to pinch-hit for the fourth Senator pitcher, Bob Burke. Harris hit a looper over shortstop Heinie Schuble's head and Bridges' dream of a perfect game was over. At that time, there had been only four perfect games pitched in modern-day baseball. Milt Wilcox came within one pitch of a perfect game against the Chicago White Sox in 1983 when Jerry Hairston got a pinch-hit single.

BATTING RECORDS

	B	G	AB	R	H	HR	SB	AVE	RBI
Gehringer, Charles	L	150	610	123	201	19	11	.330	108
Greenberg, Henry	R	152	619	121	203	36	4	.328	170
Fox, Pete	R	131	517	116	166	15	14	.321	73
Cochrane, Gordon	L	115	411	93	131	5	5	.319	47
Hayworth, Raymond	R	51	175	22	54	0	0	.309	22
Walker, Gerald	R	98	362	52	109	7	6	.301	53
Goslin, Goose	L	147	590	88	172	9	5	.292	109
Rogell, William	B	150	560	88	154	6	3	.275	71
Owen, Martin	R	134	483	52	127	2	1	.263	71
Clifton, Flea	R	43	110	15	28	0	2	.255	9
Schuble, Henry	R	11	8	3	2	0	0	.250	0
White, Joyner	L	114	412	82	99	2	19	.240	32
Morgan, Chester	L	14	23	2	4	0	0	.174	1

Less than 10 games: Frank Reiber, Harvey Walker and Hubert Shelley.

PITCHING RECORDS

	T	G	IP	W	L	PCT	ERA
Sullivan, Joe	L	25	126	6	6	.500	3.50
Bridges, Tommy	R	36	274	21	10	.677	3.51
Hogsett, Chief	L	40	97	6	6	.500	3.53
Rowe, Schoolboy	R	42	276	19	13	.594	3.68
Auker, Eldon	R	36	195	18	7	.720	3.83
Sorrell, Vic	R	12	51	4	3	.571	4.06
Crowder, General	R	33	241	16	10	.615	4.26

Less than 45 innings: Roxie Lawson, Fred Marberry and Clyde Hatter. Carl Fischer pitched in 3 games for Detroit and 24 for Chicago.

1935 WORLD SERIES

Home Team	Date	Winning Team	Winning Pitcher	Losing Pitcher	Score
Detroit	October 2	Chicago	Warneke	Rowe	3-0
Detroit	October 3	Detroit	Bridges	Root	8-3
Chicago	October 4	Detroit	Rowe	French	6-5 (11 inn.)
Chicago	October 5	Detroit	Crowder	Carleton	2-1
Chicago	October 6	Chicago	Warneke	Rowe	3-1
Detroit	October 7	Detroit	Bridges	French	4-3

The Detroit Tigers entered the 1935 World Series facing the hottest club of the National League: Charlie Grimm's Chicago Cubs. Chicago was virtually unbeaten in the final month of play. They reeled off 21 consecutive victories after losing on Labor Day. The winning streak continued through September 27 with a doubleheader victory over St. Louis that clinched the pennant for the Cubs.

The Cubs took the Series opener at Detroit, 3-0, on Lon Warneke's four-hitter defeating Schoolboy Rowe. The Tigers won the next game, 8-3, but lost the services of first baseman hank Greenberg.

Detroit chased Cubs' starter Charlie Root in the opening inning with four quick runs. Jo-Jo White blooped a single and scored on Mickey Cochran's double. Then, Hank Greenberg blasted a long home run, ending Root's mound duty for the afternoon.

The Tigers added three more runs off reliefer southpaw Roy Henshaw in the fourth frame.

In the seventh, Cochrane walked but was forced at second by Gehringer. Greenberg was hit by a pitched ball. Goslin flied out. Pete Fox singled off pitcher Fabian Kowalik's shins, the ball continued to right field. Gehringer raced home and Greenberg followed in with a tough slide into catcher Gabby Hartnett but was called out. Greenberg was injured on the play but stayed in the game.

Post-game examination indicated a broken wrist, sidelining Greenberg for the remainder of the Series. Manager Cochrane shifted Marvin Owen to first base and replaced Greenberg with Herman "Flea" Clifton at third base.

The Series moved to Chicago and the Tigers edged the Cubs, 6-5, in 11 innings with Schoolboy Rowe getting the win in four innings of relief duty.

The Tigers made it three in a row as General Crowder tossed a nifty five-hitter in a 2-1 victory over Tex Carleton.

Lon Warneke hurled six scoreless innings then had to leave the game due to a muscle injury in the fifth game. Left-hander Bill Lee finished. The Cubs won, 3-1, with Schoolboy Rowe being tagged with his second loss in the Series.

The Series returned to Detroit's Navin Field setting the stage for ninth inning heroics in the final game. Tommy Bridges and Larry French hooked up in a pitcher's duel for eight innings and a 2-2 tie. Stan Hack opened the Cub's ninth inning with a rousing triple. The Tigers' fans watched in virtual silence as Bridges faced Billy Jurges.

Statistics

Jurges struck out and the quietness turned to cheers aplenty. They now awaited Grimm's pinch-hitter for pitcher French. However, Grimm decided to let French, a .141 hitter during the season, bat for himself. French bounced an easy grounder to Bridges as Hack stayed on third. Hack was stranded as Augie Galan flied to left fielder Goslin and the Tigers' fans responded with hearty applause for pitcher Bridges.

Flea Clifton opened the Tigers' ninth and became French's seventh strike-out victim. Cochrane came through with his third hit of the contest, a hard smash that second baseman Bill Herman stopped but could not throw. Gehringer bounded to first baseman Phil Cavaretta who did not try for a force at second and retired Gehringer unassisted as Cochrane stopped at second.

Once again, Cubs' manager Grimm decided to pitch to Goose Goslin rather than set up a possible force play with an intentional pass.

Goslin stroked a single and Cochrane raced across the plate with the winning run, giving the Tigers their first World Series Championship in five attempts.

The Tigers' fans went wild in celebration and the enthusiasm spread across Metropolitan Detroit areas until the wee hours of Tuesday morning.

Pete Fox was the Series' batting champ with a .385 on 10 hits in 26 times at bat. Billy Herman topped the Cubs with a .333 on an 8-for-24.

A sad note followed the World Series success of the Detroit Tigers within five weeks. Frank J. Navin, president of the Detroit ball club, died suddenly on November 13 while he was horseback riding.

Walter O. Briggs Sr. later purchased Navin's interest from his widow and became the sole owner of the Detroit Tigers. Briggs expanded Mickey Cochrane's duties, naming him vice president along with his managerial title.

WORLD SERIES INDIVIDUAL AVERAGES

	G	AB	R	H	HR	SB	PCT	RBI
White	5	19	3	5	0	0	.263	1
Cochrane	6	24	3	7	0	0	.292	1
Gehringer	6	24	4	9	0	1	.375	4
Greenberg	2	6	1	1	1	0	.167	2
Goslin	6	22	2	6	0	0	.273	3
Fox	6	26	1	10	0	0	.385	4
Rogell	6	24	1	7	0	0	.292	1
Owen	6	20	2	1	0	0	.050	1
Clifton	4	16	1	0	0	0	.000	0
Rowe	3	8	0	2	0	0	.250	0
Bridges	2	8	1	1	0	0	.125	1
Auker	1	2	0	0	0	0	.000	0
Hogsett	1	0	0	0	0	0	.000	0
Crowder	1	3	1	1	0	0	.333	0
Walker, G.	3	4	1	1	0	0	.250	0

PITCHING RECORDS

	G	IP	W	L	PCT	R	H	BB	SO
Bridges	2	18	2	0	1.000	6	18	4	9
Crowder	1	9	1	0	1.000	1	5	3	5
Rowe	3	21	1	2	.333	8	19	1	14
Auker	1	6	0	0	.000	3	6	2	1
Hogsett	1	1	0	0	.000	0	0	0	0

LARCO'S ★★★
645 Big Beaver Road, Troy
680-0066

A classic list of Italian pasta, veal, chicken and beef dishes with well-made sauces served by an efficient staff in crisp black and white.

Lunch — 11-4 Mon.-Fri.
Dinner — 4-10 Mon.-Thurs., 5-11 Fri.-Sat., 3-9 Sun.

1936

FINAL STANDINGS

	W	L	PCT
New York	102	51	.667
DETROIT	83	71	.539
Chicago	81	70	.5364
Washington	82	71	.5359
Cleveland	80	74	.519
Boston	74	80	.481
St. Louis	57	95	.375
Philadelphia	53	100	.346

Manager: Mickey Cochrane

The 1936 Detroit Tigers' spring training opened in Lakeland, Florida with great optimism. Two successive pennants and a World Series crown contributed to the happy-go-lucky atmosphere. But once the season began, dark clouds appeared. After two wins in five game, Detroit grabbed five straight victories before they suffered double-trouble—a snapped win string and a key loss of slugging first baseman Hank Greenberg—out for the season with a broken wilst. Greenberg was hitting .348 in the 12 games.

This was a tough break for the Tigers. They were without the services of their power hitter and runs batted in specialist.

The Tigers sought a replacement for the powerful Greenberg. They finally negotiated a player deal with the St. Louis Browns, sending southpaw reliefer Chief Hogsett in exchange for Irving "Jack" Burns, a five-year major league first sacker.

Burns had big shoes to fill—replacing a .328 hitter along with 36 home runs and 170 rbi was not an easy task. The Tigers' new first baseman finished the season with a .281 mark and hit only four home runs.

Detroit's distressing season continued. Manager Mickey Cochrane was sidelined with a nervous breakdown and went to a ranch in Wyoming for a health recovery program while coach Del Baker ran the ball club in his absence. The Tigers lost their dynamic leader and it reflected on the baseball diamond.

Cochrane returned as manager in the final month of the season and aroused the team, but it was too late.

Joe McCarthy's New York Yankees dominated the American League and clinched the title on September 9—a record for the earliest pennant clinching date in the history of the league. The Tigers finished second, 19 1/2 games behind the Yankees.

Detroit was lucky to take runner-up honors with an 83-71 won-loss record and a .5389 percentage on a full schedule. Both the Chicago White Sox and Washington Senators did not play the 154 games due to rainouts.

The Tigers' team hitting finished at an even .300 mark, third best in the league. Charlie Gehringer paced the Tigers with a .354, good for fourth high in the circuit. Shortstop Luke Appling of the Chicago White Sox led the American League with a robust .388 figure.

Outfielder Gee Walker was next on the Tigers' list with .353 while outfielder Al Simmons, who Detroit obtained from Chicago for $75,000 in the winter of 1935, batted .327 and veteran Goose Goslin hit .315.

Four Tigers reached the 100 rbi plateau. Goslin led the quartet with 125 rbi, Gehringer drove in 116, Simmons 112 and third baseman Marvin Owen had 105. Goslin topped the Tigers' home run output with 24.

The Tigers' pitching staff missed manager Cochrane's guidance behind the plate. They allowed a team earned run average of 5.00 per game for the season.

Only Tommy Bridges posted a good record, winning 23 games and losing 11 on a 3.60 e.r.a., while hurling 26 complete games.

Schoolboy Rowe, although hampered by arm troubles all season, compiled a 19-10 mark, aided by three two-hit games. Eldon Auker slipped to a 13-16 record and General Crowder pitched only 44 innings on a 4-3 mark before retiring in July.

Once again, the Tigers headed the American League in team fielding, this time on a .975 percentage. Gehringer led the league's second basemen with a .974 and Bill Rogell topped the shortstops with .965 for repeat performances as defense percentage leaders.

New York's Joe McCarthy replaced the ailing Mickey Cochrane as manager of the American Leaguers in the fourth annual All-Star Game at Boston's National League Park. The NL team edged the AL stars 4-3 for their first win of the mid-summer classic.

Gehringer had a single and a double in three at bats, along with two bases on balls. Goslin singled in a pinch-hitting appearance while Schoolboy Rowe was touched for two runs and four hits in two innings.

Baseball's Hall of Fame at Cooperstown, N.Y. announced its first list of inductees following initial balloting by the Baseball Writers Association of America. Only five players from the 1900 to 1935 era qualified for Hall of Fame honors, receiving the mandatory three-quarters votes of the 226 ballots cast. Ty Cobb, 12-time batting champion of the American League with the Detroit Tigers led the Hall of Fame balloting with 222 votes. Babe Ruth and Honus Wagner, long-time Pittsburgh Pirates shortstop, tied with 215 votes each. New York Giant Christy Mathewson followed with 205 votes and Washington Senator Walter Johnson got 180 votes to round out the inaugural Hall of Fame list.

Statistics

BATTING RECORDS

	B	G	AB	R	H	HR	SB	AVE	RBI
Gehringer, Charles	L	154	641	144	227	15	4	.354	116
Walker, Gerald	R	134	550	105	194	12	17	.353	93
Greenberg, Henry	R	12	46	10	16	1	1	.348	16
Simmons, Aloysius	R	143	568	96	186	13	6	.327	112
Goslin, Leon Goose	L	147	572	122	180	24	14	.315	125
Fox, Pete	R	73	220	46	67	4	1	.305	26
Tebbetts, Birdie	R	10	33	7	10	0	0	.303	4
Owen, Marvin	R	154	583	72	172	9	9	.295	105
Burns, Jack (9 St. Louis, 138 Det.)	L	147	572	98	161	4	4	.281	64
Parker, Salty	R	11	25	6	7	0	0	.280	4
White, Joyner	L	58	51	11	14	0	2	.275	6
Rogell, William	B	146	585	85	160	6	14	.274	0
Reiber, Frank	R	20	55	7	15	1	0	.273	5
Cochrane, Mickey	L	44	126	24	34	2	1	.270	17
Hayworth, Raymond	R	81	250	31	60	1	0	.240	30
Myatt, Glenn	L	27	78	5	17	0	0	.218	5
Clifton, Flea	R	13	26	5	5	0	0	.192	1

Less than 10 games: Gilbert English.

PITCHING RECORDS

	T	G	IP	W	L	PCT	ERA
Bridges, Tommy	R	39	295	23	11	.676	3.60
Rowe, Schoolboy	R	41	245	19	10	.655	4.52
Kimsey, Chad	R	22	52	2	3	.400	4.85
Auker, Eldon	R	35	215	13	16	.448	4.90
Sorrell, Vic	R	30	131	6	7	.462	5.29
Wade, Jake	L	13	78	4	5	.444	5.31
Lawson, Roxie	R	41	128	8	6	.571	5.48
Phillips, Clarence	R	22	87	2	4	.333	6.52
Sullivan, Joe	L	26	80	2	5	.286	6.75

Less than 45 innings: General Crowder. Chief Hogsett pitched 3 games with Detroit and 39 with St. Louis.

TY COBB WOULD HAVE LOVED
THE OLD BALL PARK®
America's Largest Sports Memorabilia Stores!

OVER 500,000 CARDS IN STOCK
COMPLETE SETS . . . TOPPS-FLEER-DONRUSS
(Plus some cards like those your mother threw away!)

ALWAYS IN STOCK!
YEARBOOKS • MAGAZINES • PHOTOS (OLD & NEW)
COMPLETE HOBBY SUPPLIES •
POSTERS • MAJOR LEAGUE UNIFORMS •
JACKETS • FULL HATS • PLUS MUCH MORE . . .

★ SPORTS ★ CELEBRITIES

Ernie Harwell   **Alan Trammell**
Rick Leach   **Brooks Robinson**
Mickey Lolich   **Billy Hoeft**

. . . are just a few of the stars who have made appearances at The Old Ball Park during the past two years . . . many more are scheduled this year . . .

★ **FEATURED ON CHANNELS 2, 4 & 7** ★
OVER 100,000 FANS HAVE VISITED THIS "ONE-OF-A-KIND" BALL PARK.

SEND FOR OUR FREE MAJOR LEAGUE CATALOG

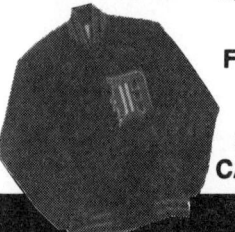

FRANCHISES NOW AVAILABLE
FRANCHISE OFFICE: (313) 851-9110

THE OLD BALL PARK®

31134 FIVE MILE RD.
(Merri-Five Shopping Ctr.)
LIVONIA, MI 48154
(313) 261-8140

42807 FORD RD.
(Ford Rd. & Lilley)
CANTON, MI 48187
(313) 981-7505

OLD BALL PARK
(Arborland Mall)
ANN ARBOR, MI 48104
(313) 677-4050

NOVI TOWN CENTER
Corner I-96 and Novi Rd.
(Between Highland Appliance and T.J. Maxx)
NOVI, MI 48050 — (313) 349-4466

1937

FINAL STANDINGS

	W	L	PCT
New York	102	52	.662
DETROIT	89	65	.578
Chicago	86	68	.558
Cleveland	83	71	.539
Boston	80	72	.526
Washington	73	80	.477
Philadelphia	54	97	.358
St. Louis	46	108	.299

Managers: Mickey Cochrane and Del Baker

The 1937 Detroit Tigers, although bedeviled by the injury jinx, were able to finish in second place, this time 13 games behind the pennant winning New York Yankees.

Schoolboy Rowe, bothered by some-arm problems, pitched in only 10 games and 31 innings. He left the team early for his home in Arkansas with a disappointing 1-4 record.

On May 25 at Yankee Stadium, New York's Bump Hadley accidentally hit Tigers' manager Mickey Cochrane with a pitched ball in the left temple, fracturing his skull. Cochrane lay near death for three days. He was later brought to Detroit and hospitalized for six weeks. The beaning injury ended Cochrane's playing career.

Del Baker subbed as Tigers' manager for the second time. Cochrane's loss affected the Tigers play on the ball field. In the closing weeks of the season, Cochrane returned following a recovery period in Europe.

With Cochrane directing the activity, Detroit became the fighting Tigers once again, but it was too late for a pennant drive. They moved into second place on August 14 and remained there until the final day of the season. On opening day, April 20, Tigers' outfielder Gee Walker had the fans cheering at Navin Field. He hit for the cycle, leading Detroit to a 4-3 win over the Cleveland Indians. Walker started with a home run, followed with a triple, double and a single.

Walker then continued to hit safely in 27 games for the league's longest hitting streak of the season. Washington's Buck Newsom halted the streak on May 24 at Griffith Stadium.

Another hitting star blossomed for the Tigers. Rookie Rudy York was tested at third base but was too erratic and was optioned to Toledo in the American Association. On that same day, Tigers' third baseman Marvin Owen was injured and York was immediately recalled to fill in. Later, York was tried as a catcher where he looked better and was kept in the job behind the plate.

Playing in 104 games, York displayed long-ball power, hitting .307 and slamming 35 home runs. York caught national attention in August when he shattered Babe Ruth's record of 17 home runs in one month. York connected for a total of 18 homers, one better than Ruth's mark in September of 1927. York hit nine at home and nine on the road.

The Tigers led the league in hitting with a team average of .292. Charlie Gehringer, at the age of 34 playing in his 14th season, topped the American League with a .371 average—20 points higher than runner-up Lou Gehrig of the New York Yankees.

Hank Greenberg, recovered from his 1936 injury and bounced back with 40 home runs, second to New York Yankees' Joe DiMaggio's league-leading 46 home runs. Greenberg batted .337 and drove in 183 runs—one behind the league record 184 posted by Lou Gehrig in 1931.

Gee Walker batted .335 and Pete Fox checked in with .331 while Marvin Owen hit .288 and Bill Rogell .276.

Goose Goslin had a bad year with a .238 and was released.

With the loss of Rowe, the Tigers' pitching staff added several newcomers. Roxie Lawson topped the Detroit hurlers with an 18-7 won-loss record but had a big 5.27 e.r.a. Eldon Auker was next with 17-9 and Tommy Bridges showed a 15-12. Rookie George Gill won 11 and lost four while newcomer Cletus "Boots" Poffenberger won 10 and lost five. He became the talk of the town with his eccentricities. [WHAT ECCENTRICITIES?]

Rookie southpaw Jake Wade won seven and lost 10 but saved his best effort for the final game of the season. He fired a two hitter in a 1-0 victory at Navin Field over the Cleveland Indians. It was a significant triumph—the Tigers' victory stopped Indians' right-hander John Allen's 15-game winning streak and tagged the first loss of the season onto the veteran hurler.

The Tigers led the American League in team fielding for the fourth straight year. This time with a .976 mark. The reliable Gehringer topped the league's second baseman, also for the fourth straight time with a .986 figure, while Bill Rogell's .968 earned him best mark for shortstops for the third year in a row, and Marvin Owen's .970 was tops for the circuit's third basemen.

Two of the four Tigers selected—Charlie Gehringer, Hank Greenberg, Tommy Bridges and Gee Walker for the American League team—saw action in the fifth annual All-Star Game as the AL stars defeated the NL stars, 8-3, on July 7 at Washington's Griffith Stadium.

Gehringer had three singles in five trips to the plate while Bridges gave up three runs and seven hits in three innings of play.

Charlie Gehringer was voted American League Most Valuable Player of 1937 by the Baseball Writers Association of America. He edged New York Yankees' outfielder Joe DiMaggio by a four-point margin in the balloting, giving the Tigers their third MVP winner in four years.

BATTING RECORDS

	B	G	AB	R	H	HR	SB	AVE	RBI
Gehringer, Charles	R	144	564	133	209	14	11	.371	96
Greenberg, Henry	R	154	594	137	200	40	8	.337	183
Walker, Gerald	R	151	635	105	213	18	23	.335	118
Fox, Pete	R	148	628	116	208	12	12	.331	82
York, Rudy	R	104	375	72	115	35	3	.307	103
Cochrane, Mickey	L	27	98	27	30	2	0	.306	12
Herman, Babe	L	17	20	2	6	0	2	.300	3
Owen, Marvin	R	107	396	48	114	1	3	.288	45
Rogell, William	B	146	536	85	148	8	5	.276	64
Hayworth, Raymond	R	30	78	9	21	1	0	.269	8
Bolton, Clifford	L	27	57	6	15	1	0	.263	7
English, Gilbert	R	18	65	6	17	1	1	.262	8
White, Joyner	L	94	305	50	75	0	12	.246	21
Laabs, Chet	R	72	242	31	58	8	6	.240	37
Goslin, Goose	L	79	181	30	43	4	0	.238	35
Tebbetts, Birdie	R	50	162	15	31	2	0	.191	16
Clifton, Flea	R	15	43	4	5	0	3	.116	2
Gelbert, Chas	R	20	47	4	4	0	0	.085	12

PITCHING RECORDS

	T	G	IP	W	L	PCT	ERA
Auker, Eldon	R	39	253	17	9	.654	3.88
Bridges, Tommy	R	34	245	15	12	.556	4.08
Coffman, Slicker	R	28	101	7	5	.583	4.37
Gill, George	R	31	128	11	4	.733	4.50
Poffenberger, Boots	R	29	137	10	5	.667	4.66
Lawson, Roxie	R	37	217	18	7	.720	5.27
Wade, Jake	L	33	165	7	10	.412	5.40

Less than 45 innings: Vic Sorrell, Clyde Hatter, Robert Logan, Schoolboy Rowe, Patrick McLaughlin and Jack Russell.

Dunleavy'z Riverplace

267 Jos Campau
Detroit, Michigan
(313) 259-0909

*Banquet Room
For 20 to 200*

Jack Dunleavy
and
Paul Zosel

Shuttle Service to All Events

1938

FINAL STANDINGS

	W	L	PCT
New York	99	53	.651
Boston	88	61	.591
Cleveland	86	66	.566
DETROIT	84	70	.545
Washington	75	76	.497
Chicago	65	83	.439
St. Louis	55	97	.362
Philadelphia	53	99	.349

Manager: Mickey Cochrane and Delmar Baker

The 1938 season was the fifth term for Tigers' manager Mickey Cochrane but the first as bench-manager. His playing career ended with the accidental 'beaning' injury in 1937.

The season took on a new look as manager Cochrane began to phase out some of the veteran players.

A December 1937 trade with the Chicago White Sox saw the departure of popular outfielder Gee Walker and third baseman Marvin Owen, along with minor league catcher Mike Tresh in exchange for pitcher Vern Kennedy, outfielder Fred "Dixie" Walker and infielder Tony Piet. The trade proved to be very unpopular with the Tigers' fans.

The Tigers opened the season in a remodeled Navin Field. The ballpark was expanded from 36,000 seating to 56,000 and a new name, Briggs Stadium.

Detroit lost the opener, then faltered with only five victories in 14 games and continued in the second division despite a couple of bright spots: newcomer Kennedy's pitching and Hank Greenberg's long-ball hitting.

Then on August 6 came the surprise firing of manager Cochrane. Coach Del Baker was Cochrane's replacement. He managed to work the team to a fourth-place finish, 16 games behind the pennant-winning New York Yankees.

Slugging first baseman Greenberg flirted with Ruth's record before settling for 58 homers for the league leadership. His 146 rbi total was good for runner-up honors to Boston's Jimmie Foxx, who topped the league with 175 rbi.

Greenberg's .315 batting average was best among Tigers. Dixie Walker was next with .308 and Charlie Gehringer hit .306, while Rudy York just missed the coveted .300 mark with a .298 but slammed 33 homers and had 127 rbi.

The Tigers team batting average dropped to .272, seventh in the league. Detroit tied a major league season record of 10 grand slam home runs, including four by Rudy York, who hit three of them in May.

For the fifth straight year, the Tigers' defense was tops in the league: .976. Two new Tigers were at the head of the defensive line. Catcher Rudy York topped the league with a .990 in 116 games while Peter Fox paced the outfielders at .994 in 155 games.

The Tigers' pitching statistics indicated its roller-coaster season performance as Tommy Bridges led the staff with a 13-9 record but had a 4.59 e.r.a.

The Tigers were victims of Indians' fireballing Bob Feller's record-setting 18 strikeouts in the season finale at Cleveland, however, Detroit won the game, collecting seven hits in a 4-1 victory. Harry Eisenstat hurled a four-hitter on a winning note.

Five Tigers were named to represent Detroit in the sixth annual All-Star Game at Cincinnati's Crosley Field on July 6, won by the National Leaguers, 4-1. First baseman Hank Greenberg, second baseman Charlie Gehringer, catcher Rudy York, pitcher Vern Kennedy and coach Del Baker joined the American League squad. Only Gehringer played the complete game; he had one single in three trips to the plate, also one walk. York struck out in a pinch-hitting appearance.

BATTING RECORDS

	B	G	AB	R	H	HR	SB	AVE	RBI
Greenberg, Henry	R	155	556	144	175	58	7	.315	146
Walker, Dixie	L	127	454	84	140	6	5	.308	43
Gehringer, Charles	L	152	568	133	174	20	14	.306	107
York, Rudy	R	135	463	85	138	33	1	.298	127
Tebbetts, Birdie	R	53	143	16	42	1	1	.294	25
Fox, Pete	R	155	634	91	186	7	16	.293	96
Morgan, Chester	L	74	306	50	87	0	5	.284	27
Cullenbine, Roy	B	25	67	12	19	0	2	.284	9
White, Joyner	L	78	206	40	54	0	3	.262	15
Ross, Donald	R	77	265	22	69	1	1	.260	30
Rogell, William	B	136	501	76	130	3	9	.259	55
Christman, Mark	R	95	318	35	79	1	5	.248	44
Laabs, Chet	R	64	211	26	50	7	3	.237	37
Piet, Tony	R	41	80	9	17	0	2	.213	14

Less than 10 games: Raymond Hayworth, Benjamin McCoy and George Archie.

PITCHING RECORDS

	T	G	IP	W	L	PCT	ERA
Benton, Al	R	19	95	5	3	.625	3.32
Eisenstat, Harry	L	32	125	9	6	.600	3.74
Gill, George	R	24	164	12	9	.571	4.12
Bridges, Tommy	R	25	151	13	9	.591	4.59
Poffenberger, Boots	R	25	125	6	7	.462	4.82
Kennedy, Vern	R	33	190	12	9	.571	5.07
Auker, Eldon	R	27	161	11	10	.524	5.25
Lawson, Roxie	R	27	127	8	9	.471	5.46
Coffman, Slicker	R	39	96	4	4	.500	6.00
Wade, Jake	L	27	70	3	2	.600	6.56

Less than 45 innings: Robert Harris, Joseph Rogalski, Woodrow Davis and Schoolboy Rowe.

1939
FINAL STANDINGS

	W	L	PCT
New York	106	45	.702
Boston	89	62	.589
Cleveland	87	67	.565
Chicago	85	69	.552
DETROIT	81	73	.526
Washington	65	87	.428
Philadelphia	55	97	.362
St. Louis	43	111	.279

Manager: Delmar Baker

The 1939 season was one of frustration for manager Del Baker, serving his first full term after three partial seasons as fill-in for side-lined Mickey Cochrane. However, it was a productive year for score-card vendors at Briggs Stadium.

Before the season began, the Tigers obtained third baseman Mike "Pinky" Higgins and pitcher Archie McKain from the boston Red Sox in return for pitchers Eldon Auker, Jake Wade and outfielder Chet Morgan. Detroit also procured the Pacific Coast League's sensational pitcher Fred Hutchinson from Seattle for four players: outfielder Jo-Jo White, infielder Tony Piet, first baseman George Archie, and pitcher Ed Selway.

Following a slow start, the Tigers worked out a 10-player deal in May with the St. Louis Browns in an effort to shake off a series of slumps. Manager Del Baker used 19 hurlers in an attempt to locate a winner.

The Tigers dropped into the second division for the first time in six years with a fifth-place finish.

However, there were several bright and memorable events along the lengthy trial of disappointments.

A 20-year-old rookie, Ted Williams of Boston, became the first player to hit a fair ball out of the rebuilt Briggs Stadium. He powered an over-the-roof home run off Tigers' Bob Harris on May 4 as the Red Sox edged Detroit 7-6.

On May 14, Tigers' Rudy York hit a grand slam pinch-hit home run to give Detroit a 7-4 win over the St. Louis Browns and complete a sweep of a doubleheader at Sportman's Park.

Charlie Gehringer became the fourth player in Tigers' history to hit for the cycle as Detroit walloped the St. Louis Browns 12-5 on May 27.

Night baseball made its American League debut in three ballparks: Philadelphia's Shibe Park, Cleveland's Municipal Stadium and Chicago's Comiskey Park.

The Detroit Tigers' involvement in its first-ever night game ended with the Tigers defeating Connie Mack's Philadelphia Athletics, 5-0, on June 20 at Shibe Park. One week later, Cleveland unveiled its floodlights, attracting

55,305 fans as Bob Feller blanked the visiting Tigers, 5-0, in the Indians' historical contest on June 27.

Three Detroit Tigers were selected on the American League squad for the seventh annual All-Star Game at New York's Yankee Stadium: pitchers Tommy Bridges, Buck Newsom and first baseman Hank Greenberg. Greenberg played the full game, had one single in three official at bats and drew one free pass. Bridges hurled two and one-third scoreless innings, allowed two hits and was the winning pitcher as the American Leaguers defeated the Nationals, 3-1.

While the Detroit pitching declined during the season, the Tigers came up with 'spoiler role' performances against formidable mound opponents. New York's Atley Donald won his first 12 games but the Tigers stopped the young right-hander's streak, 7-2, at Yankee Stadium.

Five weeks later, the Tigers beat Chicago White Sox right-hander John Rigney, who had reeled off 11 straight wins.

Charlie Gehringer topped the Detroit hitters with a .325 for the season, Hank Greenberg hit .312 with 33 home runs and 112 rbi, rookie Barney McCosky batted .311, and Rudy York posted a .307 with 20 homers.

Tommy Bridges paced the Tigers' pitching on a 17-7 record with a 3.50 e.r.a. Newsom won 17 and lost 10 for the Tigers and had a 3-1 mark with the Browns before coming to Detroit in the big trade, totalling a 20-11 record for the season.

BATTING RECORDS

	B	G	AB	R	H	HR	SB	AVE	RBI
Gehringer, Charlie	L	118	406	86	132	16	4	.325	86
Greenberg, Henry	R	138	500	112	156	33	8	.312	112
McCosky, Wm. Barney	L	147	611	120	190	4	20	.311	58
York, Rudy	R	102	329	66	101	20	5	.307	68
Walker, Dixie	L	43	154	30	47	4	4	.305	19
McCoy, Benjamin	L	55	192	38	58	1	3	.302	33
Fox, Pete	R	141	519	69	153	7	23	.295	66
Higgins, Michael F.	R	132	489	57	135	8	7	.276	76
Croucher, Frank	R	97	324	38	87	5	2	.269	40
Averill, Earl (24 Clev., 87 Det.)	L	111	364	66	96	11	4	.264	65
Tebbetts, Birdie	R	106	341	37	89	4	2	.261	53
Kress, Red (13 St. Louis, 51 Det.)	R	64	200	24	50	1	3	.250	30
Cullenbine, Roy	B	75	179	31	43	6	0	.240	23
Bell, Beau (11 St. Louis, 54 Det.)	R	65	166	18	39	1	0	.235	29
Rogell, William	B	74	174	24	40	2	3	.230	23

Less than 10 games: Mervyn Shea, Ed Parsons, Chet Laabs and Mark Christman.

Statistics

PITCHING RECORDS

	T	G	IP	W	L	PCT	ERA
Bridges, Tommy	R	29	198	17	7	.708	3.50
Newson, Bobo (6 St. Louis, 35 Det.)	R	41	292	20	11	.645	3.58
Trout, Dizzy	R	33	162	9	10	.474	3.61
McKain, Archie	L	32	130	5	6	.455	3.67
Eisenstat, Harry (10 Det., 26 Clev.)	L	36	133	8	9	.471	4.13
Benton, Al	R	37	150	6	8	.429	4.56
Rowe, Schoolboy	R	28	164	10	12	.455	4.99
Hutchinson, Fred	R	13	85	3	6	.333	5.19
Thomas, Luther (2 Phil., 4 Wash., 27 Det)	R	33	60	7	1	.875	5.25

Less than 45 innings: Leslie Fleming, Floyd Giebell, James Lynn, Hal Newhouser, James Walkup, Robert Harris and Roxie Lawson. Vern Kennedy and George Gill pitched in less than 45 innings with Detroit and completed season with St. Louis. Henry Pippin pitched in 25 games with Philadelphia and 3 with Detroit.

DAYS INN
DOWNTOWN DETROIT
231 Michigan Avenue
Detroit, Michigan 48226
(313) 965-4646

TIGERS PACKAGE

- *A deluxe guest room for one night*
- *2 Tiger tickets*
- *Complimentary shuttle service to/from Tiger Stadium*
- *Complimentary continental breakfast served Monday-Friday*
- *Special Tiger souvenir*
- *Use of the rooftop indoor swimming pool*
- *Advance reservations with deposit or credit card guarantee required*

This rate and offer is not applicable to groups, coupons or other discounted rates. Offer does not include taxes or parking.
- Total package price is $89.00 + 12% tax.

Please call reservations between 9:00 a.m. and 5:00 p.m.

1940

FINAL STANDINGS

	W	L	PCT
DETROIT	90	64	.584
Cleveland	89	65	.578
New York	88	66	.571
Chicago	82	72	.532
Boston	82	72	.532
St. Louis	67	87	.435
Washington	64	90	.416
Philadelphia	54	100	.351

Manager: Delmar Baker

The Detroit Tigers were active on the trading market prior to the 1940 season in another attempt to improve the ball club.

Detroit drafted pitcher Tom Seats from the Sacramento team of the Pacific Coast League. The Tigers traded infielder Benny McCoy and pitcher George Coffman to the Philadelphia Athletics for outfielder Wally Moses. One month later, the deal was nullified by Judge Landis after the Commissioner ruled Detroit was covering up transfer of players' contracts. Detroit lost six players as a result of this ruling.

During spring training, manager Del Baker switched first baseman Hank Greenberg to left field and assigned Rudy York to first base.

The double shuffle worked wonders for the Tigers in one of the closest and most interesting races in American League history. Long-shot Detroit captured the pennant, ending the New York Yankees' four-year reign, in a photo finish.

The Tigers won 90 and lost 64 games, squeezing past the Cleveland Indians by a slim one-game margin, the defending champion Yankees by two games, while the Chicago White Sox and Boston Red Sox tied for fourth spot, eight games behind Detroit.

The Tigers arrived in Cleveland with a two-game lead over the Indians for the final three games of the season. Detroit's 'Big Three' pitchers: Tommy Bridges, Buck Newsom and Schoolboy Rowe were all ready to apply the clincher.

However, Tiger manager Del Baker decided to pitch rookie Floyd Giebell against the Indians' ace right-hander Bob Feller.

Giebell blanked the Indians on a six-hitter for his second victory of the season. The Tigers collected only three hits off fireballing Feller, but one of them was a home run by Rudy York and the Tigers clinched the pennant, 2-0.

Ironically, Giebell was ineligible to pitch in the World Series. By the way, this was Giebell's last win as a major leaguer.

The Tigers' one-two batting punch was supplied by Greenberg and York. Greenberg led the league in home runs with 41, including 25 in the

September pennant drive. He also topped the AL circuit in the runs batted in column with 150, doubles with 50, total bases with 384 and compiled a .340 batting average.

Centerfielder Barney McCoskey hit .340 and led the league in triples with 19. Charlie Gehringer batted .313 and Billy Sullivan hit .309.

The Tigers established a new American League record in September by hitting at least one home run in 17 consecutive games with a total of 26 between September 4 and 19.

Pitcher Schoolboy Rowe staged a comeback. He won 16 games and lost only three times. Buck Newsom lost his opening game, then won 13 games in a row en route to a 21-5 season mark and a 2.83 e.r.a., despite missing three weeks of action due to a broken thumb. Bridges posted a 12-9 record while Hal Newhouser had a 9-9 mark.

Four Tigers represented Detroit in the eighth annual All-Star Game on July 10 at St. Louis Sportsman's Park: pitchers Tommy Bridges and Buck Newsom, left fielder Hank Greenberg and Tiger manager Del Baker served as coach.

Newsom hurled three scoreless innings, allowing one hit. Greenberg fouled out to the catcher twice in two turns at bat. The American Leaguers dropped a 4-0 decision to the National League team.

On August 2, Boston Red Sox manager Joe Cronin joined the hit-for-the cycle club, leading his team to a 12-9 victory at Detroit's Briggs Stadium.

The Tigers were victims of an abbreviated no-hit game performance, a six-inning pitching gem by St. Louis Browns' John Whitehead in a 4-0 triumph in the second game of a twin-bill at Sportsman's Park. It was Whitehead's only victory of the season.

Hank Greenberg was voted Most Valuable Player in the American League by the Baseball Writers Association of America. This was Greenberg's second MVP honor. His first came in 1935.

Walter O. Briggs Sr., president of the Detroit Tigers, was named Major League Executive of the Year.

Howard Ehmke was a Tiger pitcher from 1916 through 1922. In 1927, pitching for the Philadelphia Athletics, he gave up the first of Babe Ruth's 60 home runs.

BATTING RECORDS

	B	G	AB	R	H	HR	SB	AVE	RBI
McCosky, Wm. Barney	L	143	589	123	200	4	13	.340	57
Greenberg, Henry	R	148	573	129	195	41	6	.340	150
York, Rudy	R	155	588	105	186	33	3	.316	134
Gehringer, Charles	L	139	515	108	161	10	10	.313	81
Sullivan, Billy	L	78	220	36	68	3	2	.309	41
Tebbetts, Birdie	R	111	379	46	112	4	4	.296	46
Fox, Pete	R	93	350	49	101	5	7	.289	48
Campbell, Bruce	L	103	297	56	84	8	2	.283	44
Averill, Earl	L	64	118	10	33	2	0	.280	20
Higgins, Michael F.	R	131	480	70	130	13	4	.271	76
Meyer, Dutch	R	23	58	12	15	0	2	.259	6
Metha, Frank	R	26	37	6	9	0	0	.243	3
Bartell, Dick	R	139	528	76	123	7	12	.233	53
Stainback, Tucker	R	15	40	4	9	0	0	.225	1
Kress, Red	R	33	99	13	22	1	0	.222	11
Croucher, Frank	R	37	57	3	6	0	0	.105	2

Less than 10 games: Patrick Mullin and Frank Secory.

PITCHING RECORDS

	T	G	IP	W	L	PCT	ERA
Giebell, Floyd	R	2	18	2	0	1.000	1.00
McKain, Archie	L	27	51	5	0	1.000	2.82
Newsom, Bobo	R	36	264	21	5	.808	2.83
Bridges, Tommy	R	29	198	12	9	.571	3.36
Rowe, Schoolboy	R	27	169	16	3	.842	3.46
Gorsica, John	R	29	160	7	7	.500	4.33
Benton, Al	R	42	79	6	10	.375	4.44
Trout, Dizzy	R	33	101	3	7	.300	4.46
Seats, Tom	L	26	56	2	2	.500	4.66
Newhouser, Hal	L	28	133	9	9	.500	4.87
Hutchinson, Fred	R	17	76	3	7	.300	5.68

Less than 45 innings: Robert Uhle, Bud Thomas, Richard Conger and Henry Pippen.

1940 WORLD SERIES

Home Team	Date	Winning Team	Winning Pitcher	Losing Pitcher	Score
Cincinnati	October 2	Detroit	Newsom	Derringer	7-2
Cincinnati	October 3	Cincinnati	Walters	Rowe	5-3
Detroit	October 4	Detroit	Bridges	Turner	7-4
Detroit	October 5	Cincinnati	Derringer	Trout	5-2
Detroit	October 6	Detroit	Newsom	Thompson	8-0
Cincinnati	October 7	Cincinnati	Walters	Rowe	4-0
Cincinnati	October 8	Cincinnati	Derringer	Newsom	2-1

The Detroit Tigers faced Cincinnati, who won their second National League pennant in a row, in the 1940 World Series. The Reds won the NL title on a 12-game margin over the Brooklyn Dodgers.

The 1940 Series was a see-saw affair, going the limit of seven games.

The Tigers won the opener, 7-2, in Cincinnati as Buck Newsom scattered eight hits in an easy victory over the Red's Paul Derringer. Newsom's father, who witnessed his son's victory, died early the next morning.

Next day, the Reds evened the Series, 5-3, behind three-hit pitching by converted infielder Bucky Walters.

Home runs by Rudy York and Pinky Higgins in the seventh inning broke up a pitching duel between Tommy Bridges and Jim Turner in the third game. The Tigers moved ahead in the Series, 7-4, before their home town fans.

The Series was tied once again with Derringer limiting the Tigers to five hits. The Reds chased Tigers' starter Dizzy Trout in the third inning and continued on to a 5-2 victory in the fourth game.

Backed by a 13-hit attack, Detroit bounced back. Newsom hurled a three hit 8-0 shutout highlighted by Greenberg's four runs batted in on a homer and a pair of singles.

The Series returned to the Ohio city and Walters matched Newsom's shutout pitching performance with a nifty five-hitter. The Reds chased Schoolboy Rowe in the opening stanza and ended up with a 4-0 win and an even Series once more.

The finale pitted Newsom, working with only one day's rest, and Paul Derringer, pitching with two days' rest.

Detroit broke the scoring ice with an unearned run in the third inning. Billy Sullivan reached first on an infield hit and took second on Newsom's sacrifice bunt. Dick Bartell popped out and Barney McCosky walked. Charlie Gehringer hit a hard smash to third baseman Bill Werber, who knocked the ball down, but threw low to first baseman Frank McCormick. Sullivan rounded third and reached home ahead of McCormick's recovered throw.

Newsom kept Cincinnati scoreless until the seventh inning. McCormick opened with a double to left. Jim Ripple followed with a double off the top of the right field screen, bringing in the tying run. Jimmy Wilson sacrificed Ripple to third. Ernie Lombardi batted for Eddie Joost and was walked in-

Statistics

tentionally. Billy Myers drove centerfielder Barney McCosky to the fence and Ripple crossed the plate after the catch. The next two innings remained scoreless and Cincinnati won the game, 2-1, giving the Reds the 1940 World Series crown and the first National League triumph since the St. Louis Cardinals downed the Detroit Tigers in the 1934 Series.

WORLD SERIES INDIVIDUAL AVERAGES

	G	AB	R	H	HR	SB	PCT	RBI
Campbell	7	25	4	9	1	0	.360	5
Greenberg	7	28	5	10	1	0	.357	6
Higgins	7	24	2	8	1	0	.333	6
McCosky	7	23	5	7	0	0	.304	1
Bartell	7	26	2	7	0	0	.269	3
York	7	26	3	6	1	0	.231	2
Gehringer	7	28	3	6	0	0	.214	1
Sullivan	5	13	3	2	0	0	.154	0
Newsom	3	10	1	1	0	0	.100	0
Tebbetts	4	11	0	0	0	0	.000	0
Gorsica	2	4	0	0	0	0	.000	0
Bridges	1	3	0	0	0	0	.000	0
Averill	3	3	0	0	0	0	.000	0
Fox	1	1	0	0	0	0	.000	0
Trout	1	1	0	0	0	0	.000	0
Smith	1	1	0	0	0	0	.000	0
Rowe	2	1	0	0	0	0	.000	0
McKain	1	0	0	0	0	0	.000	0
Croucher	1	0	0	0	0	0	.000	0
Hutchinson	1	0	0	0	0	0	.000	0

PITCHING RECORDS

	G	IP	W	L	PCT	R	H	BB	SO
Bridges	1	9	1	0	1.000	4	10	1	5
Newsom	3	26	2	1	.667	4	18	4	17
Gorsica	2	11⅓	0	0	.000	1	6	4	4
Smith	1	4	0	0	.000	1	1	3	1
Rowe	2	3⅔	0	2	.000	7	12	1	1
Trout	1	2	0	1	.000	3	6	1	1
McKain	1	3	0	0	.000	1	4	0	0
Hutchinson	1	1	0	0	.000	1	1	1	1

TROY STAMP & COIN, INC.
3275 Rochester Rd.
Troy, MI 48083
528-1181

All Sports Cards — New & Old
Singles, Sets & Cases

Complete Stock of All Minor League Cards
From TCMA, Best Card, Pro Card & Many Others

Bats, Autographed Baseballs, Figurines
and Collectors Plates
of Your Favorite Player.

Complete Line of Supplies.

Statistics

1941

FINAL STANDINGS

	W	L	PCT
DETROIT	90	64	.584
Cleveland	89	65	.578
New York	88	66	.571
Chicago	82	72	.532
Boston	82	72	.532
St. Louis	67	87	.435
Washington	64	90	.416
Philadelphia	54	100	.351

Manager: Delmar Baker

The 1941 season saw the collapse of the Detroit Tigers. The team record dipped under the .500 mark: 75 games won and 79 games lost. That earned a tie for fourth place with the Cleveland Indians, 26 games behind the pennant-winning New York Yankees.

During spring training, manager Del Baker turned the shortstop job to Frank Croucher, replacing veteran Dick Bartell. The Tigers lost Hank Greenberg to the U.S. armed services after 19 games. He was discharged in December, but was called back on December 8, the day after the Pearl Harbor attack. Detroit once again went to the St. Louis Browns for a Greenberg replacement. This time they purchased outfielder Ray "Rip" Radcliff's contract.

Detroit hosted the ninth annual All-Star Game. Boston Red Sox outfielder Ted Williams provided a dramatic finish for an American League victory at Briggs Stadium on July 8. The American Leaguers went into the bottom of the ninth, trailing 5-3. Claude Passeau was on the National League's mound. After one out, Ken Keltner batted for pitcher Edgar Smith and scratched an infield hit to shortstop Eddie Miller. Joe Gordon singled and Cecil Travis walked to fill the bases. Joe DiMaggio forced Travis, with Keltner scoring and Gordon taking third.

Williams then homered into the upper right field stands and danced merrily around the bases for an American League, 7-5, come-from-behind triumph.

The American League regular season activity was highlighted by New York Yankees outfielder Joe DiMaggio's 56-game hitting streak between May 15 and July 16.

The Tigers' pitchers supplied hits in seven games during DiMaggio's continuous spree. Al Benton, Schoolboy Rowe, Archie McKain, Dizzy Trout, Hal Newhouser and Buck Newsom served up the hit-streak pitches.

Ted Williams drew additional national attention with his amazing hitting as he won the American League batting title with a sizzling .406 average. Williams was the first batter in the majors to hit over .400 since 1923 when Detroit outfielder Harry Heilmann won the AL crown with a .403 mark.

Dick Wakefield, an outfielder, was one of baseball's first players signed off the campus of the University of Michigan—he got a reported $52,000 bonus and a new automobile. Outfielder Barney McCosky topped the Detroit hitters with a .324 average and Greenberg's replacement, Radcliff, ended up with a season mark of .311. Rudy York slipped to a .259 average, but drove in 111 runs and slammed 27 home runs. Charlie Gehringer, reaching the end of his brilliant career, batted only .220 in 127 games.

The Tigers' pitching staff failed to reach expectations with Al Benton's 15-6 with a 2.96 e.r.a., Schoolboy Rowe's 8-6 and Dizzy Trout's 9-9 mark, the only trio to reach the .500 mark.

Tommy Bridges slumped to a 9-12 record and Buck Newsom won 12 games but lost 20 times and his earned run average zoomed to 4.61.

BATTING RECORDS

	B	G	AB	R	H	HR	SB	AVE	RBI
McCosky, Wm. Barney	L	143	589	123	200	4	13	.340	57
Greenberg, Henry	R	148	573	129	195	41	6	.340	150
York, Rudy	R	155	588	105	186	33	3	.316	134
Gehringer, Charles	L	139	515	108	161	10	10	.313	81
Sullivan, Billy	L	78	220	36	68	3	2	.309	41
Tebbetts, Birdie	R	111	379	46	112	4	4	.296	46
Fox, Pete	R	93	350	49	101	5	7	.289	48
Campbell, Bruce	L	103	297	56	84	8	2	.283	44
Averill, Earl	L	64	118	10	33	2	0	.280	20
Higgins, Michael F.	R	131	480	70	130	13	4	.271	76
Meyer, Dutch	R	23	58	12	15	0	2	.259	6
Metha, Frank	R	26	37	6	9	0	0	.243	3
Bartell, Dick	R	139	528	76	123	7	12	.233	53
Stainback, Tucker	R	15	40	4	9	0	0	.225	1
Kress, Red	R	33	99	13	22	1	0	.222	11
Croucher, Frank	R	37	57	3	6	0	0	.105	2

Less than 10 games: Patrick Mullin and Frank Secory.

PITCHING RECORDS

	T	G	IP	W	L	PCT	ERA
Giebell, Floyd	R	2	18	2	0	1.000	1.00
McKain, Arc hie	L	27	51	5	0	1.000	2.82
Newsom, Bobo	R	36	264	21	5	.808	2.83
Bridges, Tommy	R	29	198	12	9	.571	3.36
Rowe, Schoolboy	R	27	169	16	3	.842	3.46
Gorsica, John	R	29	160	7	7	.500	4.33
Benton, Al	R	42	79	6	10	.375	4.44
Trout, Dizzy	R	33	101	3	7	.300	4.46
Seats, Tom	L	26	56	2	2	.500	4.66
Newhouser, Hal	L	28	133	9	9	.500	4.87
Hutchinson, Fred	R	17	76	3	7	.300	5.68

Less than 45 innings: Robert Uhle, Bud Thomas, Richard Conger and Henry Pippen.

1942

FINAL STANDINGS

	W	L	PCT
New York	103	51	.669
Boston	93	59	.612
St. Louis	82	69	.543
Cleveland	75	79	.487
DETROIT	73	81	.474
Chicago	66	82	.446
Washington	62	89	.411
Philadelphia	55	99	.357

Manager: Delmar Baker

Baseball for 1942 was approved by President Franklin D. Roosevelt.

In a letter to Commissioner Judge Landis on January 15, the nation's Chief Executive emphasized that people working longer and harder than ever "ought to have a chance for recreation and for taking their minds off their work even more than ever before. Baseball provides a recreation, which does not last over two or two hours and a half and which can be got for very little cost I believe it best for the country to keep baseball going."

Before the season started, the Detroit Tigers selected outfielder Don Ross from the International League in the annual major league draft.

Then, the Tigers traded outfielder Bruce Campbell and shortstop Frank Croucher to the Washington Senators for outfielder Doc Cramer and second baseman Jimmy Bloodworth. Buck Newsom was a holdout and his contract was sold to the Washington Senators.

Two major league All-Star Games were played with the receipts going to the Armed Forces Service Relief and the Ball and Bat Fund.

In the first, at New York's Polo Grounds, the American Leaguers scored all of its runs in the opening inning and won, 3-1. First baseman Rudy York, catcher Birdie Tebbets, and pitcher Al Benton represented the Detroit Tigers. York slammed a two-run homer off NL starter Mort Cooper, Tebbetts went hitless in four times at bat, while Benton allowed the lone Nationals' run, a pinch-hit homer by Mickey Owen. He was touched for four hits in five innings of relief pitching.

During 1942 regular season play, the Detroit Tigers tumbled into the second division, winning 73 and losing 81 for a fifth place finish, 30 games behind the pennant-winning New York Yankees.

Boston's Ted Williams captured his second American League batting title, this time on a .356 average.

Not a single Detroit Tigers' regular player reached the charmed circle .300 batting average. Outfielder Barney McCosky came close with .293 mark in 154 games. However, the Tigers' pitching staff had five hurlers below the 3.00 e.r.a.

Southpaw Hal Newhouser posted a nifty 2.45 e.r.a. with an 8-14 won-loss record. Virgil Trucks was next with a 2.73 e.r.a. on a winning 14-8 mark, while Tommy Bridges showed a 9-7 record with a 2.74 e.r.a. Al Benton won only seven and lost 13 on a 2.89 e.r.a., Hal White showed a 12-12 record and a 2.90 e.r.a. and Dizzy Trout came up with a 12-18 with a 3.43 e.r.a. Schoolboy Rowe was ineffective and after only two games and 10 innings of mound duty was sold to the Brooklyn Dodgers.

BATTING RECORDS

	B	G	AB	R	H	HR	SB	AVE	RBI
Meyer, Dutch	R	14	52	5	17	2	0	.327	9
Riebe, Harvey	R	11	35	1	11	0	0	.314	2
McCosky, Wm. Barney	L	154	600	75	176	7	11	.293	50
Ross, Donald	R	87	226	29	62	3	2	.274	30
Harris, Ned	L	121	398	53	108	9	5	.271	45
Higgins, Michael F.	R	143	499	65	133	11	3	.267	79
Gehringer, Charles	L	45	45	6	12	1	0	.267	7
Cramer, Roger	L	151	630	71	166	0	4	.263	43
York, Rudy	R	153	577	81	150	21	3	.260	90
Franklin, Murray	R	48	154	24	40	2	0	.260	16
Radcliff, Raymond	L	62	144	13	36	1	0	.250	20
Tebbetts, Birdie	R	99	308	24	76	1	4	.247	27
Bloodworth, James	R	137	533	62	129	13	2	.242	57
Hitchcock, William	R	85	280	27	59	0	2	.211	29
McNair, Boob (26 Det., 34 Phil.)	R	60	171	13	36	1	1	.211	8
Parsons, Dixie	R	63	188	8	37	2	1	.197	11
Lipon, John	R	34	131	5	25	0	1	.191	9

Less than 10 games: Al Unser and Bob Patrick

PITCHING RECORDS

	T	G	IP	W	L	PCT	ERA
Newhouser, Hal	L	38	184	8	14	.364	2.45
Trucks, Virgil	R	28	168	14	8	.636	2.73
Bridges, Tommy	R	23	174	9	7	.563	2.74
Benton, Al	R	35	227	7	13	.350	2.89
White, Hal	R	34	217	12	12	.500	2.90
Trout, Dizzy	R	35	223	12	18	.400	3.43
Henshaw, Roy	L	23	62	2	4	.333	4.06
Gorsica, John	R	28	53	3	2	.600	4.75

Less than 45 innings: Emil Fuchs, Schoolboy Rowe and Hal Manders. Jack Wilson pitched in 12 games for Washington and in 9 for Detroit.

Statistics — 43

1943

FINAL STANDINGS

	W	L	PCT
New York	98	56	.636
Washington	84	69	.549
Cleveland	82	71	.536
Chicago	82	72	.532
DETROIT	78	76	.506
St. Louis	72	80	.474
Boston	68	84	.447
Philadelphia	49	105	.318

Manager: Stephen O'Neill

The Detroit Tigers opened the 1943 season with a new manager and a new spring training site.

Steve O'Neill was signed to manage the Tigers. He was a catcher in the major leagues for 17 years, 1911-1928, and managed the Cleveland Indians for two and a half seasons, 1935-1937.

At a special meeting called by Commissioner Judge Landis on January 5, Landis ruled all spring training sites must be north of the Ohio and Potomac Rivers and east of the Mississippi, except in the case of the two St. Louis clubs. It was estimated there was a saving of 400,000 miles of travel by the shift.

In abiding by the Judge Landis ruling, following a request by Joseph Eastman, director of the Office of Defense Transportation, for curtailment of travel, the Detroit Tigers set up Evansville, Indiana for their spring conditioning as the major league moved their spring training camps north.

Barney McCosky, Birdie Tebbetts, Charlie Gehringer, Al Benton and John Lipon joined the U.S. armed forces.

The Tigers improved their season record by five games, winning 78 and losing 76, but again finished in fifth place, 20 games behind the pennant-winning New York Yankees.

The 11th annual All-Star Game was played at night on July 13 at Philadelphia's Shibe Park. The American Leaguers came through with their eighth victory, a 5-3 decision, and the third in a row in the midsummer classic. Tigers' Dick Wakefield collected a double and single in four trips to the plate, Rudy York had one-for-three, while Hal Newhouser hurled three scoreless innings, allowing three hits.

Chicago White Sox shortstop Luke Appling won the American League batting title with a .328 average. Detroit Tigers' outfielder Wakefield's slump in the final weeks cost him a chance for the batting crown and he settled for runner-up honors with a .316 mark.

Doc Cramer ended the season with a .300 average while Rudy York batted .271, but he led the league in home runs with 34 and runs batted in with 118.

The Tigers finally came up with a 20-game winner with Dizzy Trout compiling a 20-12 won-loss record on a 2.48 e.r.a. Tommy Bridges posted a 12-7 mark and a 2.39 e.r.a., while Virgil Trucks showed a 16-10 and a 2.84 e.r.a. Southpaw Frank "Stubby" Overmire had 7-6, Hal White 7-12 and Hal Newhouser an 8-17 with a 3.03 e.r.a.

BATTING RECORDS

	B	G	AB	R	H	HR	SB	AVE	RBI
Wood, Joseph	R	60	164	22	53	1	2	.323	17
Wakefield, Dick	L	155	633	91	200	7	4	.316	79
Cramer, Roger	L	140	606	79	182	1	4	.300	48
Higgins, Michael F.	R	138	523	62	145	10	2	.277	84
York, Rudy	R	155	571	90	155	34	5	.271	118
Outlaw, Jimmy	R	20	67	8	18	1	0	.269	6
Ross, Donald	R	89	247	19	66	0	2	.267	18
Radcliff, Raymond	L	70	115	3	30	0	1	.261	10
Harris, Ned	L	114	354	43	90	6	6	.254	32
Unser, Albert	R	38	101	14	25	0	0	.248	4
Hoover, Joseph	R	144	575	78	140	4	6	.243	38
Bloodworth, James	R	129	474	41	114	6	4	.241	52
Richards, Paul	R	100	313	32	69	5	1	.220	33
Metro, Charlie	R	44	40	12	8	0	1	.200	2
Parsons, Dixie	R	40	106	2	15	0	0	.142	4

Less than 10 games: John McHale.

PITCHING RECORDS

	T	G	IP	W	L	PCT	ERA
Bridges, Tommy	R	25	192	12	7	.632	2.39
Trout, Dizzy	R	44	247	20	12	.625	2.48
Trucks, Virgil	R	33	203	16	10	.615	2.84
Newhouser, Hal	L	37	196	8	17	.320	3.03
Overmire, Stubby	L	29	147	7	6	.538	3.18
Gorsica, John	R	35	96	4	5	.444	3.38
White, Hal	R	32	178	7	12	.368	3.39
Henshaw, Roy	L	26	71	0	2	.000	3.80

Less than 45 innings: Prince Oana, Rufus Gentry and Joe Orrell.

1944

FINAL STANDINGS

	W	L	PCT
St. Louis	89	65	.578
DETROIT	88	66	.571
New York	83	71	.539
Boston	77	77	.500
Cleveland	72	82	.468
Philadelphia	72	82	.468
Chicago	71	83	.461
Washington	64	90	.416

Manager: Stephen O'Neill

The Detroit Tigers just missed winning the 1944 American League pennant in a thrilling down-to-the-wire finish.

As the race entered the final two days, Detroit and the St. Louis Browns were tied for first place with identical 87-65 records. On September 30, St. Louis made it three in a row over the New York Yankees on a 2-0 shutout and Denny Galehouse's five-hitter.

Meanwhile, Tigers' southpaw Hal Newhouser won his 29th game on a 7-3 victory over the Washington Senators.

On the closing afternoon, Tigers' manager Steve O'Neill selected Dizzy Trout to face Senators' knuckleball specialist Dutch Leonard. Leonard baffled the Tigers with his slow pitches and limited Detroit to four hits while Washington outfielder Stan Spence provided the winning blows with a pair of home runs en route to a 4-1 victory.

The St. Louis-New York game started one hour later and the Yankees' rookie Mel Queen held the Browns hitless for three innings as N.Y. moved ahead, 2-0.

In the fourth, Mike Kreevich singled and Chet Laabs, former Detroit Tigers' outfielder, tied the score with a left-field home run. After two outs in the fifth inning, Kreevich again singled. Laabs ran the count to three balls and one strike, then slammed a long home run into the bleachers for his second homer of the game and only his fifth of the year.

Vern Stephens added the Browns' final tally on a home run in the eighth while St. Louis rookie Sig Jakucki blanked the Yankees the rest of the game for his 13th win of the season on a pennant-winning 5-2 victory.

The dramatic finish gave the St. Louis Browns their first American League pennant. By the way, the Browns started the season with nine victories in a row while the Tigers lost 12 of 13 games at home.

Detroit Tigers' rookie catcher James "Hack" Miller hit a home run in his first major league time at bat on April 23 at Cleveland.

Tigers' Jimmy Bloodworth, Rip Radcliff, Virgil Trucks, Hal White and Tommy Bridges joined the U.S. armed forces.

Four Tigers represented Detroit in the 12th annual All-Star Game at Pittsburgh on July 11: pitchers Hal Newhouser and Dizzy Trout, first baseman Rudy York, and third baseman Pinky Higgins. Only Newhouser saw action, allowing two earned runs and three hits in one and two thirds innings of relief pitching as the National Leaguers defeated the American League, 7-1.

Cleveland Indians' manager Lou Boudreau won the American League batting title with a .327 average, the lowest league-leading mark since 1908, when Detroit's Ty Cobb took the batting crown with .324. Not a Detroit regular reached the coveted .300 figure, although outfielder Dick Wakefield, honorably discharged from the U.S. Navy preflight program in July, hit .355 in 78 games. Pinky Higgins topped the Tigers' regulars with a .297 in 148 games.

The Tigers' duo of Hal Newhouser and Dizzy Trout ran one-two in the leading pitching statistics of the season. Trout registered a 27-14 won-loss record on a league-leading 2.12 e.r.a., while Newhouser posted a 29-9 mark and a 2.22 e.r.a. They were the league's only 20-game winners. Trout topped the league with most complete games, 33, and seven shutouts.

Newhouser was voted Most Valuable Player in the annual balloting by the Baseball Writers Association of America. It was a close vote, Newhouser gaining the honors by a four-point margin, 236-232, over teammate Dizzy Trout.

BATTING RECORDS

	B	G	AB	R	H	HR	SB	AVE	RBI
Wakefield, Dick	L	78	276	53	98	12	2	.355	53
Hostetler, Chuck	L	90	265	42	79	0	4	.298	20
Higgins, Michael F.	R	148	543	79	161	7	4	.297	76
Cramer, Roger	L	143	578	69	169	2	6	.292	42
York, Rudy	R	151	583	77	161	18	5	.276	98
Outlaw, Jimmy	R	139	535	69	146	3	7	.273	57
Swift, Bob	R	80	247	15	63	1	2	.255	19
Mayo, Eddie	L	154	607	76	151	5	9	.249	63
Richards, Paul	R	95	300	24	71	3	8	.237	37
Hoover, Joseph	R	120	441	67	104	0	7	.236	29
Ross, Donald	R	66	167	14	35	2	2	.210	15
Orengo, Joseph	R	46	154	14	31	0	1	.201	10
Metro, Charles (38 Det., 24 Phil.)	R	62	118	12	19	0	1	.161	6
Unser, Albert	R	11	25	2	3	1	0	.120	5

Less than 10 games: Leslie Floyd, Donald Heffner, James Miller, Red Borom, Jack Sullivan and John McHale.

Statistics

PITCHING RECORDS

	T	G	IP	W	L	PCT	ERA
Trout, Dizzy	R	49	352	27	14	.659	2.12
Newhouser, Hal	L	47	312	29	9	.763	2.22
Overmire, Stubby	L	32	200	11	11	.500	3.06
Beck, Boom-Boom	R	28	74	1	2	.333	3.89
Gorsica, John	R	34	162	6	14	.300	4.11
Gentry, Rufus	R	37	204	12	14	.462	4.24

Less than 45 innings: Zeb Eaton, Chief Hogsett, Joe Orrell and Jake Mooty.

Where Good Friends Meet

German Specialities —

Knackwurst
Bratwurst
Kassler Rippchen
Eishein
Wiener Schnitzel
Sauerbraten

Kurz's Dakota Inn Rathskeller

17324 JOHN R. DETROIT, MI. • 867-9722

"THE BEST SING ALONG BAR IN TOWN!"
Live Entertainment Tuesday through Saturday

1945

FINAL STANDINGS

	W	L	PCT
DETROIT	88	65	.575
Washington	87	67	.565
St. Louis	81	70	.536
New York	81	71	.533
Cleveland	73	72	.503
Chicago	71	78	.477
Boston	71	83	.461
Philadelphia	52	98	.347

Manager: Stephen O'Neill

Baseball elected a new Commissioner, Albert "Happy" Chandler, a Senator from Kentucky, on April 24, 1945, replacing Judge Kenesaw Mountain Landis, who died in 1944. Chandler served as Commissioner without pay while holding his office in the U.S. Senate from April until November 1, 1945, when he resigned to devote full time to baseball.

Commissioner Chandler appointed Herold "Muddy" Ruel, 19-year veteran American League catcher, as special assistant to the Commissioner. Ruel caught for the Detroit Tigers in 1932.

A very dramatic finish on the final day of the season gave the Detroit Tigers their seventh pennant.

In an unusual arrangement, the pennant-contending Washington Senators completed their schedule one week earlier than the Tigers. They waited and kept in shape at the Bainbridge Naval Training Station in Maryland, hoping for St. Louis to knock off Detroit.

The Tigers faced the St. Louis Browns in a doubleheader finale. It rained beginning at noon, delaying the start of the twin-bill.

Manager Steve O'Neill picked Virgil Trucks as the starting pitcher. The right-hander just joined the team after being honorably discharged from the U.S. Navy. He opposed Nelson Potter, who had shut out the Tigers in his previous start.

The Tigers trailed by one in the eighth when Hubby Walker stroked a pinch-hit single. He took second on Skeeter Webb's bunt hit. Both runners advanced on Eddie Mayo's sacrifice. Potter walked Doc Cramer intentionally, bringing up Hank Greenberg with the bases jammed amidst falling raindrops.

With the count one and one, Greenberg blasted his 13th homer of the season into the left field stands for a pennant-winning grand slam. Newhouser's strong relief pitching earned him the win.

The second game was called after the Tigers batted in the opening frame, giving the Tigers an 88-65 record for the year, which was then the lowest winning percentage (.575) in major league history and a one and one half game margin over runner-up Washington.

One of the major cancellations of the 1945 wartime campaign was the shelving of the major league All-Star Game, scheduled for Pittsburgh's Forbes Field. War-time travel restrictions forced the call-off of the midsummer classic.

On July 21, the Detroit Tigers and Philadelphia Athletics set an American League record with a 24-inning, 1-1 contest at Shibe Park, stopped by darkness after four hours and 48 minutes of weary play.

The A's scored in the fourth. The Tigers knotted it in the seventh in the longest game played timewise and matched a 39-year mark for the most innings played.

Second baseman George Stirnweiss of the New York Yankees won the American League batting crown with a low .309 average. Greenberg paced the Tigers with a .311 in only 78 games. He rejoined the Tigers in July, following release from the U.S. armed forces. Mayo led the Tigers' regulars with a .285 mark.

Hal Newhouser dominated American League pitching with a 25-9 record and an amazing 1.81 e.r.a. He also led the league in strikeouts with 212 and most innings pitched.

Although Detroit finished third in team fielding with .975, four Tigers topped the individual defense percentages. Eddie Mayo headed the second basemen with .980 in 140 games. Paul Richards topped the catchers on a .995 in 83 games and pitcher Hal Newhouser fielded flawlessly, handling 82 chances in 40 games.

Hal Newhouser became only the second American Leaguer to win the coveted Most Valuable Player award two years in a row. Newhouser joined Philadelphia A's Jimmie Foxx, who won the laurels in 1932 and 1933. Newhouser gained the 1945 MVP honors with 236 points over runner-up teammate Eddie Mayo, who received 164 points from a 24-man committee of the Baseball Writers Association of America.

Baseball added ten names to the national Baseball Hall of Fame in Cooperstown, N.Y., including Hughie Jennings, who managed the Detroit Tigers for 14 seasons, 1907-1920 and three American League pennants, 1907-08-09.

⚾ ⚾ ⚾

Harold Newhouser is the only pitcher in major league history to win two straight Most Valuable Player awards. He won the honors in 1944 and 1945 when pitching for the Tigers. He had a 29-9 record in 1944 and 25-9 in 1945.

Statistics

BATTING RECORDS

	B	G	AB	R	H	HR	SB	AVE	RBI
Greenberg, Henry	R	78	270	47	84	13	3	.311	60
Mayo, Eddie	L	134	501	71	143	10	7	.285	54
Cramer, Roger	L	141	541	62	149	6	2	.275	58
Cullenbine, Roy (8 Clev., 146 Det.)	B	154	536	83	146	18	2	.272	93
Outlaw, Jimmy	R	132	446	56	121	0	6	.271	34
Borom, Red	L	55	130	19	35	0	4	.269	9
York, Rudy	R	155	595	71	157	18	6	.264	87
Maier, Bobby	R	132	486	58	128	1	7	.,263	34
Hoover, Joseph	R	74	222	33	57	1	6	.257	17
Richards, Paul	R	83	234	26	60	3	4	.256	32
Swift, Bob	R	95	279	19	65	0	1	.233	24
Webb, James Skeeter	R	118	407	43	81	0	8	.199	21
Hostetler, Chuck	L	42	44	3	7	0	0	.159	2
McHale, John	L	19	14	0	2	0	0	.143	1
Mierkowicz, Ed	R	10	15	0	2	0	0	.133	2
Walker, Hubby	L	28	23	4	3	0	1	.130	1

Less than 10 games: James Miller, Milton Welch, Carl McNabb and Russell Kerns. Donald Ross played 8 games with Detroit and 106 with Cleveland.

PITCHING RECORDS

	T	G	IP	W	L	PCT	ERA
Newhouser, Hal	L	40	313	25	9	.735	1.81
Benton, Al	R	31	192	13	8	.619	2.02
Orrell, Joe	R	12	48	2	3	.400	3.00
Trout, Dizzy	R	41	246	18	15	.545	3.15
Tobin, Jim	R	14	58	4	5	.444	3.57
Mueller, Les	R	26	135	6	8	.429	3.67
Overmire, Stubby	L	31	162	9	9	.500	3.89
Eaton, Zeb	R	17	53	4	2	.667	4.08
Caster, George (10 St. Louis, 22 Det.)	R	32	67	6	3	.667	4.57
Wilson, Jack	R	25	72	1	3	.250	4.63

Less than 45 innings: Tommy Bridges, Art Houtteman, Henry Oana, Billy Pierce, Patrick McLaughlin and Virgil Trucks.

1945 WORLD SERIES

Home Team	Date	Winning Team	Winning Pitcher	Losing Pitcher	Score
Detroit	October 3	Chicago	Borowy	Newhouser	9-0
Detroit	October 4	Detroit	Trucks	Wyse	4-1
Detroit	October 5	Chicago	Passeau	Overmire	3-0
Chicago	October 6	Detroit	Trout	Prim	4-1
Chicago	October 7	Detroit	Newhouser	Borowy	8-4
Chicago	October 8	Chicago	Borowy	Trout	8-7 (12 inn.)
Chicago	October 10	Detroit	Newhouser	Borowy	9-3

The Detroit Tigers' 1945 World Series opponents were Charlie Grimm's Chicago Cubs, who ended a three-year National League pennant reign of the St. Louis Cardinals in a down-to-the-wire showdown.

Before the home-town Tigers' fans settled down in their Briggs Stadium seats, the Cubs started with a four-run bang in the opening stanza off Detroit star left-hander Hal Newhouser. They chased him with three more in the third. Meanwhile, Chicago's Hank Borowy blanked the Tigers on six hits, all singles, as the Cubs marched to a 9-0 triumph.

Detroit evened the Series the next day on Virgil Truck's pitching and Hank Greenberg's three-run homer in a come-from-behind 4-1 victory.

Chicago moved ahead on the next afternoon as Claude Passeau silenced the Tigers with a superb one-hit shutout, a second inning single by Rudy York en route to the Cub's 3-0 win.

The Series shifted to Chicago's Wrigley Field and once again the Tigers evened the Series, 4-1. Dizzy Trout hurled a five-hitter, sparked by Detroit's four-run rally in the fourth inning.

The Tigers took the Series lead on a Borowy-Newhouser pitching rematch with reversed results. This time, the Tigers chased Borowy in the sixth stanza with a four-run outburst and went on to an 8-4 victory. Greenberg's three doubles led an 11-hit attack off five Cubs' hurlers.

Detroit missed a chance to clinch the Series crown in a wild extra-inning contest, flawed by Chuck Hostetler's embarrassing fall after rounding third base. Hostetler led off the seventh inning in a pinch-hitting role for shortstop Skeeter Webb and was safe on an error. He reached second as Eddie Mayo bounced out. Doc Cramer singled to left but Hostetler stumbled and fell to the ground between third and home and was an easy out at the plate. The Tigers did score two runs, but the fall proved costly.

After one out in the 12th inning, Frank Secory, batting for Len Merullo, singled. Bill Schuster ran for him. Borowy struck out but Stan Hack looped a hit in front of left-fielder Greenberg. The ball bounced crazily over Greenberg's shoulder and Schuster raced home with the winning run. The play was scored a hit along with an error for Greenberg. But, five hours later, the official scorers changed the ruling. They credited Hack with a double, a run batted in, and took the error away from Greenberg.

The decisive game proved to be a breeze for the Tigers.

Working with just one day's rest, Borowy's return to the mound was very brief. The Cub's right-hander faced only three batters—Skeeter Webb, Eddie

Statistics

Mayo and Doc Cramer hit successive singles to produce a run, a quick shower for Borowy and an early relief pitching call for Paul Derringer.

Greenberg sacrificed the two runners along and a base on balls to Roy Cullenbine jammed the sacks. Jimmy Outlaw also walked, forcing a run and setting the stage for Paul Richard's bases-clearing double climaxing a five-run explosion and a 9-3 victory. The 1945 World Series Championship belonged to the Detroit Tigers.

Cubs' first baseman Phil Cavaretta paced the World Series hitters with a .423 average at 11-for-26, while Doc Cramer topped the Tigers at .379 via 11-for-29.

WORLD SERIES INDIVIDUAL AVERAGES

	G	AB	R	H	HR	SB	PCT	RBI
Webb	7	27	4	5	0	0	.185	1
Hoover	1	3	1	1	0	0	.333	1
Mayo	7	28	4	7	0	0	.250	2
Cramer	7	29	7	11	0	1	.379	4
Greenberg	7	23	7	7	2	0	.304	7
Mierkowicz	1	0	0	0	0	0	.000	0
Cullenbine	7	22	5	5	0	1	.227	4
York	7	28	1	5	0	0	.179	3
Outlaw	7	28	1	5	0	1	.179	3
Richards	7	19	0	4	0	0	.211	6
Swift	3	4	1	1	0	0	.250	0
Newhouser	3	8	0	0	0	0	.000	1
Benton	3	0	0	0	0	0	.000	0
Tobin	1	1	0	0	0	0	.000	0
Mueller	1	0	0	0	0	0	.000	0
Trucks	2	4	0	0	0	0	.000	0
Overmire	1	1	0	0	0	0	.000	0
Bridges	1	0	0	0	0	0	.000	0
Trout	2	6	0	1	0	0	.167	0
Caster	1	0	0	0	0	0	.000	0
Eaton	1	1	0	0	0	0	.000	0
Hostetler	3	3	0	0	0	0	.000	0
Borom	2	1	0	0	0	0	.000	0
McHale	3	3	0	0	0	0	.000	0
Walker	2	2	1	1	0	0	.500	0
Maier	1	1	0	1	0	0	1.000	0

PITCHING RECORDS

	G	IP	W	L	PCT	R	H	BB	SO
Trucks	2	13 1/3	1	0	1.000	5	14	5	7
Newhouser	3	20 2/3	2	1	.667	14	25	4	22
Trout	2	13 2/3	1	1	.500	2	9	3	9
Overmire	1	6	0	1	.000	2	4	2	2
Benton	3	4 2/3	0	0	.000	1	6	0	5
Tobin	1	3	0	0	.000	2	4	1	0
Bridges	1	1 2/3	0	0	.000	3	3	3	1
Mueller	1	2	0	0	.000	0	0	1	1
Caster	1	2/3	0	0	.000	0	0	0	1

Come to Sheraton for Time of Your Life Weekends

Sheraton's got it all. The place... The package... The price!

Sheraton-Oaks

Hotels, Inns & Resorts Worldwide

The hospitality people of **ITT**

27000 SHERATON DRIVE
NOVI, MICHIGAN 48050
313/348-5000

1946

FINAL STANDINGS

	W	L	PCT
Boston	104	50	.675
DETROIT	92	62	.597
New York	87	67	.565
Washington	76	78	.494
Chicago	74	80	.481
Cleveland	68	86	.442
St. Louis	66	88	.429
Philadelphia	49	105	.318

Manager: Stephen O'Neill

After four years of northern spring sessions at Evansville, Indiana, the Tigers returned to Lakeland, Florida for preseason training.

Injuries to a couple of key players prevented Steve O'Neill's Detroit Tigers from repeating as American League pennant winners. They settled for a second place finish, despite a 92-52 record.

Joe Cronin's Boston Red Sox won 104 games and lost only 50 times to capture the 1946 AL honors, 12 games ahead of the Tigers.

Centerfielder Walter "Hoot" Evers collided with second baseman Eddie Mayo, sending the Tigers' duo to the sidelines for most of the season.

The Tigers obtained shortstop Eddie Lake from the Boston Red Sox for first baseman Rudy York in a preseason transaction. In an early season deal in May, Detroit traded outfielder Barney McCosky to the Philadelphia A's for third baseman George Kell. The Tigers also released third baseman Pinky Higgins and he signed with the Red Sox.

Detroit had only one representative in the major league All-Star Game renewal on July 9 at Boston's Fenway Park. Pitcher Hal Newhouser hurled three scoreless innings, yielding one hit, a single to pinch-hitter Peanuts Lowery. Newhouser also connected for a single off Kirby Higbe as the American Leaguers routed the Nationals, 12-0.

The Tigers enjoyed good pitching in 1946. Newhouser won 26 and lost nine while leading the American League hurlers with a 1.94 e.r.a.

Washington's Mickey Vernon gained the American League batting title with a rousing .353 average. Roy Cullenbine led the Tigers with a .335, while newcomer George Kell batted .322 and Doc Cramer hit .294.

Greenberg returned to his first-base position and paced the league with 44 home runs and 127 rbi while batting .277. Kell headed the league's third basemen defensively with a .983 mark in 131 games at the hot corner.

BATTING RECORDS

	B	G	AB	R	H	HR	SB	AVE	RBI
Cullenbine, Roy	B	113	328	63	110	15	3	.335	56
Kell, George (26 Phil., 105 Det.)	R	131	521	70	168	4	3	.322	52
McCosky, Wm. Barney (25 Det., 92 Phil.)	L	117	399	44	127	2	2	.318	45
Lipon, John	R	14	20	4	6	0	0	.300	1
Cramer, Roger	L	68	204	26	60	1	3	.294	26
Greenberg, Henry	R	142	523	91	145	44	5	.277	127
Wakefield, Dick	L	111	396	64	106	12	3	.268	59
Evers, Hoot	R	81	304	42	81	4	7	.266	33
Higgins, Michael F. (18 Det., 64 Bos.)	R	82	260	20	68	2	0	.262	36
Outlaw, Jimmy	R	92	299	36	78	2	5	.261	31
Lake, Eddie	R	155	587	105	149	8	15	.254	31
Mayo, Eddie	L	51	202	21	51	0	6	.252	22
Mullin, Pat	L	93	276	34	68	3	3	.246	35
Bloodworth, James	R	76	249	26	61	5	3	.245	36
Tebbetts, Birdie	R	87	280	20	68	1	1	.243	34
Swift, Bob	R	42	107	13	25	2	0	.234	10
Webb, James Skeeter	R	64	169	12	37	0	3	.219	17
Moore, Anse	L	51	134	16	28	1	1	.209	8
Richards, Paul	R	57	139	13	28	0	2	.201	11

Less than 10 games: John Groth and Ned Harris. Billy Hitchcock appeared in 3 games with Detroit and 98 with Washington.

PITCHING RECORDS

	T	G	IP	W	L	PCT	ERA
Newhouser, Hal	L	37	293	26	9	.743	1.94
Trout, Dizzy	R	38	276	17	13	.567	2.35
Hutchinson, Fred	R	28	207	14	11	.560	3.09
Trucks, Virgil	R	32	237	14	9	.609	3.23
Benton, Al	R	28	141	11	7	.611	3.64
Overmire, Stubby	L	24	97	5	7	.417	4.64

Less than 45 innings: John Gorsica, Hal White, George Caster, Louis Kretlow, Thomas Bridges, Ted Gray, Art Houtteman, Hal Manders and Rufus Gentry.

1947

FINAL STANDINGS

	W	L	PCT
New York	97	57	.630
DETROIT	85	69	.552
Boston	83	71	.539
Cleveland	80	74	.519
Philadelphia	78	76	.506
Chicago	70	84	.455
Washington	64	90	.416
St. Louis	59	95	.383

Manager: Stephen O'Neill

On January 17, the Detroit Tigers completed a waiver deal sending Hank Greenberg to the Pittsburgh Pirates for an estimated $35,000.

The 1947 Detroit Tigers, managed by Steve O'Neill, won 85 and lost 69 games for a second-place finish, 12 games behind the American League pennant-winning New York Yankees, piloted by Bucky Harris. The Yanks' success was insured by a 19-game winning streak in July. The Tigers snapped the Yankees' victory string on July 18 with Fred Hutchinson pitching a two-hit shutout, 8-0, at Briggs Stadium.

In a midseason trade of catchers, the Tigers sent Birdie Tebbetts to the Boston Red Sox in exchange for Hal Wagner.

Four Tigers were selected to the July 8 All-Star Game at Chicago's Wrigley Field: third baseman George Kell, outfielder Pat Mullin, pitchers Hal Newhouser and Dizzy Trout. Kell played seven innings, going 0-for-4 while Newhouser started the game and hurled three scoreless frames, allowing one hit, a single to pinch-hitting Bert Haas as the American Leaguers edged the Nationals, 2-1.

A Sunday doubleheader on July 20 against the New York Yankees attracted a record crowd of 58,369 fans at Briggs Stadium.

On September 14, Vic Wertz hit for the cycle in the first game of a twin-bill at Washington's Griffith Stadium.

Boston Red Sox outfielder Ted Williams won the American League batting crown with a .343 average. George Kell paced the Tigers on a .320 mark, Hoot Evers batted .296, Vic Wertz .288, Dick Wakefield .283 and Eddie Mayo .279. Fred Hutchinson topped the AL pitchers in the hitting department with a .302 average on 32 hits in 106 trips to the plate.

Newhouser won 17 and dropped 17 games and finished fifth in the league with a 2.87 e.r.a. Hutchinson posted an 18-10 record on a 3.03 e.r.a., while rookie Art Houtteman won seven and lost twice.

Mickey Cochrane was voted to Baseball's Hall of Fame by the Baseball Writers Association of America.

BATTING RECORDS

	B	G	AB	R	H	HR	SB	AVE	RBI
Kell, George	R	152	588	75	188	5	9	.320	93
Evers, Hoot	R	126	460	67	136	10	8	.296	67
Wertz, Vic	L	102	333	60	96	6	2	.288	44
Wakefield, Dick	L	112	368	59	104	8	1	.283	51
Mayo, Eddie	L	142	535	66	149	6	3	.279	48
Wagner, Hal (21 Bos., 71 Det.)	L	92	256	24	70	5	0	.273	39
Cramer, Roger	L	73	157	21	42	2	0	.268	30
Tebbetts, Birdie (20 Det., 90 Bos.)	R	110	344	23	92	1	2	.267	30
Mullin, Pat	L	116	398	62	102	15	3	.256	21
Swift, Bob	R	97	279	23	70	1	2	.251	62
Outlaw, Jimmy	R	70	127	20	29	0	3	.228	15
Cullenbine, Roy	B	142	464	82	104	24	3	.224	78
Lake, Eddie	R	158	602	96	127	12	11	.211	46
McHale, John	L	39	95	10	20	3	1	.211	11
Webb, Skeeter	R	50	79	18	16	0	3	.203	6
Mierkowicz, Ed	R	21	42	6	8	1	1	.190	1

Less than 10 games: John Groth, Harvey Riebe and Ben Steiner.

PITCHING RECORDS

	T	G	IP	W	L	PCT	ERA
Newhouser, Hal	L	40	285	17	17	.500	2.87
Hutchinson, Fred	R	33	220	18	10	.643	3.03
Houtteman, Art	R	23	111	7	2	.778	3.41
Trout, Dizzy	R	32	186	10	11	.476	3.48
White, Hal	R	35	85	4	5	.444	3.60
Gorsica, John	R	31	58	2	0	1.000	3.72
Overmire, Stubby	L	28	141	11	5	.688	3.77
Benton, Al	R	36	133	6	7	.462	4.40
Trucks, Virgil	R	36	181	10	12	.455	4.52

Less than 45 innings: Rufus Gentry.

1948

FINAL STANDINGS

	W	L	PCT
Cleveland	97	58	.626
Boston	96	59	.619
New York	94	60	.610
Philadelphia	84	70	.545
DETROIT	78	76	.506
St. Louis	59	94	.386
Washington	56	97	.366
Chicago	51	101	.336

Manager: Stephen O'Neill

The 1948 season was climaxed with the first pennant playoff in American League history. The Cleveland Indians and Boston Red Sox tied for first place. In a one-game playoff, manager Lou Boudreau's two home runs and rookie Gene Bearden's five-hit pitching gave Cleveland an 8-3 triumph and their first AL pennant since 1920.

Feeling the prolonged absence of star third baseman George Kell from the lineup with injuries twice — first with a broken wrist and later with a fractured jaw—Steve O'Neill's Tigers finished fifth, 18 1/2 games behind the Indians.

Tigers' rookie first baseman George Vico joined an elite list when, in his first turn at bat in the majors, Vico hit the first pitch offered by Chicago's Joe Haynes for a long home run as Detroit downed the White Sox, 5-2, on opening day at Comiskey Park on April 20.

The Detroit Tigers finally played night ball at home, becoming the last AL club to install lights.

The first game under the lights at Briggs Stadium on June 15 was a winner, a 4-1 victory over the Philadelphia Athletics viewed by 54,480 fans.

Cleveland Indians' Bob Lemon hurled a no-hit game against the Tigers on June 30. A night game crowd of 49,628 watched Lemon's masterpiece at Briggs Stadium. He faced only 30 batters, issuing three bases on balls. The Indians scored two unearned runs in the opening inning off Art Houtteman for their only tallies in a 2-0 victory.

Four Tigers were selected for the July 13 All-Star Game at St. Louis' Sportsman's Park: George Kell, Hoot Evers, Pat Mullin and Hal Newhouser. Evers played the complete game in centerfield. He homered off Ralph Branca as the American Leaguers won, 5-2.

Detroit entered the high-bidding market for standout amateur ball players and signed catcher Frank House of Bessemer, Alabama to a Flint Central League contract for a $45,000 bonus and two automobiles.

Boston's Ted Williams repeated as American League batting champion, this time on a .369 average. Evers led the Tigers with .314, Kell was next on

.304, while Johnny Lipon batted .290, Pat Mullin .288, Jimmy Outlaw .283 and Dick Wakefield .276.

Newhouser won 21, lost 12 and finished with a 3.01 e.r.a., third best in the AL. Hutchinson showed a 13-11 and Dizzy Trout 10-14 with a 3.42 e.r.a, fifth in the league.

Hutchinson topped the AL pitchers on defense with a perfect fielding percentage, handling 64 chances without an error.

Detroit Tigers' manager Steve O'Neill was released at the end of the season.

On October 27, ten Tiger minor leaguers were declared free agents by Commissioner Happy Chandler for Detroit contract mishandling procedures.

BATTING RECORDS

	B	G	AB	R	H	HR	SB	AVE	RBI
Ginsberg, Joe	L	11	36	7	13	0	0	.361	0
Evers, Hoot	R	139	538	81	169	10	3	.314	103
Kell, George	R	92	368	47	112	2	2	.304	44
Lipon, John	R	121	458	65	133	5	4	.290	52
Mullin, Pat	L	138	496	91	143	23	1	.288	80
Outlaw, Jimmy	R	74	198	33	56	0	0	.283	25
Wakefield, Dick	L	110	322	50	89	11	0	.276	53
Vico, George	L	144	521	50	139	8	2	.267	58
Berry, Neil	R	87	256	46	68	0	1	.266	16
Campbell, Paul	L	59	83	15	22	1	0	.265	11
Lake, Eddie	R	64	198	51	52	2	3	.263	18
Mayo, Eddie	L	106	370	35	92	2	1	.249	42
Wertz, Vic	L	119	391	49	97	7	0	.248	67
Swift, Bob	R	113	292	23	65	4	1	.223	33
Wagner, Hal	L	54	109	10	22	0	1	.202	10
Riebe, Harvey	R	25	62	0	12	0	0	.194	5

Less than 10 games: John Groth, Edward Mierkowicz, John Bero, Roger Cramer and John McHale.

PITCHING RECORDS

	T	G	IP	W	L	PCT	ERA
Newhouser, Hal	L	39	272	21	12	.636	3.01
Trout, Dizzy	R	32	184	10	14	.417	3.42
Trucks, Virgil	R	43	212	14	13	.519	3.78
Gray, Ted	L	26	85	6	2	.750	4.24
Hutchinson, Fred	R	33	221	13	11	.542	4.32
Houtteman, Art	R	43	164	2	16	.111	4.66
Overmire, Stubby	L	37	66	3	4	.429	6.00
Pierce, Billy	L	22	55	3	0	1.000	6.38

Less than 45 innings: Al Benton, Hal White, Louis Kretlow and Rufus Gentry.

1949

FINAL STANDINGS

	W	L	PCT
New York	97	57	.630
Boston	96	58	.623
Cleveland	89	65	.578
DETROIT	87	67	.565
Philadelphia	81	73	.526
Chicago	63	91	.409
St. Louis	53	101	.344
Washington	50	104	.325

Manager: Red Rolfe

Robert "Red" Rolfe, ten-year veteran third baseman for the New York Yankees, was named manager of the Detroit Tigers for 1949.

The Tigers selected pitcher Marv Grissom from the Pacific Coast League's Sacramento team in the annual major league draft. Detroit obtained infielder Don Kolloway from the Chicago White Sox in a trade for outfielder Earl Rapp.

Pitcher Art Houtteman was seriously injured in a car accident during spring training at Lakeland, Florida.

The Tigers were involved in a torrid American League pennant race right up to the final weeks. They took 18 out of the first 20 games in August, including 10 straight. Detroit won 87 and lost 67, but finished fourth, 10 games behind the pennant-winning New York Yankees managed by Casey Stengel.

Three Tigers represented Detroit in the major league All-Star Game on July 12 at Brooklyn's Ebbets Field: George Kell, Vic Wertz and Virgil Trucks. Kell, a third-base starter, reached base four times on two singles, a walk and an error, while Wertz went 0-for-2 playing right field, following a pinch-hitting role. Trucks was the winning pitcher as the American Leaguers defeated the Nationals, 11-7, in a hitters' contest. Trucks hurled two innings, yielding two runs and three hits.

George Kell squeezed past Boston Red Sox outfielder Ted Williams for the American League batting title by .00016 point on the final day of the season. Williams went hitless in two official trips to the plate while Kell had two hits in three at-bats to grab the crown, .34291 to .34275 average.

Vic Wertz batted .304, Hoot Evers .303 and John Groth .293 for the Tigers.

Virgil Trucks paced the Tigers' hurlers with a 19-11 record and a 2.81 e.r.a., second best earned run average in the league.

Young Houtteman, returning in May from his injury, won 15 and lost 10 in a popular comeback.

Charlie Gehringer was voted to Baseball's Hall of Fame in balloting by the Baseball Writers Association of America.

BATTING RECORDS

	B	G	AB	R	H	HR	SB	AVE	RBI
Kell, George	R	134	522	97	179	3	7	.3429	59
Wertz, Vic	L	155	608	96	185	20	2	.304	133
Evers, Hoot	R	132	432	68	131	7	6	.303	72
Groth, John	R	103	348	60	102	11	3	.293	73
Kolloway, Donald (4 Chi., 126 Det.)	R	130	487	71	142	2	7	.292	47
Campbell, Paul	L	87	255	38	71	3	3	.278	30
Robinson, Aaron	L	110	331	38	89	13	0	.269	56
Mullin, Pat	L	104	310	55	83	12	1	.268	59
Lipon, John	R	127	439	57	110	3	2	.251	59
Swift, Bob	R	74	189	16	45	2	0	.238	18
Berry Neil	R	109	329	38	78	0	4	.237	18
Wakefield, Dick	L	59	126	17	26	6	0	.206	19
Lake, Eddie	R	94	240	38	47	1	2	.196	15
Vico, George	L	67	142	15	27	4	0	.190	18
Riebe, Harvey	R	17	33	1	6	0	1	.182	2

Less than 10 games: Jimmy Outlaw, Don Lund and Bobby Mavis. Earl Rapp appeared in one game with Detroit and in 19 with Chicago.

PITCHING RECORDS

	T	G	IP	W	L	PCT	ERA
Trucks, Virgil	R	41	275	19	11	.633	2.81
Hutchinson, Fred	R	33	189	15	7	.682	2.95
Newhouser, Hal	L	38	202	18	11	.621	3.36
Gray, Ted	L	34	105	10	10	.500	3.51
Houtteman, Art	R	34	204	15	10	.600	3.71
Trout, Dizzy	R	33	59	3	6	.333	4.42
Kretlow, Lou	R	25	76	3	2	.600	6.16

Less than 45 innings: Marvin Grissom, Saul Rogovin, Hal White, Stubby Overmire and Marlin Stuart.

1950
FINAL STANDINGS

	W	L	PCT
New York	98	56	.636
DETROIT	95	59	.617
Boston	94	60	.610
Cleveland	92	62	.597
Washington	67	87	.435
Chicago	60	94	.390
St. Louis	58	96	.377
Philadelphia	52	102	.338

Manager: Red Rolfe

Manager Red Rolfe's Detroit Tigers were in the thick of the American League pennant race until the final week of the schedule when they lost three games in a row to the Cleveland Indians.

As the season wound down, Detroit southpaw Ted Gray and Cleveland's right-hander Bob Lemon were engaged in a nifty pitchers' duel on a 1-1 tie extending into overtime.

Lemon opened the Tribe's 10th inning with a lusty triple. Manager Rolfe ordered the next two batters to be walked intentionally and fill the bases.

After Larry Doby popped out, Luke Easter bounced a grounder along the first base line. Don Kolloway fielded the ball near the base, touched the bag with his foot and threw to catcher Robinson, who stepped on the plate, thinking he had retired Lemon on a force out. Lemon slid across the plate with the winning run.

Robinson's view of Kolloway touching first base had been blocked out by the running Easter en route to first so instead of tagging the sliding Lemon, the catcher had simply stepped on home plate.

The tough 2-1 loss hurt the Tigers' pennant chances, they were 2 1/2 games behind the Yanks who won the pennant with a 98-56 record while the Tigers finally settled for runner-up honors, three games behind with a 95-59 mark.

In preseason deals, the Tigers had traded outfielder Dick Wakefield to the New York Yankees for first baseman Dick Kryhoski and purchased pitcher Paul Calvert from the Washington Senators. Detroit also obtained second baseman Gerry Priddy from the St. Louis Browns for pitcher Lou Kretlow and $100,000.

In mid-May, the Tigers lost pitcher Virgil Trucks with a sore arm and he was out for the season. Detroit purchased pitcher Hank Borowy from the Pittsburgh Pirates in an August waiver deal.

Two Tigers hit for the cycle. George Kell accomplished his feat on June 2 at Philadelphia, while Hoot Evers joined the elite club on September 7 at Cleveland.

In a battle of home runs, the Tigers downed the New York Yankees, 10-9, on June 23 at Briggs Stadium. The game was highlighted by a four home run outburst in the fourth inning as pitcher Dizzy Trout, Gerry Priddy, Vic Wertz and Hoot Evers connected for circuit smashes.

Four Tigers were selected and played in the major league All-Star Game at Chicago's Comiskey Park on July 11. Kell went 0-for-6 at third base while Evers was 0-for-2 with one walk, playing right field. Art Houtteman pitched three innings, allowing one run and three hits. Ted Gray was tagged for the same stats in one and one-third innings of mound duty as the National Leaguers edged the American stars, 4-3, in a thrilling 14-inning contest.

Billy Goodman of the Boston Red Sox won the American League batting title with a .354 average. George Kell was runner-up with a .340 mark. Hoot Evers batted .323, Vic Wertz .308, John Groth .306, Johnny Lipon .293 and Don Kolloway .289 for the Tigers.

Art Houtteman posted a 19-12 pitching record, Dizzy Trout was 13-5, Fred Hutchinson 17-8 and Hal Newhouser 15-13.

Kell led the league's third basemen in fielding with .982, Evers paced the outfielders on .997 and pitcher Trout was flawless, handling 58 chances without an error for best showing among the league's hurlers.

Red Rolfe was named major league manager of the year by The Sporting News.

Jim Campbell was named business manager at the Detroit-owned Thomasville, Georgia club. The Georgia-Florida League team's Municipal Stadium was ravaged by fire five hours after the April 15 season opener, completely destroying the playing facilities.

The Thomasville home schedule was shifted to the opponents' ballparks until temporary stands were constructed.

BATTING RECORDS

	B	G	AB	R	H	HR	SB	AVE	RBI
Kell, George	R	157	641	114	218	8	3	.340	101
Evers, Hoot	R	143	526	100	170	21	5	.323	103
Keller, Charlie	L	50	51	7	16	2	0	.314	16
Wertz, Vic	L	149	559	99	172	27	0	.308	123
Groth, John	R	157	566	95	173	12	1	.306	85
Lipon, John	R	147	601	104	176	2	9	.293	63
Kolloway, Don	R	125	467	55	135	6	1	.289	62
Priddy, Jerry	R	157	618	104	171	13	2	.277	75
Berry, Neil	R	38	39	9	10	0	0	.256	7
Ginsberg, Joe	L	36	95	12	22	0	1	.232	12
Swift, Bob	R	67	132	14	30	2	0	.227	9
Robinson, Aaron	L	107	283	37	64	9	0	.226	37
Kryhoski, Dick	L	53	169	20	37	4	0	.219	19
Mullin, Pat	L	69	142	16	31	6	1	.218	23
Lake, Eddie	R	20	7	3	0	0	0	.000	1

Less than 10 games: Frank House and Paul Campbell.

Statistics

PITCHING RECORDS

	T	G	IP	W	L	PCT	ERA
Houtteman, Art.................................	R	41	275	19	12	.613	3.53
Trucks, Virgil...................................	R	7	48	3	1	.750	3.54
Trout, Dizzy....................................	R	34	185	13	5	.722	3.75
Hutchinson, Fred.............................	R	39	232	17	8	.680	3.96
Newhouser, Hal...............................	L	35	214	15	13	.536	4.33
Gray, Ted..	L	27	149	10	7	.588	4.41
White, Hal.......................................	R	42	111	9	6	.600	4.54
Calvert, Paul...................................	R	32	51	2	2	.500	6.35

Less than 45 innings: Hank Borowy, Saul Rogovin, Marlin Stuart and Ray Herbert. Bill Connelly was in 2 games with Chicago and 2 with Detroit.

June 23, 1950

On June 23, 1950, the Tigers and Yankees played one of the most dramatic games of all time. The Yankees got off to a 6-0 lead. In the fourth inning, Dizzy Trout hit a grand slam homer; then Jerry Priddy homered, George Kell singled and came home on Vic Wertz' homer. Hoot Evers hit the fourth home run of the inning for the Tigers and they led 8-6. The Yankees came back and led 9-8 when, with one on, Hoot Evers got his second home run of the game in the ninth (this one was inside the park) and the Tigers won, 10-9. All runs for both teams had come from home runs: the Yankees had six homers and the Tigers five.

For Happy Holidays...
"It's gotta be a HoneyBaked™ brand ham."

It's a cut above the imitations!

- Hickory-smoked
- Fully-cooked for 30 hours
- Spiral-sliced around the bone
- Topped with crunchy glaze
- Ready-to-serve
- Perfect for personal and corporate gifts

*"So Good
It Will 'Haunt' You
'Til It's Gone"*®

AVAILABLE ONLY AT HONEYBAKED™ STORES

DETROIT
3741 Fenkell
(313) 862-8622

LIVONIA
31450 W. Five Mile Road
(313) 525-2994

BIRMINGHAM
31190 Southfield Road
(313) 540-0404

ROSEVILLE
29888 Gratiot
(313) 775-7900

DEARBORN HEIGHTS
23300 Ford Road
(313) 274-9600

WEST BLOOMFIELD
33270 W. Fourteen Mile Road
(313) 851-2400

TROY
1081 E. Long Lake Road
(313) 689-4890

TAYLOR
23143 Eureka Road
(313) 374-2600

GRAND RAPIDS
3756 28th Street, S.E.
(616) 957-3430

To send HONEYBAKED brand hams anywhere in the continental U.S.A., call our toll-free numbers: In Michigan: 1-800-732-HAMS — Elsewhere: 1-800-892-HAMS.

HONEYBAKED®
The *original* spiral-sliced ham...since 1957.

1951

FINAL STANDINGS

	W	L	PCT
New York	98	56	.636
Cleveland	93	61	.604
Boston	87	67	.565
Chicago	81	73	.526
DETROIT	73	81	.474
Philadelphia	70	84	.455
Washington	62	92	.403
St. Louis	52	102	.338

Manager: Red Rolfe

Baseball elected a new Commissioner, Ford C. Frick, who had been the National League president. He succeeded Happy Chandler, who resigned on July 15 after being denied an extension of his contract by a minority group of major league owners.

The 1951 season was a most disappointing one for Detroit sports fans. The Tigers lost pitchers Art Houtteman and Ray Herbert to the U.S. armed forces. Hal Newhouser went on the disabled list in July due to a sore arm. Hoot Evers languished in a season-long batting slump, dropping 99 points to a dismal .224 average.

The Tigers slipped to below the .500 mark on a 73-81 record for a fifth place result for Red Rolfe's team, 25 games behind Casey Stengel's pennant-winning New York Yankees.

Pitcher Gene Bearden was purchased from the Washington Senators. Then in mid-May, the Tigers traded pitcher Saul Rogovin to the Chicago White Sox for pitcher Bob Cain. In August, the Tigers sold catcher Aaron Robinson to the Boston Red Sox.

Hoot Evers came within two games of tying the American League record of 120 consecutive errorless games for outfielders when he fumbled a single for an extra base on April 21 at Chicago's Comiskey Park.

The Tigers were victimized on a no-hit pitching gem by Cleveland's fireballing Bob Feller on July 1 at Cleveland's Municipal Stadium in a 2-1 loss.

Hoot Evers temporarily emerged from his batting slump on July 7 with a perfect 5-for-5 performance against the Cleveland Indians. The four singles and a double helped the Tigers win, 13-3 at Briggs Stadium. Two months later, Johnny Lipon duplicated Evers' 5-for-5 exploit in an 8-6 victory over Philadelphia on September 18 at Shibe Park.

The Tigers hosted the major league All-Star Game on July 10 at Briggs Stadium and had three representatives in the midsummer classic: George Kell, Vic Wertz and Fred Hutchinson.

The National League used home run power to win 8-3. Stan Musial, Bob Elliott, Gil Hodges and Ralph Kiner slammed homers for the winners while

Kell and Wertz connected for home runs in a losing cause. Hutchinson was tagged for three runs and three hits in three innings of mound duty.

On August 10, Charlie Gehringer returned to baseball after nine years of absence from the game—this time to the Detroit Tigers' front office as vice president and general manager succeeding Billy Evans. Muddy Ruel was appointed minor league director.

St. Louis Browns' new owner Bill Veeck displayed a flair for showmanship by signing Eddie Gaedel, a 3-foot seven-inch midget, to a player's contract. On August 19, Gaedel made his big-league debut and only appearance in a game against the Detroit Tigers at Sportsman's Park. Manager Zach Taylor called Gaedel to pinch-hit and Tigers' pitcher Bob Cain walked him on four pitches.

Philadelphia's Ferris Fain won the American League batting title with a .344 average. George Kell was the Tigers' lone .300 hitter, attaining the .319 mark. John Groth just missed with a .299.

Virgil Trucks paced the Tiger hurlers with a 13-8, Hutchinson posted a 10-10, Dizzy Trout showed a 9-14, Ted Gray 7-14 and Bob Cain 12-12, including 11-10 in a Tiger uniform.

Kell topped the AL third basemen defensively on a .960 percentage, while Groth led the outfielders with a .993 figure.

BATTING RECORDS

	B	G	AB	R	H	HR	SB	AVE	RBI
Kell, George	R	147	598	92	191	2	10	.319	59
Groth, John	R	118	428	41	128	3	1	.299	49
Kryhoski, Dick	L	119	421	58	121	12	1	.287	57
Wertz, Vic	L	138	501	86	143	27	0	.285	94
Mullin, Pat`	L	110	295	41	83	12	2	.281	51
Lipon, John	R	129	487	56	129	0	7	.265	38
Priddy, Jerry	R	154	584	73	152	8	4	.260	57
Ginsberg, Joe	L	102	304	44	79	8	0	.260	37
Keller, Charlie	L	54	62	6	16	3	0	.258	21
Kolloway, Don	R	78	212	28	54	1	2	.255	17
Souchock, Steve	R	91	188	33	46	11	0	.245	28
Berry, Neil	R	67	157	17	36	0	4	.229	9
Evers, Hoot	R	116	393	47	88	11	5	.224	46
House, Frank	L	18	41	3	9	1	1	.220	4
Robinson, Aaron (36 Det., 26 Bos.)	L	62	156	12	32	2	0	.205	16
Swift, Bob	R	44	104	8	20	0	0	.192	5

Less than 10 games: Russ Sullivan, Al Federoff and Hal Daugherty.

PITCHING RECORDS

	T	G	IP	W	L	PCT	ERA
Rogovin, Saul (5 Det., 22 Chi.)	R	27	217	12	8	.600	2.78
Hutchinson, Fred	R	31	188	10	10	.500	3.69
Stuart, Marlin	R	29	124	4	6	.400	3.77
Newhouser, Hal	L	15	96	6	6	.500	3.94
Trout, Dizzy	R	42	192	9	14	.391	4.03
Gray, Ted	L	34	197	7	14	.333	4.07
Trucks, Virgil	R	37	154	13	8	.619	4.32
Cain, Bob (4 Chi., 35 Det.)	L	39	176	12	12	.500	4.55
Bearden, Gene (1 Wash., 37 Det.)	L	38	109	3	4	.429	4.62
White, Hal	R	38	76	3	4	.429	4.74
Borowy, Hank	R	26	45	2	2	.500	7.00

Less than 45 innings: Ray Herbert, Wayne McLeland, Earl Johnson, Paul Calvert and Dick Marlowe.

YOU'RE SAFE!

With insurance through AAA Michigan.
Auto · Boat · Home · Life

AAA Michigan
You can't do better than all A's.®

Insurance underwritten by the Auto Club Insurance Association and affiliated companies.

1952
FINAL STANDINGS

	W	L	PCT
New York	95	59	.617
Cleveland	93	61	.604
Chicago	81	73	.526
Philadelphia	79	75	.513
Washington	78	76	.506
Boston	76	78	.494
St. Louis	64	90	.416
DETROIT	50	104	.325

Managers: Red Rolfe and Fred Hutchinson

The death of Walter O. Briggs Sr. on January 17, 1952 resulted in a major front office change. The 74-year-old Briggs had directed the Detroit Tigers since 1935 when he bought out his late partner Frank J. Navin. Walter O. "Spike" Briggs Jr. succeeded his father as president of the Detroit club.

The Tigers were very active on the trading market in an effort to improve the team. In preseason activity, Detroit drafted shortstop Alex Garbowski from the Pacific Coast League Sacramento team. Then, a seven-player swap brought outfielder Cliff Mapes, first baseman Ben Taylor, catcher Matt Batts and pitcher Dick Littlefield in exchange for first baseman Dick Kryhoski, pitchers Bob Cain and Gene Bearden to the St. Louis Browns. The Tigers also purchased pitcher Ken Johnson from the Philadelphia Phillies.

Losing their first eight games and 10 out of 13, the Tigers dropped to the league cellar on May 2.

One month later, the Tigers signed outfielder John Hopp, who was released by the New York Yankees. Next day, June 3, the Tigers turned to the Boston Red Sox for help via a nine-player deal.

The Tigers obtained first baseman Walt Dropo, third baseman Fred Hatfield, shortstop Johnny Pesky, outfielder Don Lenhardt and pitcher Bill Wight for third baseman George Kell, shortstop Johnny Lipon, outfielder Hoot Evers, and pitcher Dizzy Trout.

The Tigers' recession continued. On July 5, manager Red Rolfe was relieved of his duties and released. The job was turned over to pitcher Fred Hutchinson.

Detroit's misfortunes lingered on. Second baseman Gerry Priddy broke his ankle. Al Federoff was brought up from the Buffalo team in the International League, replacing injured Priddy.

The Tigers had difficulties getting out of the basement, so general manager Charlie Gehringer arranged another multiplayer waiver transaction with the St. Louis Browns. On August 14, outfielders Vic Wertz and Don Lenhardt, along with pitchers Dick Littlefield and Marlin Stuart, packed their bags for St. Louis, while pitchers Ned Garver, Dave Madison and Bud Black, and outfielder Jim Delsing joined the Tigers.

All the player maneuverings failed to help the Tigers. They won 27 and lost 55 under Hutchinson's guidance and finished in last place for the first time in Detroit history—45 games behind the pennant-winning New York Yankees and 14 games behind seventh place St. Louis Browns.

Despite the losing campaign, the Tigers were involved in several memorable events.

Pitcher Virgil Trucks experienced a roller-coaster season. He lost his first eight games and finished with a frustrating 5-19 record. However, two of his victories were no hitters.

On May 15, Trucks no-hit the Washington Senators at Briggs Stadium, winning 1-0 on Vic Wertz' two-out home run in the ninth inning off Bob Porterfield. Trucks' second no-hitter came on August 25 at New York's Yankee Stadium via another 1-0 victory. Walt Dropo's double and Steve Souchock's single off left-hander Bill Miller in the seventh inning produced the game's lone tally.

Only one Tiger, Vic Wertz, represented Detroit in the major league All-Star Game on July 8 at Philadelphia's Shibe Park. Wertz failed to see action in the five-inning contest, called off because of rain, and won by the National Leaguers, 3-2.

Walt Dropo enjoyed a record two-day batting spree, July 14 and 15. He started his consecutive hitting streak at Yankee Stadium with five singles in five trips off Jim McDonald and Bobby Hogue.

Next stop was a twi-nighter at Washington. Dropo opened with four successive singles off Walt Masterson to make it nine hits in a row.

In the nightcap, Dropo tripled off Bob Porterfield in his initial time at bat. Two innings later, Dropo made it 11-in-a-row with a single off Porterfield. The record-tying hit, a double, came off left-hander Lou Sleater. Dropo was finally stopped on his next time at bat when he fouled out to catcher Mickey Grasso.

Philadelphia's Ferris Fain won the American League batting title on a .327 average. John Groth topped the Tiger regulars with a .284 mark.

Harry Heilmann was voted to Baseball's Hall of Fame by the Baseball Writers Association of America.

Statistics

BATTING RECORDS

	B	G	AB	R	H	HR	SB	AVE	RBI
Sullivan, Russ	L	15	52	7	17	3	1	.327	5
Kuenn, Harvey	R	19	80	2	26	0	2	.325	8
Kell, George (39 Det., 75 Bos.)	R	114	418	52	133	7	0	.311	57
Groth, John	R	141	524	56	149	4	2	.284	51
Priddy, Jerry	R	75	279	37	79	4	1	.283	20
Wertz, Vic (85 Det., 37 St. L.)	L	122	415	68	115	23	1	.277	70
Dropo, Walt (37 Bos., 115 Det.)	R	152	591	69	163	29	2	.276	97
Evers, Hoot (1 Det., 106 Bos.)	R	107	402	53	106	14	5	.264	59
Delsing, Jim (93 St. L., 33 Det.)	L	126	411	48	107	4	4	.260	49
Mullin, Pat	L	97	255	29	64	7	4	.251	35
Souchock, Steve	R	92	265	40	66	13	1	.249	45
Kolloway, Don	R	65	173	19	42	2	0	.243	21
Federoff, Al	R	74	231	14	56	0	1	.242	14
Hatfield, Fred (19 Bos., 112 Det.)	L	131	466	48	112	3	2	.240	28
Lenhardt, Don (30 Bos., 45 Det., 18 St. L.)	R	93	297	41	71	11	0	.239	42
Batts, Matt	R	56	173	11	14	3	1	.237	13
Berry, Neil	R	73	189	22	43	0	1	.228	13
Pesky, John (25 Bos., 69 Det.)	L	94	244	36	55	1	1	.225	11
Ginsberg, Joe	L	113	307	29	68	6	1	.221	36
Lipon, John (39 Det., 79 Bos.)	R	118	370	42	78	0	4	.211	30
Mapes, Cliff	L	86	193	26	38	9	0	.197	23
Hopp, John (15 NY, 42 Det.)	L	57	71	9	14	0	2	.197	5
Lerchen, George	R	14	32	1	5	1	1	.156	3
Swift, Bob	R	28	58	3	8	0	0	.138	4

Less than 10 games: Don Lund, Bill Tuttle, Ben Taylor, Carl Linhart and Alex Garbowski.

PITCHING RECORDS

	T	G	IP	W	L	PCT	ERA
Littlefield, Dick (28 Det., 7 St. L.)	L	35	94	2	6	.250	3.54
Garver, Ned (21 St. L., 1 Det.)	R	22	158	8	10	.444	3.59
White, Hal	R	41	63	1	8	.111	3.71
Newhouser, Hal	L	25	154	9	9	.500	3.74
Wight, Bill (10 Bos., 23 Det.)	L	33	168	7	10	.412	3.75
Trout, Dizzy (10 Det., 26 Bos.)	R	36	161	10	13	.435	3.91
Trucks, Virgil	R	35	197	5	19	.208	3.97
Gray, Ted	L	35	224	12	17	.414	4.14
Hoeft, Billy	L	34	125	2	7	.222	4.32
Houtteman, Art	R	35	221	8	20	.286	4.36
Stuart, Marlin (30 Det., 12 St. L.)	R	42	117	4	4	.500	4.77
Madison, Dave (31 St. L., 10 Det.)	R	41	93	5	3	.625	4.94

Less than 45 innings: Fred Hutchinson, Wayne McLeland, Ken Johnson, Bill Black and Dick Marlowe.

John Laffrey's
STEAKS on the HEARTH

• **AT 7 MILE & TELEGRAPH** •

CHOICE...STEAKS, CHOPS, SEAFOOD
& CATCH OF THE DAY

TRY LAFFREY'S FAMOUS "HOUSE
DRESSING" AT THE SALAD BAR!

LUNCHEONS SERVED...MON. THRU FRI.
DINNERS SERVED...
TILL 11 PM MON. THRU THURS.
TIL MIDNIGHT FRI. AND SAT.
5 PM TIL 10 PM SUNDAYS

*Banquet Facilities
Up to 65 People*

538-4688

24201 W. 7 Mile Rd.
At Telegraph Rd. Detroit

MC,VISA,AMEX,DC
Valet Parking

1953

FINAL STANDINGS

	W	L	PCT
New York	99	52	.656
Cleveland	92	62	.597
Chicago	89	65	.578
Boston	84	69	.549
Washington	76	76	.500
DETROIT	60	94	.390
Philadelphia	59	95	.383
St. Louis	54	100	.351

Manager: Fred Hutchinson

The shake-up of Detroit Tigers player personnel continued in 1953, beginning on two preseason deals with the St. Louis Browns.

First, the Tigers sent outfielder Cliff Mapes and infielder Neil Berry for outfielder Jake Crawford. Then, Detroit traded outfielder John Groth, along with pitchers Virgil Trucks and Hal White for outfielder Bob Nieman, infielder Owen Friend and catcher J. W. Porter.

Detroit obtained infielder Billy Hitchcock from the Philadelphia A's for infielder Don Kolloway. They also purchased third baseman George Freese from the St. Louis Browns.

Additional player changes were made during the season. The Tigers purchased pitcher Earl Harrist from the Chicago White Sox in May. Then, in a major trade on June 15, the Tigers received three pitchers: Steve Gromek, Al Aber and Dick Weik, along with infielder Ray Boone from the Cleveland Indians for pitchers Art Houtteman and Bill Wight, catcher Joe Ginsberg and infielder Owen Friend.

On June 18, the Boston Red Sox blasted the three new Tiger pitchers, Gromek, Weik and Harrist, for 17 runs in the seventh inning at Fenway park. Gene Stephens connected for three hits in the explosive merry-go-round frame as the Red Sox rolled to an easy 23-3 victory.

In a July waiver transaction, the Tigers purchased pitcher Ralph Branca from the Brooklyn Dodgers.

Shortstop Harvey Kuenn was the lone Tiger representative in the major league All-Star Game on July 14 at Cincinnati's Crosley Field. He pinch-hit for pitcher Allie Reynolds and lined out to right field. The Nationals won the game, 5-1.

Detroit invested $120,000 in the acquisition of three bonus babies off the sandlots: Bob Miller, a 17-year-old left-handed pitcher, signed a three-year pact for a reported $60,000; 18-year-old outfielder Al Kaline from Baltimore, Maryland received $35,000; and Reno Bertoia, an 18-year-old infielder from Windsor, Canada, agreed to a $25,000 bonus.

The trio saw limited action during the season. Miller appeared in 13 games, Kaline in 30 games, mainly in pinch-hitting and late-inning outfield replacement roles, and Bertoia batted only once while filling in at second base.

Detroit won only 27 out of their first 87 games, then were victorious 33 times in the remaining 67 to finish in sixth place, 40 1/2 games behind the pennant-winning New York Yankees.

The 35-year-old Mickey Vernon of the Washington Senators grabbed the American League batting honors with a .337 average. Kuenn led the Tigers with .308 and topped the American League in hits with a 209 total. Kuenn also gained the American League's Rookie of the Year award in balloting by the Baseball Writers Association of America.

The BBWAA Voted Al Simmons to Baseball's Hall of Fame in Cooperstown, New York.

BATTING RECORDS

	B	G	AB	R	H	HR	SB	AVE	RBI
Kuenn, Harvey	R	155	679	94	209	2	6	.308	48
Souchock, Steve	R	89	278	29	84	11	5	.302	46
Boone, Ray (34 Clev., 101 Det.)	R	135	497	94	147	26	3	.296	114
Pesky, John	L	103	308	43	90	2	3	.292	24
Ginsberg, Joe (18 Det., 46 Clev.)	L	64	162	16	47	0	0	.290	13
Delsing, Jim	L	138	479	77	138	11	1	.288	62
Nieman, Bob	R	142	508	72	143	15	0	.281	69
Batts, Matt	R	116	374	38	104	6	2	.278	42
Mullin, Pat	L	79	97	11	26	4	0	.268	17
Carswell, Frank	R	16	15	2	4	0	0	.267	2
Lund, Don	R	131	421	51	108	9	3	.257	47
Hatfield, Fred	L	109	311	41	79	3	3	.254	19
Sullivan, Russ	L	23	72	7	18	1	0	.250	6
Kaline, Al	R	30	28	9	7	1	1	.250	2
Dropo, Walt	R	152	606	61	150	13	2	.248	96
Priddy, Jerry	R	65	196	14	46	1	1	.235	24
Bucha, John	R	60	158	17	35	1	1	.222	14
Hitchcock, Billy	R	22	38	8	8	0	0	.211	0
Friend, Owen (31 Det., 34 Clev.)	R	65	164	17	33	5	0	.201	23

Less than 10 games: Bob Swift, John Baumgartner, George Freese and Reno Bertoia.

Bob Lemon, of the Cleveland Indians, pitched a no-hitter against the Detroit Tigers on June 30, 1948 at Briggs Stadium. It was the first no-hitter pitched at night in the American League.

Statistics

PITCHING RECORDS

	T	G	IP	W	L	PCT	ERA
Branca, Ralph	R	17	102	4	7	.364	4.15
Gromek, Steve (5 Clev., 19 Det.)	R	24	137	7	9	.438	4.40
Garver, Ned	R	30	198	11	11	.500	4.45
Gray, Ted	L	30	176	10	15	.400	4.60
Houtteman, Art (16 Det., 22 Clev.)	R	38	178	9	13	.409	4.60
Scarborough, Ray (25 NY, 13 Det.)	R	38	75	2	4	.333	4.68
Aber, Al (6 Clev., 17 Det.)	L	23	73	5	4	.556	4.68
Hoeft, Billy	L	29	198	9	14	.391	4.82
Herbert, Ray	R	43	88	4	6	.400	5.22
Marlowe, Dick	R	42	120	6	7	.462	5.25
Wight, Bill (13 Det., 20 Clev.)	L	33	52	2	4	.333	6.23
Madison, Dave	R	32	62	3	4	.429	6.82

Less than 45 innings: Hal Newhouser, Bob Miller, Dick Weik, Fred Hutchinson, Hal Erickson, Paul Foytack and Milt Jordan. Earl Harrist was in 7 games with Chicago and 8 games with Detroit.

Detroit News Dec. 22-1991

Obituaries

Wilma Garner was seamstress for Tigers

By Kate DeSmet
THE DETROIT NEWS

The Detroit Tigers won the World Series in 1968 with pitching, hitting and base running. They also won it in uniforms tailored by Wilma Martin Garner, a widowed seamstress with only one arm.

Mrs. Garner died Thursday, Dec. 19, 1991 of cancer at her home in Berkley. She was 82.

"She was a remarkable woman," said her son, John Martin of Huntington Woods.

Martin said his mother's right hand was amputated when she was a toddler. Since she was born right-handed, she was forced to learn to do everything with her left hand.

"She was determined to sew and paint and not let her amputation be a handicap for her," Martin said.

Mrs. Garner, the mother of three children, became a professional seamstress during World War II. She tailored military uniforms for soldiers and high-ranking naval officers in Detroit and Washington, D.C.

Later, after becoming a widow, she was hired by the Tigers to repair uniforms and tailor them to individual players. She worked for the team from 1964 to 1972. Although the Tigers wanted her to accompany them on road games, Mrs. Garner declined.

"She thought she was too old for that, and she still had a daughter living at home," Martin said.

Her favorite Tiger was pitcher Denny McLain, he said.

"When she started doing their uniforms, she became a baseball fan for the first time in her life," Martin said. "And the few times she went to the games she really liked watching McLain."

Mrs. Garner was also a member of the Daughters of the American Revolution (DAR), Ezra Palmer chapter in Pleasant Ridge.

She is survived by her son, Frank; a sister and two grandchildren.

A funeral service is scheduled for 11 a.m. Monday at the William Sullivan & Son Funeral Home, 705 W. 11 Mile, in Royal Oak.

Mrs. Garner

the best deals. Period.

Last Minute

SALE!

LIFETIME PRICE PROTECTION GUARANTEE*

It's FREE if we don't beat your best price...for life!

1954

FINAL STANDINGS

	W	L	PCT
Cleveland	111	43	.721
New York	103	51	.669
Chicago	94	60	.610
Boston	69	85	.448
DETROIT	68	86	.442
Washington	66	88	.429
Baltimore	54	100	.351
Philadelphia	51	103	.331

Manager: Fred Hutchinson

The 1954 Detroit Tigers started off with a good showing and played .500 ball in May, then faltered and finished in fifth place on a 68-86 record. They trailed the amazing pennant-winning Cleveland Indians by 43 games, who authored a fabulous record-setting 111-43 won-loss story.

The Tigers traded catcher Matt Batts to the Chicago White Sox for catcher Robert "Red" Wilson on May 29. Ten days later, the Tigers sent catcher John Bucha, first baseman Charles Kress and minor league pitcher Ernie Nevel to the Brooklyn Dodgers for first baseman Wayne Belardi. Just before the trading decline, the Tigers sold infielder Johnny Pesky to the Washington Senators.

Ray Boone and Harvey Kuenn represented the Detroit Tigers in the major league All-Star Game at Cleveland's Municipal Stadium on July 13.

Boone started at third base, collected one hit in four trips, a home run off Robin Roberts. Kuenn failed to see action. The Americans won an 11-9 slugfest.

On July 29, the Tigers reacquired outfielder Hoot Evers in a waiver purchase from the New York Giants.

Cleveland second baseman Roberta Avila won the American League batting crown with a .341 average. Harvey Kuenn paced the Tigers with .306, Ray Boone hit .295 and Al Kaline, in his first year as a regular outfielder, batted .276.

Steve Gromek won seven of his first eight games en route to an 18-16 mark with a 2.74 e.r.a., fifth best in the league. Ned Garver posted a 14-11 record with a 2.82 e.r.a.

Manager Fred Hutchinson was released at the end of the season and Bucky Harris was named manager for 1955, after getting his walking papers from the Washington Senators, who finished sixth, two games behind the Tigers.

BATTING RECORDS

	B	G	AB	R	H	HR	SB	AVE	RBI
Kuenn, Harvey	R	155	656	81	201	5	9	.306	48
Boone, Ray	R	148	543	76	160	20	4	.295	85
Hatfield, Fred	L	81	218	31	64	2	4	.294	25
Dropo, Walt	R	107	320	27	90	4	0	.281	44
Kaline, Al	R	138	504	42	139	4	9	.276	43
Wilson, Red (8 Chi., 54 Det.)	R	62	190	24	52	3	3	.274	23
Tuttle, Bill	R	147	530	64	141	7	5	.266	58
Nieman, Bob	R	91	251	24	66	8	0	.263	35
House, Frank	L	114	352	35	88	9	2	.250	38
Delsing, Jim	L	122	371	39	92	6	4	.248	38
Pesky, John (20 Det., 49 Wash.)	L	69	175	22	43	1	1	.246	10
Bolling, Frank	R	117	368	46	87	6	3	.236	38
Batts, Matt (12 Det., 55 Chi.)	R	67	179	17	42	3	0	.235	24
Belardi, Wayne	L	88	250	27	58	11	1	.232	24
King, Chick	R	11	28	4	6	0	0	.214	3
Kress, Charles	L	24	37	4	7	0	0	.189	3
Souchok, Steve	R	25	39	6	7	3	1	.179	8
Evers, Hoot (6 Bos., 30 Det.)	R	36	68	6	11	0	1	.162	5
Bertoia, Reno	R	54	37	13	6	1	1	.162	2
Lund, Don	R	35	54	4	7	0	1	.130	3

Less than 10 games: Al Lakeman, George Bullard and Walter Streuli.

PITCHING RECORDS

	T	G	IP	W	L	PCT	ERA
Miller, Bob	L	32	70	1	1	.500	2.44
Gromek, Steve	R	36	253	18	16	.529	2.74
Garver, Ned	R	35	246	14	11	.560	2.82
Zuverink, George	R	35	203	9	13	.409	3.59
Aber, Al	L	32	125	5	11	.313	3.96
Marlowe, Dick	R	38	84	5	4	.556	4.18
Hoeft, Billy	L	34	175	7	15	.318	4.58
Branca, Ralph (17 Det., 5 NY)	R	22	58	4	3	.571	5.12
Gray, Ted	L	19	72	3	5	.375	5.38
Herbert, Ray	R	42	84	3	6	.333	5.89

Less than 45 innings: Dick Weik, Dick Donovan and Frank Lary.

1955

FINAL STANDINGS

	W	L	PCT
New York	96	58	.623
Cleveland	93	61	.604
Chicago	91	63	.591
Boston	84	70	.545
DETROIT	79	75	.513
Kansas City	63	91	.409
Baltimore	57	97	.370
Washington	53	101	.344

Manager: Bucky Harris

No one knew quite what to expect from the Tigers in 1955. The experts picked them to finish anywhere from third to seventh. They were, for the most part, a young club with a new manager, Bucky Harris.

Harris, who had previously managed the Tigers from 1929 through 1933, was rehired during the off-season when Fred Hutchinson resigned. Harris, who had piloted the Washington Senators to fifth and sixth place finishes in the previous two years, and who had never finished higher than fifth during his first tour of duty at the Tiger helm, was expected to lift the Tigers into the first division.

And, in fact, Detroit did enjoy its most exciting season since 1950 when the Tigers finished second. The team spent much of the first half of the season in fourth place, teasing its fans with title hopes, however faint, as late as the first week in August.

That's when the young Tigers fell flat. Forced to duel the pennant-minded Cleveland Indians and Chicago White Sox during a rugged two-week stretch, the New York Yankees dropped 10 of 13 decisions to fall permanently out of contention and into fifth place.

Still, the '55 season was not without its bright spots—most notably a young outfielder named Al Kaline—as the Tigers topped the .500 mark (79-75) for the first time since 1950.

Kaline, well aware that it had been his gifted glove that had kept him in the lineup the year before, entered the 1955 season with one goal in mind: to beef up his performance with the bat. At the time, there were still those who wondered if the shy, slender young man would ever hit with enough power and authority to be a major league outfield star.

Kaline's goals going into 1955 were relatively modest. He wanted to hit .300 and he wanted to increase his extra base hits. Little did he or anyone else realize he would be so dramatically successful.

Kaline, wearing a new number, 6, started off with a bang, batting .453 during the month of April, and smacking five home runs, one more than he had hit during all of 1954. Overnight, people began likening Kaline to the great Joe DiMaggio.

What's more, Kaline did not cool off at the plate as the weather warmed up. He continued to hit with remarkable regularity in May and June and early July. And his efforts did not go overlooked outside of Detroit.

When the time came for the fans across the country to vote for the American League All-Stars, Kaline was elected the starting rightfielder by a whopping margin. Only two of the day's superstars—Yogi Berra of the New York Yankees and Roy Campanella of the Brooklyn Dodgers—attracted more votes from the nation's fans.

Kaline played all 12 innings of the All-Star Game and, although the Tigers dropped out of the pennant race shortly thereafter, Al continued his quest of the batting crown. In spite of an early September slump, Kaline hit .340 for the season, the best batting mark in the American League by 21 points. He also whacked 27 homers and drove in 102 runs. At the tender age of 20, he became the youngest man ever to win the AL batting crown, edging Tiger immortal Ty Cobb for that distinction by one day.

Harvey Kuenn, whom many people thought might overtake Kaline in his pursuit of the batting title, finished the season at .306, while Ray Boone tied the Boston Red Sox' Jackie Jensen for league-leadership in runs batted in with 116.

Lefthander Billy Hoeft, finally living up to expectations, won 16 games and lost 7 to lead the pitching staff, which included Frank Lary, a young righthander (14-15) who would soon acquire a reputation as a Yankee killer.

Prior to the 1955 season, the Tigers sold outfielder Hoot Evers to the Baltimore Orioles, and during the year they purchased outfielder Charlie Maxwell from those same Birds.

Following the season they traded outfielder Bubba Phillips, who had batted .234, to the Chicago White Sox for pitcher Virgil Trucks, who had toiled for the Tigers from 1941 through 1953, with time out for military service.

⚾ ⚾ ⚾

Al Kaline had many great games as a Tiger during his illustrious 22-year career, but probably the finest was on April 17, 1955. Al hit three home runs, two in one inning and had four straight hits. He drove in six runs as the Tigers beat Kansas City 16-0 at Briggs Stadium behind Steve Gromek.

BATTING RECORDS

	B	G	AB	R	H	HR	SB	AVE	RBI
Kaline, Al	R	152	588	121	200	27	6	.340	102
Phillips, Jack	R	55	117	15	37	1	0	.316	20
Kuenn, Harvey	R	145	620	101	190	8	8	.306	62
Boone, Ray	R	135	500	61	142	20	1	.284	116
Torgeson, Earl	L	89	300	58	85	9	9	.283	50
Tuttle, Bill	R	154	603	102	168	14	6	.279	78
Fain, Ferris (58 Det., 56 Clev.)	L	114	258	32	67	2	5	.260	31
House, Frank	L	102	328	37	85	15	0	.259	53
Maxwell, Charlie (4 Balt., 55 Det.)	L	59	113	19	29	7	0	.257	18
Delsing, Jim	L	114	356	49	85	10	2	.239	60
Porter, J. W.	R	24	55	6	13	0	0	.236	3
Phillips, Bubba	R	95	184	18	43	3	2	.234	23
Hatfield, Fred	L	122	413	51	96	8	3	.232	33
Wilson, Red	R	78	241	26	53	2	1	.220	17
Malmberg, Harry	R	67	208	25	45	0	0	.216	19
Bertoia, Reno	R	38	68	13	14	1	0	.206	10
Small, Jim	L	12	4	2	0	0	0	.000	0

Less than 10 games: Steve Souchock, Walter Streuli, Ron Stamford, Wayne Belardi and Chick King.

PITCHING RECORDS

	T	G	IP	W	L	PCT	ERA
Hoeft, Billy	L	32	220	16	7	.696	2.99
Lary, Frank	R	36	235	14	15	.483	3.10
Zuverink, George (14 Det., 28 Balt.)	R	42	115	4	8	.333	3.37
Aber, Al	L	39	80	6	3	.667	3.38
Garver, Ned	R	33	231	12	16	.429	3.97
Gromek, Steve	R	28	181	13	10	.565	3.98
Birrer, Babe	R	36	80	4	3	.571	4.16
Maas, Duke	R	18	87	5	6	.455	4.86
Foytack, Paul	R	22	50	0	1	.000	5.22
Bunning, Jim	R	15	51	3	5	.375	6.35

Less than 45 innings: Leo Cristante, Dick Marlowe, Bill Black, Van Fletcher, Ben Flowers, Bob Miller, Bill Froats, and Bob Schultz. Joe Coleman appeared in 6 games with Baltimore and 17 with Detroit.

1956
FINAL STANDINGS

	W	L	PCT
New York	97	57	.630
Cleveland	88	66	.571
Chicago	85	69	.552
Boston	84	70	.545
DETROIT	82	72	.532
Baltimore	69	85	.448
Washington	59	95	.383
Kansas City	52	102	.338

Manager: Bucky Harris

The 1956 season was a particularly frustrating one for the Tigers and their faithful followers.

After all, the team, mired in the second division for the previous five years, did continue to improve, this time winning 82 games while losing 72. Furthermore, the Tigers boasted not one or two but four .300 hitters. The big guns in the Bengal attack were Harvey Kuenn at .332, Charley Maxwell at .326, Al Kaline at .314 and Ray Boone at .308 as the Tigers led the league in batting with a .279 mark.

Maxwell, who seemed to excel on Sundays, broke the club record for home runs by a left-handed slugger with 28 while Kaline continued to flex his newly found muscles by smacking 27 home runs and driving in 128 runs, second best in the AL.

The pitching improved, too, as Frank Lary, in only his second season, led the league with 21 victories, while losing 13, and Billy Hoeft was 20-14. Paul Foytack, Kaline's new roommate, was a respectable 15-13, but the failure of Ned Garver hampered by a sore elbow, to win a single game proved costly.

The Tigers even managed to win 12 of their 22 games against the hated New York Yankees, marking only the second time under Casey Stengel's tutelage that the Bronx Bombers had failed to win a season series against any American League foe.

In spite of those accomplishments, the Tigers finished fifth again—15 games behind the Yankees—in a campaign that was marred by off-the-field strife.

Ownership of the Detroit ball club had been in the hands of the trustees for the estate of the late Walter O. Briggs Sr. since Briggs died in 1952. And when those trustees decreed that the team should be sold, a spirited bidding battle ensued.

Eight separate syndicates submitted secret bids prior to the July 2 deadline and four of those bids exceeded $5 million, which at the time was a record price for a major league franchise.

Among those men who headed interested syndicates were Bill Veeck, the colorful, controversial former owner of the Cleveland Indians and St. Louis

Browns; Baltimore and Detroit beer-maker Jerry Hoffberger; Jack Kent Cooke, owner of the Toronto entry in the International League; and Chicago-based insurance man Charley Finley, who later obtained control of the Kansas City—Oakland Athletics.

The situation was a sticky one because the president of the Tigers, Walter O. "Spike" Briggs Jr. wanted to purchase his late father's franchise outright from his sisters. However, as one of the trustees of the estate, Spike was not permitted to "buy the club from himself."

In fact, were it not for the pending sale of the ball club and the uncertainty over who the new owners would be, manager Bucky Harris probably would have lost his job in midseason.

In the midst of a 10-game losing streak in late June, Spike Briggs lashed out at nearly everyone connected with his team, prompting coach Joe Gordon to resign.

Thwarted in his efforts to buy the Tigers himself, Spike ignored a bid of $5,250,000 from Veeck, whom he did not personally favor, and went to bat at a trustee meeting for an 11-man syndicate headed by Michigan radio executives Fred Knorr and John Fetzer.

Briggs argued that the two Michigan men had the local background needed to run the club properly and that they had agreed to manage the franchise under the principles established by the senior Briggs.

Besides, under the ownership of the Knorr-Fetzer group—whose winning bid included $4.2 million in cash and $1.3 million payable in five years at four percent interest—Spike Briggs would be retained as executive vice president and general manager of the ball club.

The new ownership was scheduled to take control after the 1956 season was complete but Knorr, who was named club president, let everyone connected with the Tiger club know he expected a stronger, more aggressive effort from all concerned.

That kind of talk bothered some of the players, but most admitted the idea of more hustle and aggressiveness in the organization seemed to be a sound one. And, from the All-Star break until the end of the season, the Tigers boasted the best record in the league—48 wins against 30 defeats. They were the so-called "second-half champs" but their surge of victories had come too late to save them from their third consecutive fifth place finish.

Statistics

BATTING RECORDS

	B	G	AB	R	H	HR	SB	AVE	RBI
Kuenn, Harvey	R	146	591	96	196	12	9	.332	88
Maxwell, Charlie	L	141	500	96	163	28	1	.326	87
Small, Jim	L	58	91	13	29	0	0	.319	10
Kaline, Al	R	153	617	96	194	27	7	.314	128
Boone, Ray	R	131	481	77	148	25	0	.308	81
Phillips, Jack	R	67	224	31	66	1	1	.295	20
Wilson, Red	R	78	228	32	66	7	2	.289	38
Bolling, Frank	R	102	366	53	103	7	6	.281	45
Belardi, Wayne	L	79	154	24	43	6	0	.279	15
Torgeson, Earl	L	117	318	61	84	12	6	.264	42
Hatfield, Fred (8 Det., 106 Chi.)	L	114	333	48	87	7	1	.261	35
Tuttle, Bill	R	140	546	61	138	9	5	.253	65
House, Frank	L	94	321	44	77	10	1	.240	44
Kennedy, Bob (8 Chi., 69 Det.)	R	77	190	17	42	4	2	.221	22
Brideweser, Jim (10 Chi., 70 Det.)	R	80	167	23	36	0	3	.216	11
Hicks, Buddy	B	26	47	5	10	0	0	.213	5
Bertoia, Reno	R	22	66	7	12	1	0	.182	5
Porter, J. W.	R	14	21	0	2	0	0	.095	3
Delsing, Jim (10 Det., 55 Chi.)	L	65	53	11	5	0	1	.094	2

Less than 10 games: Walter Streuli, Chick King and Charlie Lau.

PITCHING RECORDS

	T	G	IP	W	L	PCT	ERA
Lary, Frank	R	41	294	21	13	.618	3.15
Aber, Al	L	42	63	4	4	.500	3.43
Foytack, Paul	R	43	256	15	13	.536	3.59
Bunning, Jim	R	15	53	5	1	.833	3.74
Trucks, Virgil	R	22	120	6	5	.545	3.83
Hoeft, Billy	L	38	248	20	14	.588	4.06
Masterson, Walt	R	35	50	1	1	.500	4.14
Gromek, Steve	R	40	141	8	6	.571	4.28
Maas, Duke	R	26	63	0	7	.000	6.57

Less than 45 innings: Ned Garver, Jim Brady, Gene Host, Pete Wojey, Bob Miller, Bill Black and Hal Woodeshick. Dick Marlowe appeared in 7 games with Detroit and 1 with Chicago.

TOM HOLZER

TOM HOLZER FORD, INC.
39300 W. Ten Mile Rd.
Farmington Hills, MI 48018

Phone
(313) 474-1234

⚾ ⚾ ⚾

In this day and age when starting pitchers rarely go the route, it is hard to imagine two pitchers pitching 20 innings. On May 24, 1929, the Tigers and the Chicago White Sox battled 21 innings before the Tigers won 6 to 5. Ted Lyons pitched the entire 21 innings for Chicago and George Uhle pitched 20 innings for the Tigers. The Tigers won the game in the 21st when Roy Johnson scored the winning run on Charlie Gehringer's long fly. In the Tiger lineup that day were Gehringer, Johnson, Dale Alexander, Harry Rice, Rocky Stone, Heinie Schuble, Bob Fothergill and Marty McManus among others. The White Sox had Willie Kamm, Bill Cissell, Carl Reynolds and Bud Clancy. The score had been tied from the sixth inning on. George Uhle, the winning pitcher, recently passed away in Cleveland, Ohio and Ted Lyons is now living in his native Louisiana.

1957
FINAL STANDINGS

	W	L	PCT
New York	98	56	.636
Chicago	90	64	.584
Boston	82	72	.532
DETROIT	78	76	.506
Baltimore	76	76	.500
Cleveland	76	77	.497
Kansas City	59	94	.386
Washington	55	99	.357

Manager: Jack Tighe

The Tigers had high hopes when the 1957 season dawned. Under new manager Jack Tighe, who had replaced Bucky Harris, they saw themselves as legitimate pennant contenders for the first time in many years.

In truth, their chances of catching the mighty New York Yankees were slim. The New Yorkers simply were stronger and deeper than any other team in the league. But some of the other league powers, namely Cleveland, Chicago and Boston, seemed to be on their way down while the Tigers were definitely headed upwards.

The signing and development of bonus babies Harvey Kuenn and Al Kaline had been the beginning of building a winning nucleus. In addition, they had infielders Ray Boone, Frank Bolling and Reno Bertoia, outfielders Charlie Maxwell and Bill Tuttle, catcher Frank House, plus pitchers Jim Bunning, Frank Lary, Paul Foytack, and Billy Hoeft. The Tigers seemed set to finally give their long-suffering fans something substantial to cheer about.

What the Tigers did not count on was a prolonged early-season slump by several of their key players, a problem which was compounded and, perhaps, in part caused by more front office turmoil.

The trouble began during the winter when Spike Briggs sent Al Kaline a contract calling for a small raise. Kaline, who had finished strong in '56 to put together two solid seasons back-to-back, felt he deserved a larger increase, so he sent the contract back, unsigned.

A few days later, speaking at a sports banquet in Detroit, Briggs publicly attacked Kaline. "Al thinks he's as good as Mickey Mantle and wants more money than Mantle," Briggs declared. "I don't agree with him and he isn't going to get it."

When Kaline heard of Briggs' remarks, he was furious. "I definitely didn't ask for Mantle's pay," Kaline protested. "All I want is a fair raise."

Briggs shrugged the whole incident off, and Kaline soon signed with assistant general manager John McHale for the same amount he had originally requested. But the stage had been set.

After a feeble spring training performance, in which they won only nine games and lost 17, the Tigers started the season slowly. On April 26, Briggs, who had accused the new owners of the Tigers—his employers—of "trying to run the team like a factory," was replaced as general manager. Whether Briggs was fired for his remarks or whether he resigned was never made clear.

In spite of the shake-up in the front office, on the field the Tiger fortunes failed to improve. Kaline and Kuenn continued to struggle at the plate, while Lary and Hoeft, the two aces of the pitching staff, failed to produce. At the All-Star break, Lary owned only four victories and Hoeft had won just once.

Again the Tigers came on strong during the second half of the season, and again it was Kaline who led the way, collecting 17 of his 24 homers during the final 54 games to top the team with a .295 average and 90 rbi.

Bunning, in his first full season in the big leagues, picked up some of the slack on the pitching staff, with 20 victories to tie Billy Pierce of Chicago for the league lead, while losing only eight. Paul Foytack was 14-11. But Lary and Hoeft, who had won 21 and 20 games, respectively, for the Tigers the summer before, this time combined for only 20 victories between them.

Even so, by season's end, the Tigers finally climbed into the first division for the first time since 1950, finishing fourth, a distant 20 games back.

Following the season, on November 20, in one of their biggest deals ever, the Tigers traded outfielders Bill Tuttle and Jim Small, pitchers Duke Maas and John Tsitouris, catcher Frank House, infielder Kent Hadley and a player to be named later to the Kansas City Athletics for infielder Billy Martin—who years later would become the Tigers' manager—outfielders Gus Zernial and Lou Skizas, pitchers Tom Morgan and Maury McDermott, and catcher Charlie Thompson.

BATTING RECORDS

	B	G	AB	R	H	HR	SB	AVE	RBI
Kaline, Al	R	149	577	83	170	23	11	.295	90
Philley, Dave (22 Chi., 65 Det.)	B	87	244	24	72	2	4	.295	25
Torgeson, Earl (30 Det., 86 Chi.)	L	116	301	58	86	8	7	.286	51
Groth, John (55 KC, 38 Det.)	R	93	162	21	45	0	0	.278	18
Kuenn, Harvey	R	151	624	74	173	9	5	.277	44
Maxwell, Charlie	L	138	492	75	136	24	3	.276	82
Bertoia, Reno	R	97	295	28	81	4	2	.275	28
Boone, Ray	R	129	462	48	126	12	1	.273	65
Finigan, Jim	R	64	174	20	47	0	1	.270	17
Bolling, Frank	R	146	576	72	149	15	4	.259	40
House, Frank	L	106	348	31	90	7	1	.259	36
Tuttle, Bill	R	133	451	49	113	5	2	.251	47
Porter, J. W.	R	58	140	14	35	2	0	.250	18
Wilson, Red	R	59	178	21	43	3	2	.242	13
Dittmer, Jack	L	16	22	3	5	0	0	.227	2
Samford, Ron	R	54	91	6	20	0	1	.220	5
Small, Jim	L	36	42	7	9	0	0	.214	0
Olson, Karl (8 Wash., 8 Det.)	R	16	26	3	4	0	0	.154	1
Robinson, Eddie (33 Det., 19 Clev., 4 Balt.)	L	36	39	1	6	1	0	.154	3
Osborne, Bobo	L	11	27	4	4	0	0	.148	1
Boros, Steve	R	24	41	4	6	0	0	.146	2

Less than 10 games: Jack Phillips, Tom Yewcik, Bill Taylor, Mel Clark and George Thomas.

PITCHING RECORDS

	T	G	IP	W	L	PCT	ERA
Bunning, Jim	R	45	267	20	8	.714	2.70
Foytack, Paul	R	38	212	14	11	.560	3.14
Maas, Duke	R	45	219	10	14	.417	3.29
Byrd, Harry	R	37	59	4	3	.571	3.36
Hoeft, Billy	L	34	207	9	11	.450	3.48
Sleater, Lou	L	41	69	3	3	.500	3.78
Lary, Frank	R	40	237	11	16	.407	3.98

Less than 45 innings: Jim Stump, Joe Presko, Chuck Daniel, Bob Shaw, Pete Wojey, Don Lee, Steve Gromek and Jack Crimian. Al Aber appeared in 28 games with Detroit and 3 with Kansas City.

LEBOWSKI AND BRODSKY, P.C.
CERTIFIED PUBLIC ACCOUNTANTS

(313) 626-0755

Contact
STEVEN J. LEBOWSKI
C.P.A., J.D.
7125 Orchard Lake Road
Suite 302
West Bloomfield, MI 48033

Tigers with 250 or More Home Runs

The leading home run hitter of all time is Hank Aaron with 755, followed by Babe Ruth with 714. The leading Tiger in the home run department is Al Kaline with 399. Frank Howard had 382 homers but only 14 of these were hit as a Tiger. Eddie Mathews hit a total of 512 homers during his 17 years in the major leagues, but all nint were in the National League. Norm Cash hit 377, Rocky Colavito had 374 and Hank Greenberg 331. Willie Horton hit 325 homers, Al Simmons 307, Rusty Staub 292, Darrell Evans 318, including his 40 in 1985. Rudy York had 277, Vic Wertz 266, and Larry Doby hit 253, none of them during his brief tenure with the Tigers.

1958
FINAL STANDINGS

	W	L	PCT
New York	92	62	.597
Chicago	82	72	.532
Boston	79	75	.513
Cleveland	77	76	.503
DETROIT	77	77	.500
Baltimore	74	79	.484
Kansas City	73	81	.474
Washington	61	93	.396

Managers: Jack Tighe and Bill Norman

The huge 13-player swap over the winter had given the Tigers new reason to be encouraged about their prospects for 1958. The front office situation had finally stabilized with the departure of Spike Briggs and the emergence of John Fetzer as chairman of the board, and newly acquired Billy Martin was expected to stir up much-needed fire on the field.

Unfortunately, the team was still short of talent at several key positions and once again the Tigers stumbled coming out of the starting gate. Hampered by assorted aches and pains, Al Kaline was batting a mere .196 by the end of April and blamed himself for the team's sad start. In truth, Al was not alone. Two of the team's top pitchers, Billy Hoeft and Jim Bunning, were injured and out of the starting rotation and Martin was limping around with a torn leg muscle.

In late May, the Tigers embarked on a nine-game losing streak that tumbled them into the American League basement. And the fans did not hesitate to let their favorites know how they felt. One night when the Tiger Stadium public address announcer made a routine sales pitch on the availability of tickets for future games, his spiel was drowned out by a cascade of boos.

Finally, Fetzer could tolerate no more. He called a meeting of the club's top executives at his home in Kalamazoo to discuss possible solutions. John McHale, who had replaced Briggs as general manager, recommended that manager Jack Tighe be fired and replaced by Bill Norman, who was currently managing the Tigers' top farm club at Charleston. The top brass agreed, so on June 10, McHale flew to Boston to give Tighe the bad news. Under the circumstances, with the team languishing in seventh place, Tighe seemed almost relieved.

As so often happens when a team changes managers, the Tigers suddenly woke up and began playing decent baseball. Ozzie Virgil, the first black ballplayer to wear a Tiger uniform, was summoned from Charleston to plug one of the holes in the sieve-like infield. And, on June 15, with their pitching poor and their hitting virtually nonexistent, the Tigers traded veteran

Ray Boone, once one of their big stars, and ineffective pitcher Bob Shaw to the Chicago White Sox for pitcher Bill Fischer and outfielder Tito Francona. Whatever the cause, the Tigers soared from the cellar to second place on July 13, winning seven games in a row against the league-leading New York Yankees. Even so, the Yanks were still on top by 12 1/2 games, and the Tigers' sudden surge soon ran out of gas.

Eventually, the Tigers settled into fifth place again, winning 77 while losing the same number, to finish 14 1/2 lengths behind New York. It was their seventh fifth-place finish in eight years.

Harvey Kuenn, who moved to centerfield to make room for Billy Martin, proved he had no difficulty adjusting to the new position by batting .319. And Kaline, in spite of his slow start and seemingly endless string of injuries, wound up hitting .313, although he did fall off in home runs to just 16.

For the second year in a row, Kaline won the Gold Glove as the league's best rightfielder, receiving 141 votes to a scant 14 for runners-up Hank Bauer and Jackie Jensen. What's more, he had 24 assists—more than any other outfielder in either league—even though enemy runners rarely took chances on his throwing arm.

The star of the pitching staff was young Frank Lary, who beat the New York Yankees seven times while losing only once during the season, prompting Yankee manager Casey Stengel to remark, "He done splendid."

Unfortunately, Lary was not nearly so successful against the other teams in the league, and wound up with a 16-15 record for the year. Jim Bunning, a 20-game winner the season before, fell off to 14-12, but did toss a no-hitter against the Boston Red Sox.

On November 14, the Tigers were shocked by the news that their play-by-play radio announcer, Mel Ott, the former National League home run hitting star, had been killed in an automobile accident. To replace him, Fetzer hired George Kell, the former Tiger third baseman.

Former pitcher Ed Rakow was quite an athlete. At one time, he was a good football player in the Pittsburgh area. Rakow played quarterback for the semi-pro Bloomfield Rams, but he lost his job in 1956 to an up-and-coming signal caller named Johnny Unitas.

BATTING RECORDS

	B	G	AB	R	H	HR	SB	AVE	RBI
Zernial, Gus	R	66	124	8	40	5	0	.323	23
Kuenn, Harvey	R	139	561	73	179	8	5	.319	54
Kaline, Al	R	146	543	84	170	16	7	.313	85
Wilson, Red	R	103	298	31	89	3	10	.299	29
Groth, John	R	88	146	24	41	2	0	.281	11
Harris, Gail	L	134	451	63	123	20	1	.273	83
Maxwell, Charlie	L	131	397	56	108	13	6	.272	65
Bolling, Frank	R	154	610	91	164	14	6	.269	75
Veal, Coot	R	58	207	29	53	0	1	.256	16
Martin, Billy	R	131	498	56	127	7	5	.255	42
Francona, Tito (41 Chi., 45 Det.)	L	86	197	21	50	1	2	.254	20
Virgil, Ossie	R	49	193	19	47	3	1	.244	19
Boone, Ray (39 Det., 77 Chi.)	R	116	360	41	87	13	0	.242	61
Skizas, Lou	R	23	33	4	8	1	0	.242	2
Hagle, Bob	L	43	58	5	14	2	0	.241	5
Bertoia, Reno	R	86	240	28	56	6	5	.233	27
Bolling, Milt	R	24	31	3	6	0	0	.194	0
Hegan, Jim	R	45	130	14	25	1	0	.192	7
Lau, Charlie	L	30	68	8	10	0	0	.147	6

Less than 10 games: George Alusik, Steve Boros, Jack Feller, Bobo Osborne, Billy Taylor, George Thomas and Tim Thompson.

PITCHING RECORDS

	T	G	IP	W	L	PCT	ERA
Lary, Frank	R	39	260	16	15	.516	2.91
Morgan, Tom	R	39	63	2	5	.286	3.14
Foytack, Paul	R	39	230	15	13	.536	3.44
Bunning, Jim	R	35	220	14	12	.538	3.52
Moford, Herb	R	25	110	4	9	.308	3.60
Aguirre, Hank	L	44	70	3	4	.429	3.73
Susce, George (2 Bos., 27 Det.)	R	29	93	4	3	.571	3.97
Cicotte, Al (8 Wash., 14 Det.)	R	22	71	3	4	.429	4.06
Hoeft, Billy	L	36	143	10	9	.526	4.15
Shaw, Bob (11 Det., 29 Chi.)	R	40	91	5	4	.556	4.75
Valentinetti, Vito (15 Det., 23 Wash.)	R	38	114	5	6	.455	4.82
Fischer, Bill (17 Chi., 22 Det., 3 Wash.)	R	42	88	4	10	.286	6.34

Less than 45 innings: Don Lee, Mickey McDermott, Joe Presko, Herman Wehmeier and George Spencer. Lou Sleater appeared in 4 games with Detroit and 6 with Baltimore.

JOE DWYER IMPORTS

SINCE 1959

Authorized dealer for

VOLVO SUBARU®

Complete Service,
Parts and
Bump Shop Dents

24841 Grand River at 7 Mile Road
6 Blocks West of Telegraph Road
Detroit

537-2292

On June 23, 1917, Babe Ruth started a game for the Boston Red Sox. He walked the first batter and was thrown out of the game by the umpire for protesting the umpire's decision. Ernie Shore relieved Ruth and base runner Ray Morgan was out stealing. Shore retired the next 26 batters and is given credit for a perfect game. The final out of the game was made by pinch-hitter Mike Menosky. Mike, who was a Detroiter and a long-time probation officer after his baseball career, passed away in Detroit on April 11, 1983.

1959
FINAL STANDINGS

	W	L	PCT
Chicago	94	60	.610
Cleveland	89	65	.578
New York	79	75	.513
DETROIT	76	78	.494
Boston	75	79	.487
Baltimore	74	80	.481
Kansas City	66	88	.429
Washington	63	91	.409

Managers: Bill Norman and Jimmy Dykes

There were new faces all over the field as the Tigers embarked on the 1959 season. Gone were infielder Billy Martin and pitcher Al Cicotte, traded to the Cleveland Indians for pitchers Ray Narleski and Don Mossi, and infielder Ossie Alvarez. Gone were infielders Reno Bertoia and Ron Samford and outfielder Jim Delsing, traded to the Washington Senators for infielders Eddie Yost and Rocky Bridges, and outfielder Neil Chrisley. Gone was outfielder Tito Francona, dealt to Cleveland for outfielder Larry Doby.

At least no one could accuse the fifth-place Tigers of standing pat.

There had been major changes upstairs in the front office, too. General Manager John McHale had resigned in January to accept a similar position with the Milwaukee Braves and had been replaced by farm director and former major league catcher Rick Ferrell.

Hopes were high as the Tigers opened the season, confident they had solidified their leaky infield and bolstered themselves elsewhere. But again they got off to a horrendous start, losing 15 of their first 17 games. That convinced Fetzer and Ferrell to bounce Bill Norman as manager and bring in 62-year-old Jimmy Dykes, a grizzled veteran who had survived in the big leagues for 22 years as a player and 17 more as a manager.

Dykes had built a reputation for repairing down-trodden teams—and that description certainly seemed to fit the Tigers. And they responded immediately, sweeping a doubleheader from the Yankees the day Dykes arrived as Charley Maxwell belted four home runs in the twin bill. Detroit won seven of their first eight games under the new manager.

In fact, they won 32 out of 46 to soar to within a half-game of first place by late June. "I don't think Dykes can get too much praise for what he's done with this club," raved Al Kaline. "He's a ballplayer's manager."

There was, however, little that Dykes could do about the injuries that continually forced the Tigers to function at less than full strength, gradually causing them to fall back into the pack.

Kaline and Harvey Kuenn, The K-Boys, battled one another all season for the batting crown and eventually finished one-two in the race, with Kuenn outdistancing Kaline .353 to .327.

Two off-season acquisitions, Mossi and Yost, also played prominent roles in the Tigers' success. Mossi won 17 games, as did Frank Lary and Jim Bunning, while Yost led the league in walks with 135 and also hammered 21 homers, nine above his previous career high.

In addition to finishing second behind Kuenn in the batting chase, Kaline also matched his personal high with 27 home runs, won the league slugging title with a .530 mark, and earned his third consecutive Gold Glove—this one for his performance in centerfield, making him the first man ever to win that coveted award at two positions.

Even so, it was a frustrating season for the Tigers. Though they finished fourth, their 76-78 record was their worst in five years and they trailed the pennant-winning Chicago White Sox by a discouraging 18 games.

Obviously, the Tigers still had their problems. The front office, particularly the new owners, had been severely criticized in the press, depicted as bumbling baseball novices.

To correct that, following the season, Fetzer hired Bill DeWitt, a veteran baseball executive, and appointed him president and general manager of the Tigers. DeWitt, a flamboyant personality, had a reputation as being both tight-fisted with club finances and an impulsive wheeler-dealer when it came to making player trades.

The arrival of DeWitt had the Tiger players and their fans all wondering what would happen next. And DeWitt didn't keep them guessing for long.

BATTING RECORDS

	B	G	AB	R	H	HR	SB	AVE	RBI
Kuenn, Harvey	R	139	561	99	198	9	7	.353	71
Kaline, Al	R	136	511	86	167	27	10	.327	94
Lepcio, Ted (3 Bos., 76 Det.)	R	79	218	26	61	7	2	.280	25
Yost, Ed	R	148	521	115	145	21	9	.278	61
Bridges, Rocky	R	116	381	38	102	3	1	.268	35
Bolling, Frank	R	127	459	56	122	13	2	.266	55
Wilson, Red	R	67	228	28	60	4	2	.263	35
Maxwell, Charlie	L	145	518	81	130	31	0	.251	95
Groth, John	R	55	102	12	24	1	0	.235	10
Doby, Larry (18 Det., 21 Chi.)	L	39	113	6	26	0	1	.230	13
Zernial, Gus	R	60	132	11	30	7	0	.227	26
Harris, Gail	L	114	349	39	77	9	0	.221	39
Berberet, Lou	L	100	338	38	73	13	0	.216	44
Veal, Coot	R	77	89	12	18	1	0	.202	15
Osborne, Bobo	L	86	209	27	40	3	1	.191	21
Chrisley, Neil	L	65	106	7	14	6	0	.132	11
Demeter, Steve	R	11	18	1	2	0	0	.111	1

Less than 10 games: Ossie Alvarez, Charlie Lau and Ron Shoop.

PITCHING RECORDS

	T	G	IP	W	L	PCT	ERA
Mossi, Don	L	34	228	17	9	.654	3.36
Lary, Frank	R	32	223	17	10	.630	3.55
Burnside, Pete	L	30	62	1	3	.250	3.77
Bunning, Jim	R	40	250	17	13	.567	3.89
Morgan, Tom	R	46	93	1	4	.200	3.97
Sisler, Dave (3 Bos., 32 Det.)	R	35	58	1	3	.250	4.34
Foytack, Paul	R	39	240	14	14	.500	4.65
Hoeft, Billy (2 Det., 5 Bos., 16 Balt.)	L	23	68	2	5	.286	5.56
Narleski, Ray	R	42	104	4	12	.250	5.80

Less than 45 innings: Jim Stump, Bob Bruce, Jim Proctor, Bob Smith, Jerry Davie, Hank Aguirre, Bob Schultz and George Susce.

To Join
the

AAA Michigan

Please Call

**JOHN R. DUFFY
JOHN FLIS
RON LINDER**

**680-1235
3517 Rochester Road • Troy, Michigan 48084**

Life - Automobile - Homeowners - Boat - Motorcycle

1960

FINAL STANDINGS

	W	L	PCT
New York	97	57	.630
Baltimore	89	65	.578
Chicago	87	67	.565
Cleveland	76	78	.494
Washington	73	81	.474
DETROIT	71	83	.461
Boston	65	89	.422
Kansas City	58	96	.377

Managers: Jimmy Dykes and Joe Gordon

The Tiger players were on edge throughout their 1960 spring training camp. No one—not even Al Kaline—could be certain he wouldn't be traded without warning by the impulsive Bill DeWitt. And, on April 12, DeWitt made his move, dealing infielder Steve Demeter to the Cleveland Indians for Norm Cash.

But DeWitt had just begun. The day before the regular season began, the Tigers president and GM shocked the baseball world by trading Harvey Kuenn, the 1959 American League batting champion, to the Indians for Rocky Colavito, the reigning AL home run king. It marked the first time in history that a batting champ had been traded for a home run champ.

Both players were stunned. So were their teammates. So were fans on both sides of Lake Erie. Tiger fans, although happy to be receiving some much-needed home run punch, could not perceive the wisdom of parting with a hitter as consistent as Kuenn.

Five games into the season, the Tigers were still undefeated and fans were raving about Detroit's new "Murderer's Row"—Colavito, Cash and Kaline. Ten games—and 10 consecutive losses—later those same Tigers were in last place and everyone was wondering what had gone wrong.

DeWitt tried more trades: infielder Gail Harris to the Los Angeles Dodgers for outfielder Sandy Amoros; pitcher Ray Semproch to the Dodgers for pitcher Clem Labine; pitcher Tom Morgan to the Washington Senators for pitcher Bill Fischer; catcher Bob Wilson and infielder Rocky Bridges to the Cleveland Indians for catcher Hank Foiles; catcher Harry Chiti from the Kansas City Athletics for cash.

Finally, on August 3, DeWitt engineered his boldest deal of all. With the team mired in sixth place, eight games under .500, DeWitt made major league history by trading Tiger manager Jimmy Dykes to the Cleveland Indians for their manager, Joe Gordon.

Nobody had ever traded managers before. But DeWitt and his Cleveland counterpart, Frank Lane, who had swung the Kuenn-for-Colavito deal at the start of the season, had pulled off the unthinkable.

Unfortunately for the Tigers, the change in managers made more newspaper headlines than difference in the standings.

Gordon finished out the season as the Tigers compiled their worst record (71-83) since 1954, then immediately resigned. He locked the door to his apartment and refused to open it for anyone. Gordon had had enough of the Tigers. But not of baseball. A few days later he signed to manage the Kansas City Athletics.

A lot of things went wrong for the sixth-place Tigers in 1960, making it difficult to point the finger of blame at any one person. As a team, the Bengals finished last in the league in batting with an anemic .239 average. During the course of the long and difficult season, they lost 31 games by one run.

The team's two big guns, Kaline and Colavito, both failed to produce as expected. Kaline batted only .278 with 15 home runs, while Colavito hit .249, although he did lead the team with 35 home runs and 87 rbi.

Frank Lary led the pitching staff with a 15-15 record while Jim Bunning was a disappointing 11-14, although he did finish second in the league in earned run average with 2.79.

For the record, Dykes didn't do any better with the Indians than Gordon did with the Tigers and Kuenn batted only .308, although he was the Tribe's only .300 hitter.

Perturbed by the abrupt departure of Gordon, who blamed DeWitt's meddling for his decision to quit, John Fetzer bought controlling interest of the Tigers from his business partners in October and immediately assumed the position of president. Fetzer offered DeWitt a role as his assistant, but DeWitt resigned rather than accept.

In an effort to wipe the slate clean and make a new beginning, Fetzer then renamed Briggs Stadium Tiger Stadium.

Bob Miller

Bob Miller has been the head coach at the University of Detroit since 1965. Bob pitched for St. Mary's of Redford High School, the University of Detroit and then went into professional baseball. He won 19 and lost nine with Terre Haute in the Three-Eye League in 1949 and then joined the Philadelphia Phillies. The Phillies won the pennant in 1950 when they were called the Whiz Kids and Bob won 11 and lost six, including a string of eight straight victories. He stayed with the Phillies for ten seasons and had a lifetime record of 42 wins and 42 losses. He was mainly a relief pitcher after the first season. He retired after the 1959 season, became an assistant to the late Lloyd Brazil, and took over as head coach after Lloyd's untimely death. Bob is a member of the University of Detroit's Hall of Fame and is an obvious candidate for Michigan's Sports Hall of Fame.

BATTING RECORDS

	B	G	AB	R	H	HR	SB	AVE	RBI
Groth, John	R	25	19	3	7	0	0	.368	2
Bridges, Rocky (10 Det., 10 Clev.)	R	20	32	1	10	0	0	.313	3
Gernert, Dick	R	21	50	6	15	1	0	.300	5
Veal, Coot	R	27	64	8	19	0	0	.297	8
Cash, Norm	L	121	353	64	101	18	4	.286	63
Foiles, Henry (6 KC, 24 Clev., 26 Det.)	R	56	131	15	37	1	1	.282	10
Kaline, Al	R	147	551	77	153	15	19	.278	68
Yost, Eddie	R	143	497	78	129	14	5	.260	47
Chrisley, Neil	L	96	220	27	56	5	2	.255	24
Bolling, Frank	R	139	536	64	136	9	7	.254	59
Colavito, Rocky	R	145	555	67	138	35	3	.249	87
Fernandez, Chico	R	133	435	44	105	4	13	.241	35
Maxwell, Charlie	L	134	482	70	114	24	5	.237	81
Virgil, Ossie	R	62	132	16	30	3	1	.227	13
Wilson, Red (45 Det., 32 Clev.)	R	77	222	22	48	2	3	.216	24
Bilko, Steve	R	78	222	20	46	9	0	.207	25
Chiti, Harry (58 KC, 37 Det.)	R	95	294	25	59	7	1	.201	33
Berberet, Lou	L	85	232	18	45	5	2	.194	23
Amoros, Sandy	L	65	67	7	10	1	0	.149	7
Wise, Casey	B	30	68	6	10	2	1	.147	5

Less than 10 games: Gail Harris, Emert Lindbeck and Dick McAuliffe.

PITCHING RECORDS

	T	G	IP	W	L	PCT	ERA
Sisler, Dave	R	41	80	7	5	.583	2.48
Bunning, Jim	R	36	252	11	14	.440	2.79
Aguirre, Hank	L	37	95	5	3	.625	2.84
Mossi, Don	L	23	158	9	8	.529	3.47
Lary, Frank	R	38	274	15	15	.500	3.51
Bruce, Bob	R	34	130	4	7	.364	3.74
Morgan, Tom (22 Det., 14 Wash.)	R	36	52	4	5	.444	4.25
Burnside, Pete	L	31	114	7	7	.500	4.26
Fischer, Bill (20 Wash., 20 Det.)	R	40	132	8	8	.500	4.30
Regan, Phil	R	17	68	0	4	.000	4.50
Foytack, Paul	R	28	97	2	11	.154	6.12

Less than 45 innings: Clem Labine, Ray Semproch and George Spencer.

1961

FINAL STANDINGS

	W	L	PCT
New York	109	53	.673
DETROIT	101	61	.623
Baltimore	95	67	.586
Chicago	86	76	.531
Cleveland	78	83	.484
Boston	76	86	.469
Minnesota	70	90	.438
Los Angeles	70	91	.435
Kansas City	61	100	.379
Washington	61	100	.379

Manager: Bob Scheffing

John Fetzer was determined to bring some order and stability to the Tiger organization in the wake of the chaos that had prevailed in recent years. To do that, he decided to try to hire the venerable Casey Stengel to manage the team.

Along with Rick Ferrell and Jim Campbell, who had emerged as Fetzer's right-hand man in the front office, the Tiger owner flew to California after the 1960 season to offer the job to Stengel, who had been cut loose by the New York Yankees.

The more the three men talked about the Tigers, the more Stengel liked the idea of managing the team. He even went so far as to name the coaches he would like to have assist him. Then Stengel's wife, Edna, entered the conversation and suggested Casey should first have a medical exam to make sure he was physically up to the task before him. The next day, Stengel's doctor decreed that it would be very unwise for the old man to return to managing at that time.

Deeply disappointed, the Tigers turned to Bob Scheffing, a former catcher and manager of the Chicago Cubs. Scheffing was both knowledgeable and affable. He seemed like an ideal choice.

And the Tiger players responded to their new manager. The Tigers were the biggest surprise in the American League in 1961, and the only real threat to the continued domination of the New York Yankees, who this year featured the home run heroics of Roger Maris and Mickey Mantle.

The Tigers set the pace during the early months of the season and alternated with the Yankees in the lead for much of the summer. On September 1, the Tigers, who had won 11 of their last 14 games to stay very much in the race, went into New York for a three-game show-down series, trailing the Yankees by just 1 1/2 games.

The three-game weekend confrontation in Yankee Stadium attracted a record 171,503 fans and ranked as one of the most thrilling in baseball history. Unfortunately, the Tigers lost all three games.

The largest crowd of the season, 65,566 showed up for the opening game and saw Tiger Don Mossi lock horns with the Yankees' Whitey Ford in a classic pitcher's duel that was eventually decided, 1-0, in favor of New York on ninth inning singles by Elston Howard, Yogi Berra and Bill Skowron.

In the second game, the Yankees hammered their old nemesis, Frank Lary, 7-2, as Maris belted home runs 52 and 53. And in Sunday's finale, before a crowd of 55,676, the Yanks came from behind in the bottom of the ninth to prevail 8-5.

For the Tigers, the season was all but over. New York went on to win its next 10 games while the Tigers dropped five more before halting their skid. The Tigers hung on to finish second, but they were eight lengths back, even though they won 101 games to match the all-time team record set in 1934 by Mickey Cochrane's champions.

Although they had been the weakest hitting outfit in the league the year before, the Tigers were first at the plate in 1960. Only in home runs were the Yankees able to overshadow them.

Norm Cash, one of the few Tigers who had ever played on a pennant winner, had a sensational season. Stormin' Norman led the league in hitting at .361 and added 41 homers and 132 rbi to establish himself as one of the AL's premier power hitters.

Al Kaline and Rocky Colavito did their share of slugging, too. Kaline finished second behind Cash in the batting race with a .324 average, that included 19 home runs and 82 rbi. Colavito hit .290 with 45 homers and 140 rbi. Rocky's 45 home runs represented the second highest such total in Tiger history.

Frank Lary was the ace of the Tigers' pitching staff, winning 23 while losing nine. Don Mossi was 15-7 and Jim Bunning was 17-11 to give Detroit a formidable Big Three. But the rest of the staff was inconsistent at best.

Still it was a season to be proud of. Kaline was named AL Comeback Player of the Year and Scheffing was named Manager of the Year for bringing the Tigers home second when many had expected them to finish fifth again.

Norm Cash

Norm batted over .300 only once in his 17 years in the American League but he won the American League batting championship in 1961 when he hit .361. Norm's next highest average was .286.

BATTING RECORDS

	B	G	AB	R	H	HR	SB	AVE	RBI
Cash, Norm	L	159	535	119	193	41	11	.361	132
Kaline, Al	R	153	586	116	190	19	14	.324	82
Colavito, Rocky	R	163	583	129	169	45	1	.290	140
Morton, Bubba	R	77	108	26	31	2	3	.287	19
Thomas, George (17 Det., 79 LA)	R	96	288	41	79	13	3	.274	59
Boros, Steve	R	116	396	51	107	5	4	.270	62
Brown, Dick	R	93	308	32	82	16	0	.266	45
Wertz, Vic (99 Bos., 8 Det.)	L	107	323	33	84	11	0	.260	61
Wood, Jake	R	162	663	96	171	11	30	.258	69
Bruton, Billy	L	160	596	99	153	17	22	.257	63
McAuliffe, Dick	L	80	285	36	73	6	2	.256	33
Fernandez, Chico	R	133	435	41	108	3	8	.248	40
Cottier, Chuck (10 Det., 101 Wash.)	R	111	344	39	81	2	9	.233	35
Maxwell, Charlie	L	79	131	11	30	5	0	.229	18
House, Frank	L	17	22	3	5	0	0	.227	3
Bertoia, Reno (35 Minn., 39 KC, 24 Det.)	R	98	270	35	61	2	3	.226	25
Roarke, Mike	R	86	229	21	51	2	0	.223	22
Osborne, Bobo	L	71	93	8	20	2	1	.215	13
Alusik, George	R	15	14	0	2	0	0	.143	2
Virgil, Ossie (20 Det., 11 KC)	R	31	51	2	7	1	0	.137	1

Less than 10 games: Dick Gernert, Harry Chiti and Bill Freehan.

PITCHING RECORDS

	T	G	IP	W	L	PCT	ERA
Woodeshick, Hal (7 Wash., 12 Det.)	L	19	59	4	3	.571	5.19
Fischer, Bill (26 Det., 15 KC)	R	41	68	4	2	.667	4.63
Lary, Frank	R	36	275	23	9	.719	3.24
Fox, Terry	R	39	57	5	2	.714	1.42
Mossi, Don	L	35	240	15	7	.682	2.96
Bunning, Jim	R	38	268	17	11	.607	3.19
Regan, Phil	R	32	120	10	7	.588	5.25
Foytack, Paul	R	32	170	11	10	.524	3.92
Aguirre, Hank	L	45	55	4	4	.500	3.27
Kline, Ron (26 LA, 10 Det.)	R	36	161	8	9	.471	4.14
Bruce, Bob	R	14	45	1	2	.333	4.40
Staley, Gerry (16 Chi., 23 KC, 13 Det.)	R	52	61	2	5	.286	3.98
Casale, Jerry (13 LA, 3 Det.)	R	16	55	1	5	.167	6.22
Donahue, Jim (14 Det., 38 LA)	R	52	121	5	7	.417	4.17

Less than 45 innings: Howard Koplitz, Manny Montejo, Ron Nischwitz, Fred Gladding and Joe Grzenda.

Detroit:
500 Renaissance Center
Suite 1700
Detroit, MI 48243-1902
(313) 259-0200
FAX (313) 567-4381

Grand Rapids:
150 Grand Plaza Place
Grand Rapids, MI 49501-2408
(616) 456-5366

INSURANCE AND BONDING
For Michigan and the World

FRANK B. HALL & CO. OF MICHIGAN
Serving contractors & Builders since 1939

Rocky Colavito on June 24, 1962, in a 22-inning game went to bat ten times and had seven hits, one of them a triple. Jim Northrup on August 28, 1969 had two home runs and four singles. Cesar Gutuierrez, playing in the second game of a doubleheader, had seven hits at seven times at bat—six singles and one double June 21, 1970. Clancy Cutshaw had six singles on August 9, 1915 playing for Brooklyn. He played second base for Detroit in 1922 and 1923.

1962

FINAL STANDINGS

	W	L	PCT
New York	96	66	.593
Minnesota	91	71	.562
Los Angeles	86	76	.531
DETROIT	85	76	.528
Chicago	85	77	.525
Cleveland	80	82	.494
Baltimore	77	85	.475
Boston	76	84	.475
Kansas City	72	90	.444
Washington	60	101	.373

Manager: Bob Scheffing

The Tigers were convinced they had turned the corner and established themselves as perennial pennant contenders as they entered the 1962 season. After all, they had kept pace with the mighty Yankees all the way into September the previous season.

Unfortunately, they didn't figure on the absence of Yankee-killer Frank Lary, who was hampered all season with a sore arm and won only two games, or the loss of Al Kaline who missed 61 games because of a broken collar bone. Without their ace pitcher and their best hitter, the Tigers were overmatched against the top teams in the American League.

In a diving effort to catch a pop fly off the bat of New York's Elston Howard, Kaline landed on his right shoulder. Al caught the ball but had to be helped off the field and into the Tiger clubhouse where he fainted from the pain. When his teammates learned of the severity of Kaline's injury and the fact that their star rightfielder would miss at least two months, morale on the team sank. "How do you win a pennant without Kaline?" one Tiger player asked. Then, without waiting for a reply, he added, "You don't."

In the weeks that followed, the Tigers seemed to be simply going through the motions, trying to win, of course, but realizing their chances had been greatly reduced.

Indicative, perhaps, of the type of season it had become, was the Tigers' game against the Yankees on Sunday afternoon, June 24. The contest took 22 innings to complete, and lasted for seven hours, from 1:30 in the afternoon, until 8:30 in the evening. The Yankees, who eventually prevailed 9-7, used 21 of their 25 players. The Tigers employed 22. Even the Tiger Stadium concession stands had to be closed before the game ended because of a Michigan law which prohibited women from working more than 10 hours on Sunday. It went into the record books as the longest major league game ever played, up until that point—and another Tiger loss.

Kaline didn't get back into the lineup until July 23. Even so, he finished the season with a career high 29 home runs as well as a .304 average and

94 rbi. However, the Tigers couldn't help but wonder what those numbers might have looked like if Al had been healthy all season.

As a team, the Tigers led both major leagues in home runs with 209, breaking the club record of 180, set the previous season. Norm Cash was the top slugger, belting 39 home runs, just two more than teammate Rocky Colavito. Chico Fernandez contributed 20 round trippers.

However, the Tigers batted only .248 as a unit and only a solid finish, that saw them win 12 of the final 15 games, enabled them to nip the White Sox and claim fourth place. Jim Bunning was the Tigers' big winner on the mound with a 19-10 record, while Hank Aguirre was 16-8 with a league-leading 2.21 e.r.a.—the best such mark by any Tiger lefty since Hal Newhouser in 1945-46.

On September 22, Jim Campbell was named general manager of the Tigers, replacing Rick Ferrell, who retained the title of vice president in charge of evaluating player talent.

Following the season, the Tigers, along with baseball Commissioner Ford Frick, American League president Joe Cronin, and several members of the front office, made a barn-storming tour of Hawaii, Korea and Japan, winning 16, losing 4, and tying 2.

BATTING RECORDS

	B	G	AB	R	H	HR	SB	AVE	RBI
Wertz, Vic	L	74	105	7	34	5	0	.324	18
Kaline, Al	R	100	398	78	121	29	4	.304	94
Bruton, Billy	L	147	561	90	156	16	14	.278	74
Colavito, Rocky	R	161	601	90	164	37	2	.273	112
Maxwell, Charlie (30 Det., 69 Chi.)	L	99	273	35	74	10	0	.271	52
Alusik, George (2 Det., 90 KC)	R	92	211	29	57	11	1	.270	35
Kostro, Frank	R	16	41	5	11	0	0	.268	3
McAuliffe, Dick	L	139	471	50	124	12	4	.263	63
Morton, Bubba	R	90	195	30	51	4	1	.262	17
Fernandez, Chico	R	141	503	64	125	20	10	.249	59
Cash, Norm	L	148	507	94	123	39	6	.243	89
Brown, Dick	L	134	431	40	104	12	0	.241	40
Osborne, Bobo	L	64	74	12	17	0	0	.230	7
Goldy, Purnal	R	20	70	8	16	3	0	.229	12
Buddin, Don`	R	31	83	14	19	0	1	.229	4
Boros, Steve	R	116	356	46	81	16	3	.228	47
Wood, Jake	R	111	367	68	83	8	24	.226	30
Roarke, Mike	R	56	136	11	29	4	0	.213	14
Farley, Bob (35 Chi., 36 Det.)	L	71	103	16	18	2	0	.175	8

Less than 10 games: Reno Bertoia.

PITCHING RECORDS

	T	G	IP	W	L	PCT	ERA
Fox, Terry	R	44	58	3	1	.750	1.71
Aguirre, Hank	L	42	216	16	8	.667	2.21
Bunning, Jim	R	41	258	19	10	.655	3.59
Jones, Sam	R	30	81	2	4	.333	3.67
Nischwitz, Ron	L	48	65	4	5	.444	3.88
Regan, Phil	R	35	171	11	9	.550	4.05
Mossi, Don	L	35	180	11	13	.458	4.19
Kline, Ron	R	36	77	3	6	.333	4.32
Foytack, Paul	R	29	144	10	7	.588	4.38
Lary, Frank	R	17	80	2	6	.250	5.74

Less than 45 innings: Jerry Casale, Tom Fletcher, Bill Faul, Doug Gallagher, Bob Humphreys, Fred Gladding and Howie Koplitz.

Statistics

1963

FINAL STANDINGS

	W	L	PCT
New York	104	57	.646
Chicago	94	68	.580
Minnesota	91	70	.565
Baltimore	86	76	.531
DETROIT	79	83	.488
Cleveland	79	83	.488
Boston	76	85	.472
Kansas City	73	89	.451
Los Angeles	70	91	.435
Washington	56	106	.346

Managers: Bob Scheffing and Charlie Dressen

Disappointed by their fourth-place showing the previous season, the Tigers loaded their roster with new faces for 1963. Pitchers Ron Nischwitz and Gordon Seyfried were sent to the Cleveland Indians for infielder Bubba Phillips; catcher Dick Brown was dealt to the Baltimore Orioles for catcher Gus Triandos and outfielder Whitey Herzog; infielder Steve Boros was traded to the Chicago Cubs for pitcher Bob Anderson; and infielder Larry Osborne was peddled to the Washington Senators for outfielder Wayne Comer.

All of those changes, plus the expected good health of Al Kaline, convinced most of the so-called experts that the Tigers should finish second behind the New York Yankees in '63. Kaline himself, before the season began, called the '63 Tigers "the best team I've played on."

How wrong those expert were!

Plagued by woefully weak hitting on the part of most of their big guns, as well as an assortment of nagging injuries to key cogs such as Kaline, the Tigers sunk to ninth place by mid-June. Determined to try to shake the Tigers out of their slump, general manager Jim Campbell traded pitcher Paul Foytack and utility man Frank Kostro to the Los Angeles Angels for outfielder George Thomas, then turned to the farm system for pitcher Willie Smith and slugging outfielder Gates Brown.

But Campbell knew that wasn't enough. So on June 19, he fired Bob Scheffing, who had been Manager of the Year in 1961, and replaced him with 65-year-old Charlie Dressen. In addition to Scheffing, Campbell dumped the entire Tiger coaching staff of Phil Cavaretta, George Myatt and Tom Ferrick. It marked the first time that a manager and all of his coaches had been canned at midseason. Campbell declared "the move had to be made." Most observers felt Scheffing had been too easy-going with the stumbling Tigers.

Dressen, on the other hand, was anything but easy-going. A former player and manager of the Cincinnati Reds, Brooklyn Dodgers, Washington

Senators and Milwaukee Braves, Dressen brought with him a reputation as a demanding man with a sharp tongue when the situation called for it. His job was to wake the Tigers up before the season was totally lost.

It took a few games, but the Tigers gradually responded to Dressen's call for "more pep and aggressiveness on the field."

Phil Regan developed into a winning pitcher under Dressen, taking 13 out of 15 decisions after Dressen took over to finish the season as the Tigers' top winner at 15-9. Frank Lary, who spent much of the season in the minors trying to regain his earlier form, also contributed to the Tigers' late-season surge, which carried them at least to a fifth-place tie with Cleveland.

The brightest spot in an otherwise generally dismal season was the performance of Kaline who, despite a painful right knee that hampered him for the final three months of the season, finished second in the batting race behind Carl Yastrzemski with a .312 average. Al also knocked in 101 runs and topped the team with 27 homers, one more than teammate Norm Cash.

It marked the seventh time in 10 years as a regular that Kaline had batted .300 or better. In addition, he appeared in his 12th All-Star Game—a Tiger record—and won his sixth Gold Glove for defensive excellence.

And again folks couldn't help but wonder what Kaline might have accomplished had he been healthy all year, instead of hobbling on an injured knee.

Though encouraged by their fast finish under Dressen, the Tigers realized they faced a major rebuilding job if they were to prevent a repeat of their disastrous start of 1963, which had caused attendance to dip to 821,952—a 20-year low.

In their first move to remedy that situation, on November 18, Campbell traded Rocky Colavito—who had slumped to .271 with 22 homers—to Kansas City for infielder Jerry Lumpe and pitchers Ed Rakow and Dave Wickersham.

Two weeks later, the Tigers made another major change, dealing Jim Bunning and Gus Triandos to the Philadelphia Phillies for outfielder Don Demeter and pitcher Jack Hamilton.

Willie Horton picked one of the toughest pitchers of all time off which to hit his first home run in the majors. It was on September 14, 1963, at Tiger Stadium when Willie drove the ball out of the park against the Baltimore Orioles and Robin Roberts. Robin was in the twilight of his great career and Willie was just starting his.

BATTING RECORDS

	B	G	AB	R	H	HR	SB	AVE	RBI
Horton, Willie	R	15	43	6	14	1	2	.326	4
Roarke, Mike	R	23	44	5	14	0	0	.318	1
Kaline, Al	R	145	551	89	172	27	6	.312	101
Colavito, Rocky	R	160	597	91	162	22	0	.271	91
Wood, Jake	R	85	351	50	95	11	18	.270	27
Cash, Norm	L	147	493	67	133	26	2	.270	79
Brown, Gates	L	55	82	16	22	2	2	.268	14
McAuliffe, Dick	L	150	568	77	149	13	11	.262	61
Wert, Don	R	78	251	31	65	7	3	.259	25
Bruton, Billy	L	145	524	84	134	8	14	.256	48
Phillips, Bubba	R	128	464	42	114	5	6	.246	45
Freehan, Bill	R	100	300	37	73	9	2	.243	36
Triandos, Gus	R	106	327	28	78	14	0	.239	41
Kostro, Frank (31 Det., 43 LA)	R	74	151	10	34	2	0	.225	10
Thomas, George (53 LA, 49 Det.)	R	102	276	27	61	5	2	.221	26
Veal, Coot	R	15	32	5	7	0	0	.219	4
Smith, George	R	52	171	16	37	0	4	.216	17
Herzog, Whitey	L	52	53	5	8	0	0	.151	7
Fernandez, Chico	R	15	49	3	7	0	0	.143	2
Wertz, Vic (6 Det., 35 Minn.)	L	41	49	3	6	3	0	.122	7

Less than 10 games: Purnal Goldy, Bubba Morton and John Sullivan.

PITCHING RECORDS

	T	G	IP	W	L	PCT	ERA
Lary, Frank	R	16	108	4	9	.308	3.28
Anderson, Bob	R	32	60	3	1	.750	3.30
Lolich, Mickey	L	33	144	5	9	.357	3.56
Fox, Terry	R	46	80	8	6	.571	3.60
Aguirre, Hank	L	38	226	14	15	.483	3.66
Mossi, Don	L	24	123	7	7	.500	3.73
Sturdivant, Tom (28 Det., 17 KC)	R	45	108	2	4	.333	3.75
Regan, Phil	R	38	189	15	9	.625	3.86
Bunning, Jim	R	39	248	12	13	.480	3.88
Faul, Bill	R	28	97	5	6	.455	4.64
Foytack, Paul (9 Det., 25 LA)	R	34	88	5	6	.455	4.70

Less than 45 innings: Bob Dustal, Dick Egan, Larry Foster, Fred Gladding, Alan Koch, Denny McLain and Willie Smith.

A·J· DESMOND & SONS
Funeral Directors

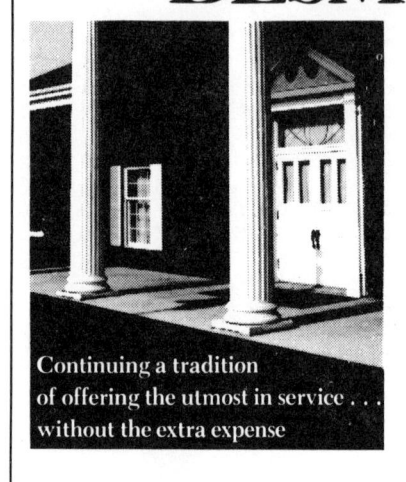

2600 Crooks Road

Between Maple and Big Beaver Roads

Phone 362-2500

Continuing a tradition of offering the utmost in service... without the extra expense

FIRST PLACE AWARD
"PURSUIT OF EXCELLENCE"
NATIONAL FUNERAL DIRECTORS ASSOCIATION

Jim Bunning

On Father's Day in 1964, Jim Bunning pitched a perfect game, beating the New York Mets 6-0. It was the seventh perfect game in modern major league baseball history. It was only fitting that Bunning pitch the game on Father's Day as he is the father of seven children. Bunning had pitched a no-hitter when he was with the Tigers against the Boston Red Sox in 1958. Jim joined the Tigers in 1955 and remained with them until 1964 when he was traded to the Philadelphia Phillies along with Gus Triandos for Don Demeter and Jack Hamilton. He spent 17 years in the big leagues and finished his career with the Phillies in 1971. He was a 20-game winner for the Tigers in 1957, the only time he won 20 games. However, on four occasions he won 19 games. He won 118 game in the American League and 106 in the National League.

1964
FINAL STANDINGS

	W	L	PCT
New York	99	63	.611
Chicago	98	64	.605
Baltimore	97	65	.599
DETROIT	85	77	.525
Los Angeles	82	80	.506
Cleveland	79	83	.488
Minnesota	79	83	.488
Boston	72	90	.444
Washington	62	100	.383
Kansas City	57	100	.352

Manager: Charlie Dressen

In spite of all their trades, the Tigers were still a team with plenty of problems as the 1964 season began. And the Tigers knew it. Nevertheless, there was reason to believe the team might finally be headed in the desired direction.

The loss of Rocky Colavito's power left the Tigers with a shortage of muscle. But General Manager Jim Campbell was convinced he had just the man to pick up the slack and supply some much-needed punch in the Tiger lineup. That was Willie Horton, a stocky, muscular young slugger from the sandlots of Detroit. But no one could be certain Horton was ready to make his presence felt in a major league lineup on a daily basis.

The Tigers also had another very promising young prospect in Bill Freehan, the bonus baby catcher from the University of Michigan. On the mound, manager Charlie Dressen was looking forward to many victories from a talented young left-handed pitcher named Mickey Lolich.

However, that wasn't nearly enough.

Even the purchase of veteran pitcher Larry Sherry from the Los Angeles Dodgers for $50,000 just before the season began was not enough to save the Tigers in '64.

Poor pitching by most of the staff, especially the men in the bullpen, plus a lack of offensive production from injury-plagued Al Kaline and disappointing Don Demeter were primarily to blame for yet another oh-so-slow start by the Tigers.

The Tigers were counting on a strong comeback by former Yankee-killer Frank Lary, but it soon became obvious that the gutsy righthander, who had won 123 games for the Tigers in his 10-year career, had lost his touch.

On May 31, the Tigers finally gave up waiting for Lary and sold him to the New York Mets for $30,000. To take Lary's place, the Tigers summoned yet another promising young player who was to figure prominently in their future success: a pitcher named Denny McLain.

Lary wasn't the only pitcher who struggled early. Hank Aguirre, Lolich and Wickersham were all having their problems, too. To make matters worse, Kaline was so hobbled by a painful foot injury that he finally had to be benched.

As the Tigers' losses continued to mount, burying them in eighth place in the American League, Dressen's patience began to wear thin and the outspoken manager became more and more open in his criticism of his players. That didn't set well with some of the Tigers. Soon the team became divided between those who respected the irascible manager and those who disliked him intensely.

By July 1, the Tigers were still mired in eighth place. So frustrated were the fans that some of them actually began to suggest the Tigers should trade Kaline.

The New York Yankees went so far as to offer outfielder Roger Maris in exchange for Kaline, but Campbell was not about to make a deal like that, not with the man Dressen had described as "the greatest player I have ever managed."

Once again, a late season surge saved some face for the Tigers, allowing them to climb to fourth place. Even so, attendance continued to fall, dipping to 816,139, the lowest since 1943.

So weak was the Tigers' pitching that only two hurlers—Wickersham and Lolich—were able to turn in more than eight victories. Wickersham, acquired in the controversial Colavito trade, won 19 and lost 12 while Lolich was 18-9 with six shutouts, giving the Tigers a formidable one-two punch in their starting rotation.

Sherry also did the job he was acquired to do until a line drive off the bat of Cleveland's Leon Wagner busted the reliever's foot on August 2, knocking him out of action for the rest of the season. But the rest of the pitching staff was a dismal disappointment.

Horton, the Tigers' slugging hope for the future, proved he wasn't quite ready, although he did return from the minors in September along with fellow outfielder Jim Northrup.

Freehan emerged as the Tigers' top hitter in only his second season in the big leagues, batting an even .300—the first Tiger catcher since Mickey Cochrane to hit .300. And shortstop Dick McAuliffe, another key cog of the future, surprised everyone by leading the team with 24 home runs.

But all of that was not sufficient to overshadow the facts that Kaline, hobbled by foot, ankle, and knee injuries at various times, slumped to .293 with 17 homers and only 68 rbi, while Demeter batted only .256 with 22 home runs.

Clearly, the Tigers still had a long way to go.

Statistics

BATTING RECORDS

	B	G	AB	R	H	HR	SB	AVE	RBI
Freehan, Bill	R	144	520	69	156	18	5	.300	80
Kaline, Al	R	146	525	77	154	17	4	.293	68
Thomas, George	R	105	308	39	88	12	4	.286	44
Bruton, Billy	L	106	296	42	82	5	14	.277	33
Brown, Gates	L	123	426	65	116	15	11	.272	54
Wert, Don	R	148	525	63	135	9	3	.257	55
Cash, Norm	L	144	479	63	123	23	2	.257	83
Lumpe, Jerry	L	158	624	75	160	6	2	.256	46
Demeter, Don	R	134	441	57	113	22	4	.256	80
Phillips, Bubba	R	46	87	14	22	3	1	.253	6
McAuliffe, Dick	L	162	557	85	134	24	8	.241	66
Wood, Jake	R	64	125	11	29	1	0	.232	7
Roarke, Mike	R	29	82	4	19	0	0	.232	7
Horton, Willie	R	25	80	6	13	1	0	.163	10

Less than 10 games: Bill Roman, George Smith, Mickey Stanley, Jim Northrup and John Sullivan.

PITCHING RECORDS

	T	G	IP	W	L	PCT	ERA
Sparma, Joe	R	21	84	5	6	.455	3.00
Gladding, Fred	R	42	67	7	4	.636	3.09
Lolich, Mickey	L	44	232	18	9	.667	3.26
Fox, Terry	R	32	61	4	3	.571	3.39
Wickersham, Dave	R	40	254	19	12	.613	3.44
Navarro, Julio (5 LA, 26 Det.)	R	31	50	2	1	.667	3.60
Sherry, Larry	R	38	66	7	5	.583	3.68
Rakow, Ed	R	42	152	8	9	.471	3.73
Aguirre, Hank	L	32	162	5	10	.333	3.78
McLain, Denny	R	19	100	4	5	.444	4.05
Regan, Phil	R	32	147	5	10	.333	5.02

Less than 45 innings: Johnnie Seale, Bill Faul, Jack Hamilton, Dick Egan, Frank Lary and Fred Fisher. Alan Koch appeared in 3 games with Detroit and 32 with Washington.

DR. H. S. SAPERSTEIN
SURGEON PODIATRIST - FOOT SPECIALIST

HOURS BY APPOINTMENT

26095 WEST SIX MILE RD.
REDFORD, MICHIGAN 48240

537-4030

Tiger Players with 200 Hits Four or More Years

There are 27 players in the major leagues who have 200 hits in a season four or more times. Pete Rose leads the majors with 10; followed by Ty Cobb, who had 200 hits or more in nine different years. Charlie Gehringer had 200 hits or more seven different times, Al Simmons six times, and Harry Heilmann and Heinie Manush four times.

The Tigers paid for their 1905 spring training rent in Augusta, Georgia by giving the local team a young pitcher, Eddie Cicotte. Cicotte won 208 games during his major league career, but he is best known for his infamous involvement in the 1919 Black Sox scandal.

1965

FINAL STANDINGS

	W	L	PCT
Minnesota	102	60	.630
Chicago	95	67	.586
Baltimore	94	68	.580
DETROIT	89	73	.549
Cleveland	87	75	.537
New York	77	85	.475
California	75	87	.463
Washington	70	92	.432
Boston	62	100	.383
Kansas City	59	103	.364

Managers: Charlie Dressen and Bob Swift

Because of the emergence of so many promising young players, there was a fresh wave of optimism in the Tigers' training camp in 1965. From the top down, the team now felt it had the nucleus to quickly develop into a legitimate contender for many years to come, instead of a perennial also-ran.

However, their exuberance was short-lived.

On March 7, Manager Charlie Dressen staged a "chili party" for the team in the clubhouse. He spent four hours making a huge batch of his famous chili, then helped the players enjoy it. Spirits had seldom been higher. At 7 a.m. the following morning, Dressen phoned Tiger coach Stubby Overmire and asked Stubby to drive him to the airport. "My wife is ill in Los Angeles and I have to fly there," Dressen explained.

Dutifully, Overmire drove the Tiger manager to the airport, where Dressen called General Manager Jim Campbell to explain the reason for his sudden departure. "I'll be back in a few days," Dressen promised. "Bob Swift can handle the team while I'm gone."

However, the following day Campbell discovered the real reason behind Dressen's hasty departure. The high-strung Tiger manager had suffered a heart attack in his room after the chili party and had checked into a hospital as soon as he arrived in California. Campbell immediately had Swift summon the Tiger players to the clubhouse, where he explained the tragic situation to the stunned team.

Campbell announced that Swift would act as manager until Dressen returned. But the Tiger GM readily admitted he didn't know how soon that would be. The Tigers were in a daze. Even those who didn't particularly like Dressen personally realized he was a very sound, knowledgeable baseball man. They also sensed that, as a team, they were on the brink of something good and they didn't want anything to disrupt or detract from that feeling.

Swift had always wanted to be a big league manager, but getting the job on a temporary basis because of another man's tragic misfortune was not his idea of achieving his goal. Likewise, the players, who liked and respected Swift, realized he was just filling a space until Dressen was able to return.

Still, the Tigers played well under Swift, winning 24 while losing 18 to occupy third place when Dressen returned to duty on May 31.

One Tiger in particular made his presence felt. During one Tiger visit to Boston, Willie Horton managed to reach base 15 times in 17 tries, slamming a couple of home runs while knocking in five runs two nights in a row.

The Tigers sputtered but nevertheless stayed in contention most of the season as Al Kaline, Dick McAuliffe and Horton were all named to the American League All-Star team.

But the Tigers were admittedly worried about Kaline's troublesome foot that seemed to hinder him each season. There was much talk of possible surgery during the off-season to try to correct the problem. As promising as the Tigers appeared to be, most everyone agreed there was no way they would ever win the pennant without a healthy No. 6.

Seven wins in eight games in mid-August lifted the Tigers into second place but they soon settled back into fourth again, for the third time in four seasons. However, this time they won 89 games along the way; only once since 1950 had they won more.

The Tigers' hopes were further buoyed by the emergence of a pair of fine young right-handed pitchers, Denny McLain and Joe Sparma. McLain, who lost three of his first four decisions, developed into the ace of the staff, winning eight in a row during one span to finish the season at 16-6. Meanwhile, Sparma was 13-8. Lolich also enjoyed another excellent season, winning 15 and losing 9, but Dave Wickersham dropped to a disappointing 9-14.

Kaline again ranked as the Tigers' No. 1 hitter at .281, in spite of his many ailments, but it was Horton and Norm Cash who made the Tiger attack one to be feared. Cash belted 30 home runs while Horton hammered 29 and led the club with 104 rbi.

Jim Bunning, who pitched for the Tigers from 1955 through 1963, was the first man to pitch for both leagues in All-Star Games. He pitched six times for the American League and twice for the National.

BATTING RECORDS

	B	G	AB	R	H	HR	SB	AVE	RBI
Wood, Jake	R	58	104	12	30	2	3	.288	7
Kaline, Al	R	125	399	72	112	18	6	.281	72
Demeter, Don	R	122	389	50	108	16	4	.278	58
Horton, Willie	R	143	512	69	140	29	5	.273	104
Sullivan, John	L	34	86	5	23	2	0	.267	11
Cash, Norm	L	142	467	79	124	30	6	.266	82
Wert, Don	R	162	609	81	159	12	5	.261	54
McAuliffe, Dick	L	113	404	61	105	15	6	.260	54
Lumpe, Jerry	L	145	502	72	129	4	7	.257	39
Brown, Gates	L	96	227	33	58	10	6	.256	43
Stanley, Mickey	R	30	117	14	28	3	1	.239	13
Freehan, Bill	R	130	431	45	101	10	4	.234	43
Thomas, George	R	79	169	19	36	3	2	.213	10
Northrup, Jim	L	80	219	20	45	2	1	.205	16
Oyler, Ray	R	82	194	22	36	5	1	.186	13
Smith, George	R	32	53	6	5	1	0	.094	1
Moore, Jackie	R	21	53	2	5	0	0	.094	2
Roman, Bill	L	21	27	0	2	0	0	.074	0

Less than 10 games: Wayne Redmond.

PITCHING RECORDS

	T	G	IP	W	L	PCT	ERA
McLain, Denny	R	33	220	16	6	.727	2.62
Fox, Terry	R	42	78	6	4	.600	2.77
Gladding, Fred	R	46	70	6	2	.750	2.83
Sherry, Larry	R	39	78	3	6	.333	3.12
Sparma, Joe	R	30	167	13	8	.619	3.18
Lolich, Mickey	L	43	244	15	9	.625	3.44
Aguirre, Hank	L	32	208	14	10	.583	3.59
Wickersham, Dave	R	34	195	9	14	.391	3.78
Pena, Orlando (12 KC, 30 Det.)	R	42	93	4	12	.250	4.16
Regan, Phil	R	16	52	1	5	.167	5.02

Less than 45 innings: Ron Nischwitz, John Hiller, Verne Holtgrave, Leo Marentette, Julio Navarro, Jack Hamilton, Ed Rakow and John Seale.

1966

FINAL STANDINGS

	W	L	PCT
Baltimore	97	63	.606
Minnesota	89	73	.549
DETROIT	88	74	.543
Chicago	83	79	.512
Cleveland	81	81	.500
California	80	82	.494
Kansas City	74	86	.463
Washington	71	88	.447
Boston	72	90	.444
New York	70	89	.440

Managers: Charlie Dressen, Bob Swift, and Frank Skaff

The Tigers had many reasons to be encouraged as they entered the 1966 season. They featured three very promising, very talented young hurlers in Denny McLain, Mickey Lolich and Joe Sparma. Their outfield, considered by many to be the best in the league, was made up of Al Kaline, Willie Horton and Mickey Stanley. Bill Freehan was now a fixture behind the plate, and the infield was set with Norm Cash at first, Jerry Lumpe at second, Dick McAuliffe at short and Don Wert at third.

However, it was no secret the Tigers were lacking in depth. And that weakness soon began to show. First Freehan and then Stanley were felled by injuries. Then on May 16, the Tigers suffered their most crippling blow of all.

The team was on the field preparing to meet the St. Louis Cardinals in an exhibition game when General Manager Jim Campbell, who rarely was ever seen in the dugout or clubhouse, suddenly appeared on the dugout steps and motioned the players into the locker room.

There, the Tiger GM told his team that Manager Charlie Dressen had suffered another heart attack, his second in 14 months. Within a few days, it became apparent Dressen probably would never be able to manage the Tigers again. For the second time in little more than a year, Bob Swift assumed the position of Tiger manager under tragic circumstances.

The Tigers placed five players—Al Kaline, Bill Freehan, Norm Cash, Dick McAuliffe and Denny McLain—on the American League All-Star team, but that failed to disguise the fact that the team was struggling.

To make matters worse, two days after the All-Star break, Bob Swift became seriously ill and had to be hospitalized. It marked the first time in history that a major league baseball team had lost two managers to illness in the same season.

At first, Swift's illness was diagnosed as "a virus infection in the lining of the stomach," and the Tigers figured he would soon be back at the helm.

Meanwhile, third base coach Frank Skaff was placed in charge of the team while Dressen and Swift recuperated.

All in all, it inevitably had a demoralizing effect on the Tiger players, who were already having their problems on the field. Then Kaline strained his right side and was sidelined for nine days. While Al was ailing, Dick McAuliffe joined Swift in the hospital with a case of food poisoning.

Out on the field, the Tiger hitters stopped hitting and the pitchers were ineffective. The fielding became sloppy. During one three-week span, the Tigers had only one complete game by a starting pitcher.

Meanwhile, speculation mounted about who the next Tiger manager would be. Al Lopez and Billy Martin were two names that received considerable mention. Yet Tiger General Manager Jim Campbell was reluctant to make any definite moves in that direction until he could be certain about the future of Dressen and Swift.

As the Tigers continued to drop farther behind the front-running Baltimore Orioles, they received word on August 5 that Dressen had re-entered the hospital, this time suffering from a kidney infection. On August 10, Charlie Dressen died.

From that point on, certainly the Tigers could be excused if it appeared they were merely going through the motions. However, in spite of everything, they remained in a battle with the Minnesota Twins for second place.

Then, on September 26, the team received word that Bob Swift, suffering a malignant tumor on his lung, had lapsed into a coma and had been placed on the critical list—in three weeks, he would succumb. On the final weekend of the season, with second place at stake, the Tigers dropped three straight to the Kansas City Athletics and were forced to settle for third place.

It had been a season marred by tragedy, yet at the same time there had been reason for encouragement.

The Tigers led the American League in home runs with 179 as Al Kaline batted .288 and hit 28 homers. Norm Cash hit .279 with 32 homers, Willie Horton contributed 27 homers and McAuliffe continued to shine as one of the league's hardest-hitting shortstops with a .274 average and 23 home runs.

Denny McLain reached the coveted 20-victory mark for the first time, and Earl Wilson won nine in a row after coming to the Tigers from the Boston Red Sox in exchange for Don Demeter.

In an effort to put the tragedies of 1966 behind them as quickly as possible, the Tigers promptly hired former Philadelphia Phillies and Cincinnati Reds manager Mayo Smith to run the club in 1967.

Statistics

BATTING RECORDS

	B	G	AB	R	H	HR	SB	AVE	RBI
Stanley, Mickey	R	92	235	28	68	3	2	.289	19
Kaline, Al	R	142	479	85	138	29	5	.288	88
Cash, Norm	L	160	603	98	168	32	2	.279	93
McAuliffe, Dick	L	124	430	83	118	23	5	.274	56
Demeter, Don (32 Det., 73 Bos.)	R	105	325	43	87	14	2	.268	41
Wert, Don	R	150	559	56	150	11	6	.268	70
Brown, Gates	L	88	169	27	45	7	3	.266	27
Northrup, Jim	L	123	419	53	111	16	4	.265	58
Horton, Willie	R	146	526	72	138	27	1	.262	100
McFarlane, Orlando	R	49	138	16	35	5	0	.254	13
Wood, Jake	R	98	230	39	58	2	4	.252	27
Freehan, Bill	R	136	492	47	115	12	5	.234	46
Lumpe, Jerry	L	113	385	30	89	1	0	.231	26
Tracewski, Dick	R	81	124	15	24	0	1	.194	7
Oyler, Ray	R	71	210	16	36	1	0	.171	9

Less than 10 games: Arlo Brunsberg and Don Pepper.

PITCHING RECORDS

	T	G	IP	W	L	PCT	ERA
Wilson, Earl (15 Det., 00 Bul.)	R	38	264	18	11	.621	3.07
Pena, Orlando	R	54	108	4	2	.667	3.08
Wickersham, Dave	R	38	141	8	3	.727	3.19
Gladding, Fred	R	51	74	5	0	1.000	3.28
Podres, Johnny	L	36	108	4	5	.444	3.42
Aguirre, Hank	L	30	104	3	9	.250	3.81
Sherry, Larry	R	55	78	8	5	.615	3.81
McLain, Denny	R	38	264	20	14	.588	3.92
Monboquette, Bill	R	30	103	7	8	.467	4.72
Lolich, Mickey	L	40	204	14	14	.500	4.76
Sparma, Joe	R	29	92	2	7	.222	5.28

Less than 45 innings: John Hiller, Julio Navarro, Terry Fox, Bill Graham and George Korince.

SANTA ANITA

Electronic Bingo

709 Ouelette Ave.   Windsor   519-252-1702

$1100 Jackpot - $2150 Must Be Won

Friday 12:30, 1:30-5:30 — 7:30-10:30
Saturday 11:00, 1:30-4:30 — 7:30-10:30

Monday, Tuesday, Wednesday, Thursday
Friday, Saturday

*Winnings will be paid in
American money if you
play with American money.*

John & Jim Ogilvy

1967

FINAL STANDINGS

	W	L	PCT
Boston	92	70	.568
DETROIT	91	71	.562
Minnesota	91	71	.562
Chicago	89	73	.549
California	84	77	.522
Baltimore	76	85	.472
Washington	76	85	.472
Cleveland	75	87	.463
New York	72	90	.444
Kansas City	62	99	.385

Manager: Mayo Smith

As the Tigers prepared for the 1967 season, there seemed to be sound reasons for optimism for the first time in many years. In spite of the emotional shock that inevitably accompanied the tragic loss of their two managers during the previous summer, the Tigers appeared to be in position to make a real run for the pennant under new manager Mayo Smith.

The talented players developed in the farm system—players such as Willie Horton, Mickey Stanley, Jim Northrup, Bill Freehan, Gates Brown and Mickey Lolich—were ready to begin producing with championship regularity. Of course, the Tigers still had the incomparable Al Kaline. And they had further bolstered themselves with the addition of Denny McLain, Fred Lasher, Daryl Patterson, Tommy Matchick and Earl Wilson.

The biggest task in the minds of many observers, belonged to the new manager, Mayo Smith. It would be up to him to restore and enhance the Tigers' confidence in themselves. Only then would they be able to prove on the field what appeared to be true on paper. He moved Dick McAuliffe from short to second base and put Ray Oyler at short.

Al Kaline got off to a sensational start, hitting safely in 11 straight games to send his average soaring to near the .400 mark, and at the end of April the Tigers were in first place.

Typical of their new-found good fortune was a game against the Baltimore Orioles on April 30.

Steve Barber, a hard-throwing but erratic Oriole left-hander was the opposing pitcher that particular day and for eight innings he held the Tigers helpless and hitless. Leading 1-0, going into the top of the ninth, Barber stood three outs away from baseball immortality. And the crowd at Baltimore's Memorial Stadium grew quiet in anticipation of history about to be made.

Barber, never known for his pin-point control, walked Norm Cash, the first Tiger to face him in the ninth. Immediately Smith sent Dick Tracewski in to run for Cash. Next up was Ray Oyler, never known for his hitting. But

Barber walked him, too. Jake Wood, who could fly, was sent into run for Oyler.

Detroit's pitcher, Earl Wilson, was up next. Wilson, although one of baseball's better-hitting pitchers, sacrificed himself for the sake of the possible win, bunting both Tiger runners into scoring position.

Up came Willie Horton, pinch-hitting for Dick McAuliffe. And the powerful Horton popped up. Barber was one-out away from a no-hitter as Mickey Stanley stepped up to the plate. Stanley watched first a ball, then a strike, go by. Then he swung at the next pitch and missed. Barber was now one pitch away.

Then disaster struck. Barber's next pitch bounced in the dirt in front of the plate and caromed off Oriole catcher Larry Haney's shoulder. While Barber and the Baltimore crowd watched in horror, Tracewski raced home from third with the tying run. Now completely flustered, Barber proceeded to walk Stanley, sending Oriole manager Hank Bauer to the mound waving for reliever Stu Miller.

Still the Tigers' luck held out. Don Wert bounced to shortstop Luis Aparicio for what looked to be a certain inning-ending force-out at second. But second baseman Mark Belanger dropped the ball and Wood scampered home with what turned out to be the winning run.

The Tigers—the first-place Tigers—had prevailed without so much as a single base hit.

As the Tigers continued to win, their confidence continued to grow. And so did the confidence of their long-suffering fans who gradually came to believe, this time, their Tigers were for real.

Then on June 27, Kaline, who had been leading the league in hitting and who was the American League's top vote-getter in the All-Star election, was felled by yet another untimely injury.

After striking out against Cleveland's Sam McDowell, Kaline returned to the dugout and, in disgust, slammed his bat into the bat rack. Immediately, he felt a sharp pain travel up his little finger. Later, doctors discovered he had broken his finger.

It was a crippling blow to the Tigers. And, as everyone readily realized, one that could have been avoided. "Of all the dumb things I've ever done," admitted Kaline, "this has got to be the dumbest."

In spite of the loss of Kaline, and later injuries to Gates Brown, Willie Horton and Don Wert, the Tigers managed to remain in the pennant race, along with Chicago, Boston and Minnesota.

The four-way chase for the league championship continued through August and September, with no team showing any signs of surrendering. It went down to the final days, indeed the final hours, of the season.

Three days of cold, rainy weather made it necessary for the Tigers to play back-to-back doubleheaders against the California Angels on the final two days of the season. If they could sweep all four games they could win the pennant outright. But the overworked Tiger pitching staff could do no better than beat California twice.

Statistics

For the second-place Tigers, the season ended as Dick McAuliffe—who had not grounded into a double play all season—accounted for the final two outs by hitting into one.

It was the Tigers' best finish since 1945, but it nevertheless left a bitter taste in the mouths of the players because they knew they could so easily have finished one notch better.

Still there were reasons to smile. Attendance was up nearly 30 percent to 1,447,143, which made the front office happy. And on the field there had been many individual performances to be proud of.

Earl Wilson enjoyed a banner year, winning 22 and losing 11 to rank as the Tigers' top winner since Hal Newhouser and Dizzy Trout back in the 1940's.

In spite of his broken finger, Kaline topped the Tigers with a .308 average, 25 home runs and 78 rbi. Bill Freehan enhanced his status as the AL's leading catcher by batting .282 with 20 homers and 74 rbi.

But it was the Tigers' pitching staff that really stole the show as Joe Sparma posted a 16-9 record and Mickey Lolich came through in the clutch, throwing three straight shutouts during the critical September pennant rush.

Denny McLain won 17 and lost 16 but, because of a mysterious foot injury, missed the final days of the season when his presence might have made a difference in the race.

In the Tiger bullpen, Fred Gladding, Fred Lasher, Mike Marshall and John Hiller carried the load.

The final result may have been terribly frustrating, but no one could deny it had nevertheless been a successful season.

BATTING RECORDS

	B	G	AB	R	H	HR	SB	AVE	RBI
Kaline, Al	R	131	458	94	141	25	8	.308	78
Freehan, Bill	R	155	517	66	146	20	1	.282	74
Tracewski, Dick	R	74	107	19	30	1	1	.280	9
Green, Lennie	L	58	151	22	42	1	1	.278	13
Horton, Willie	R	122	401	47	110	19	0	.274	67
Northrup, Jim	L	144	495	63	134	10	7	.271	61
Price, Jim	R	44	92	9	24	0	0	.261	8
Wert, Don	R	142	534	60	137	6	1	.257	40
Cash, Norm	L	152	488	64	118	22	3	.242	72
McAuliffe, Dick	L	153	557	92	133	22	6	.239	65
Lumpe, Jerry	L	81	177	19	41	4	0	.232	17
Mathews, Eddie	L	36	108	14	25	6	0	.231	19
Stanley, Mickey	R	145	333	38	70	7	9	.210	24
Oyler, Ray	R	148	367	33	76	1	0	.207	29
Landis, Jim (25 Det., 5 Bos.)	R	30	55	5	11	3	0	.200	5
Brown, Gates	L	51	91	17	17	2	0	.187	9
Heath, Bill	L	20	32	0	4	0	0	.125	4
Wood, Jake	R	14	20	2	1	0	0	.050	0

Less than 10 games: Wayne Comer, Tom Matchick and Dave Campbell.

PITCHING RECORDS

	T	G	IP	W	L	PCT	ERA
Marshall, Mike	R	37	59	1	3	.250	1.98
Gladding, Fred	R	42	77	6	4	.600	1.99
Monbouquette, Bill (2 Det., 33 NY)	R	35	135	6	5	.545	2.33
Hiller, John	L	23	65	4	3	.571	2.63
Wickersham, Dave	R	36	85	4	5	.444	2.75
Dobson, Pat	R	28	49	1	2	.333	2.94
Lolich, Mickey	L	31	204	14	13	.519	3.04
Wilson, Earl	R	39	264	22	11	.667	3.27
Pena, Orlando (2 Det., 48 Clev.)	R	50	90	0	4	.000	3.60
Sparma, Joe	R	37	218	16	9	.640	3.76
McLain, Denny	R	37	235	17	16	.515	3.79
Podres, Johnny	L	21	63	3	1	.750	3.86

Less than 45 innings: Fred Lasher, Hank Aguirre, Larry Sherry, John Klippstein and George Korince.

Statistics ——————————————————————————— 133

1968

FINAL STANDINGS

	W	L	PCT
DETROIT	103	59	.636
Baltimore	91	71	.562
Cleveland	86	75	.534
Boston	86	76	.531
New York	83	79	.512
Oakland	82	80	.506
Minnesota	79	83	.488
California	67	95	.414
Chicago	67	95	.414
Washington	65	96	.404

Manager: Mayo Smith

To a man, the Tiger players believed they had been the best team in the American League in 1967. So they couldn't wait for 1968 to begin.

They felt the race should never have gone down to the final day in '67, that with their talent they should have walked away from the pack. And they were determined to prove that at the first opportunity.

Furthermore, the Tigers had proved to themselves and to everyone else that they were no longer the type of team that folded in the clutch, when the going got tough.

It didn't take the Tigers long to show they were absolutely right about 1968 either.

They simply won, and won, and won, leading the American League for all but 15 days from April until October. Time and time again the Tigers would overwhelm the opposition in the late innings as if they refused to be denied.

Nothing—not even the loss of their leader, Al Kaline, to a broken arm in late May—could stop the Tigers. By June 12, the Tigers had won 19 games in which they had been tied or behind in the seventh inning or later. In 12 of those games, the Tigers had pushed the winning run across the plate in their final turn at bat.

There were many reasons for the Tigers' remarkably consistent success in 1968 and many players who deserved to share in the credit.

For one thing, the '68 Tigers had depth. They had guys sitting in the dugout who could come off the bench in the late innings and get the job done.

Second, they had pitching. Strong pitching. Denny McLain had suddenly become almost unbeatable on a staff that also included Mickey Lolich.

Last but certainly not least, the Tigers believed in themselves and in their ability to win. They honestly expected to win every time they set foot on the field and they were genuinely surprised when they failed to do so.

And no one displayed more of that kind of confidence than McLain. By June 13, the often-outspoken, controversial righthander had won 10 games. By mid-July, his record was 18 wins against only two losses.

Even the loss of sparkplug infielder Dick McAuliffe, who was suspended for five days following his on-the-field fight with Tommy John of the White Sox, failed to halt the Tigers' push to the pennant—although the Tigers did lose four games while McAuliffe was serving his sentence.

On September 14, McLain won for the 30th time, making him the first 30-game winner since Dizzy Dean in 1934 and the first in the American League since Lefty Grove in 1931.

Three days later, the Tigers made the inevitable official, clinching the AL pennant.

Of course, the near-capacity crowd of 46,512 at Tiger Stadium, went absolutely wild. Fans actually tore down the left- field screen in the haste to get out on the field and celebrate the Tigers' first pennant since 1945. Inside the clubhouse, the jubilant Tigers celebrated with 108 bottles of champagne, spraying most of the bubbly over one another's heads.

This was one Tiger team that no one could accuse of collapsing in the clutch.

By the season's end, they had won 103 games—a Detroit record—to finish 12 lengths ahead of the second-place Baltimore Orioles, the widest such margin in the AL since 1947.

McLain, the center of attention all summer, finished with a 31-6 record and 28 complete games out of 41 starts. Along the way, Denny struck out 280 enemy batters in 336 innings to break another all-time Detroit record.

Offensively, the Tigers led the league in home runs with 185 and runs scored with 671. They were, indeed, a team of big booming bats.

For heroes, Tiger fans had plenty of players to choose from: Willie Horton for all of his clutch runs batted in; Gates Brown for all of his record-setting pinch hits; Bill Freehan for his 25 home runs and 84 rbi; Jim Northrup for his grand slam home runs; Norm Cash for his late season surge; Mickey Stanley for his excellent defense and much improved hitting; Mickey Lolich for his 10-2 effort during the final two months; and Dick McAuliffe for his inspiration as well as his contribution at second base. And, of course, 31-game winner Denny McLain.

At long last, the Tigers were winners again. But one huge obstacle still lay ahead of them: the World Series.

Pinch-Hit Home Run Leaders

There have been 14 players who have pinch-hit ten or more home runs in their career. Gates Brown had a total of 16 homers in his career with the Tigers.

BATTING RECORDS

	B	G	AB	R	H	HR	SB	AVE	RBI
Brown, Gates	L	67	92	15	34	6	0	.370	15
Kaline, Al	R	102	327	49	94	10	6	.287	53
Horton, Willie	R	143	512	68	146	36	0	.285	85
Northrup, Jim	L	154	580	76	153	21	4	.264	90
Freehan, Bill	R	155	540	73	142	25	0	.263	84
Cash, Norm	L	127	411	50	108	25	1	.263	63
Stanley, Mickey	R	153	583	88	151	11	4	.259	60
McAuliffe, Dick	L	151	570	95	142	16	8	.249	56
Mathews, Eddie	L	31	52	4	11	3	0	.212	8
Matchick, Tom	L	80	227	18	46	3	0	.203	14
Wert, Don	R	150	536	44	107	12	0	.200	37
Price, Jim	R	64	132	12	23	3	0	.174	13
Tracewski, Dick	R	90	212	30	33	4	3	.156	15
Oyler, Ray	R	111	215	13	29	1	0	.135	12
Comer, Wayne	R	48	48	8	6	1	0	.125	3

Less than 10 games: Bob Christian, Lennie Green and Dave Campbell.

PITCHING RECORDS

	T	G	IP	W	L	PCT	ERA
McLain, Denny	R	41	336	31	6	.838	1.96
McMahon, Don (25 Chi., 20 Det.)	R	45	82	5	2	.714	1.98
Patterson, Daryl	R	38	68	2	3	.400	2.12
Hiller, John	L	39	128	9	6	.600	2.39
Wyatt, John (8 Bos., 7 NY, 22 Det.)	R	37	49	2	4	.333	2.76
Dobson, Pat	R	47	125	5	8	.385	2.66
Wilson, Earl	R	34	224	13	12	.520	2.85
Lolich, Mickey	L	39	220	17	9	.654	3.19
Lasher, Fred	R	34	49	5	1	.833	3.31
Sparma, Joe	R	34	182	10	10	.500	3.71
Ribant, Denny (14 Det., 17 Chi.)	R	31	56	2	4	.333	4.34

Less than 45 innings: Les Cain, Jim Rooker, Elroy Face and Jon Warden.

1968 WORLD SERIES

Home Team	Date	Winning Team	Winning Pitcher	Losing Pitcher	Score
St. Louis	October 2	St. Louis	Gibson	McLain	4-0
St. Louis	October 3	Detroit	Lolich	Briles	8-1
Detroit	October 5	St. Louis	Washburn	Wilson	7-3
Detroit	October 6	St. Louis	Gibson	McLain	10-1
Detroit	October 7	Detroit	Lolich	Hoerner	5-3
St. Louis	October 9	Detroit	McLain	Washburn	13-1
St. Louis	October 10	Detroit	Lolich	Gibson	4-1

The Tigers' opponents in the 1968 World Series were the reigning world champion St. Louis Cardinals. But first, Tiger manager Mayo Smith had a decision to make: he had to find a way to get Al Kaline into the Detroit lineup.

Kaline, the Tigers' only legitimate superstar for so many seasons, had broken his arm in late May; when he was ready to return to the lineup, he found there was no place for him to play.

It was a fact that the Tigers had won the pennant without Kaline. The question was: Could they win the World Series without him, too?

That was a chance Smith was not willing to take. Besides, the Tiger manager believed after all of his often-frustrating seasons of faithful service, Kaline deserved a place in the lineup now that the Tigers had finally reached the Series.

The problem was, where? Smith could not bring himself to bench any of the three young Tiger outfielders—Willie Horton, Mickey Stanley and Jim Northrup—who had performed so admirably all season in Kaline's absence. They had won the pennant; they deserved to play in the Series as much as Kaline did.

Kaline had played some first base after his return during the regular season, but Smith could not see himself removing a Norm Cash from the lineup to make room for Al. Cash certainly deserved to play in the Series. Besides, the Tigers needed his potent bat.

Aware of what had to be going through his manager's mind, Kaline approached Smith and suggested Mayo "go with the younger guys." In effect, Kaline, who had waited his entire career to play in a World Series, was volunteering to watch this one from the bench.

But Smith not only felt Kaline deserved to play in the Series, Mayo wanted Al in the lineup. Kaline, after all, was still probably the best all-around ballplayer on the team.

Finally, he found a solution: Smith would move Stanley from centerfield to shortstop, where he had never played before, shift Northrup over from rightfield to center, and start Kaline in right.

It was perhaps the boldest move any manager had ever made in any World Series. And the whole world was waiting to see if it would backfire.

They didn't have to wait long as the first ball hit in by the Cardinals in their first turn at bat in the opening game, went directly to Stanley, who fielded it cleanly. By the end of the Series, Stanley had handled 29 chances and committed only two errors, neither of which hurt the Tigers.

Game One of the Series pitted the two teams' ace pitchers, Denny McLain of the Tigers and Bob Gibson of the Cardinals against one another. That much-ballyhooed match-up belonged entirely to Gibson as the veteran righthander struck out an all-time record 17 Tigers en route to a 4-0 victory.

The next afternoon, however, the Tigers proved that their much-publicized powerhouse attack was not simply a figment of the American League's imagination as they battered the Cardinals 8-1.

Mickey Lolich, whose 17-9 record during the regular season had been overshadowed by McLain, shrugged off a groin infection to pitch a six-hit victory that even included a rare home run by the winning pitcher.

Horton and Cash also homered for the Tigers, marking the first time all season that any team had hit three home runs off St. Louis pitching in the same game.

The Tigers returned home for their first World Series game at Tiger Stadium in 23 years, but they disappointed their faithful followers by dropping a 7-3 decision to Ray Washburn of the Cardinals.

In spite of home runs by Kaline and Dick McAuliffe, the Tigers were both outhit and outrun by the Redbirds. Tim McCarver and Orlando Cepeda both smacked three-run homers for the Cardinals and speedster Lou Brock, who had stolen a total of three bases in the first two games, swiped three more.

McLain and Gibson were matched up again in Game Four and again the result was the same: a decisive victory for the Cardinals. The Cards hammered the Tigers' 31-game winner for six hits and four runs in less than three innings as they coasted to an easy 10-1 win. Twice the game was delayed by rain and the Tiger offense looked as dismal as the weather as they settled for a bases-empty Jim Northrup home run off Gibson in the fourth inning.

On the brink of elimination, the Tigers turned to Lolich in the fifth game and the Redbirds quickly jumped on Mickey with three first-inning runs. However, that was all they got as Smith stuck with Lolich and the Tiger lefthander mowed the enemy down until his teammates could catch up and win, 5-3.

The turning point in the game—indeed, in the Series—came in the fifth inning of Game Five when, with his team leading 3-2, Brock decided to try to score from second on Julian Javier's single to leftfield—without sliding.

Willie Horton's throw home to Bill Freehan, who had effectively blocked the plate, nailed Brock standing up and gave the Tigers even more momentum. The Tigers scored three times in the seventh inning, featured by a bases-loaded single by Kaline, and won the game 5-3.

McLain, back on the mound in Game Six, after two disappointing efforts, was treated to a tremendous outburst of Tiger hitting and coasted to an easy 13-1 win that evened the once-lopsided Series at three victories per side. It was the most humiliating setback in St. Louis World Series history as the Tigers rallied for 10 runs in the third inning to match or break 10 Series records. Jim Northrup belted a grand slam home run—his fifth of the year—and Kaline and Cash each collected three hits as once again the Tigers made McLain absolutely unbeatable.

The seventh and deciding game pitted Lolich against Gibson, each man seeking his third win of the Series. The two men matched pitch for pitch, out for out, inning for inning until the seventh, when Gibson, who had retired 20 of the first 21 Tigers he had faced, suddenly yielded singles to Cash and Horton. Northrup followed with a line-drive to center where the usually sure-gloved Curt Flood misjudged the ball, then slipped and misplayed it into a triple. Bill Freehan came through with a runs batted in single, and Lolich did the rest to give the Tigers their world championship.

Lolich, of course, was the Series MVP for his three critical victories along with a 1.67 Series earned run average, but the Tigers had other heroes, too.

Cash batted .385 and Kaline made his presence felt with a .379 average and two home runs, proving Mayo Smith had not merely made a sentimental decision, but a wise one as well.

What followed has been described as the wildest celebration in the history of Detroit sports. And you could hardly blame the Tigers or their fans for their uncontrolled exuberance. After all, they had waited a long, long time.

WORLD SERIES INDIVIDUAL AVERAGES

	G	AB	R	H	HR	SB	PCT	RBI
Comer	1	1	0	1	0	0	1.000	0
Cash	7	26	5	10	1	0	.385	5
Kaline	7	29	6	11	2	0	.379	8
Mathews	2	3	0	1	0	0	.333	0
Horton	7	23	6	7	1	0	.304	3
Northrup	7	28	4	7	2	0	.250	8
Lolich	3	12	2	3	1	0	.250	2
McAuliffe	7	27	5	6	1	0	.222	3
Stanley	7	28	4	6	0	0	.214	0
Wert	6	17	1	2	0	0	.118	2
Freehan	7	24	0	2	0	0	.083	2
Brown	1	1	0	0	0	0	.000	0
Wilson	1	1	0	0	0	0	.000	0
Price	2	2	0	0	0	0	.000	0
Matchick	3	3	0	0	0	0	.000	0
McLain	3	6	0	0	0	0	.000	0
Oyler	4	0	0	0	0	0	.000	0
Dobson	3	0	0	0	0	0	.000	0
Hiller	2	0	0	0	0	0	.000	0
McMahon	2	0	0	0	0	0	.000	0
Patterson	2	0	0	0	0	0	.000	0
Tracewski	2	0	1	0	0	0	.000	0
Lasher	1	0	0	0	0	0	.000	0
Sparma	1	0	0	0	0	0	.000	0

PITCHING RECORDS

	G	IP	W	L	PCT	R	H	BB	SO
Patterson	2	3	0	0	.000	0	1	1	0
Lasher	1	2	0	0	.000	0	1	0	1
Lolich	3	27	3	0	1.000	5	20	6	21
McLain	3	16⅔	1	2	.333	8	18	4	13
Dobson	3	4⅔	0	0	.000	2	5	1	0
Wilson	1	4⅓	0	1	.000	3	4	6	3
Hiller	2	2	0	0	.000	4	6	3	1
McMahon	2	2	0	0	.000	3	4	0	1
Sparma	1	⅓	0	0	.000	2	2	0	0

Tiger Spring Training Sites

1901 ————*Detroit*
1902 ————*Ypsilanti*
1903-04 ————*Shreveport, LA*
1905-07————*Augusta, GA*
1908 ————*Hot Springs, AR*
1909-10————*San Antonio, TX*
1911-12————*Monroe, LA*
1913-15————*Gulfport, MS*
1916-18————*Waxahachie, TX*
1919-20————*Macon, GA*
1921 ————*San Antonio, TX*
1922-26————*Augusta, GA*
1927-28————*San Antonio, TX*
1929 ————*Phoenix, AZ*
1930 ————*Tampa, FL*
1931 ————*Sacramento, CA*
1932 ————*Palo Alto, CA*
1933 ————*San Antonio, TX*
1934-42————*Lakeland, FL*
1943-45————*Evansville, IN*
1946-present *Lakeland, FL*

SAFFRON BILLIARD

MICHIGAN'S LARGEST BILLIARD SUPPLY

EVERYTHING FOR YOUR GAME ROOM:

- Pool Tables • Bars & Barstools
- Ping Pong Tables • Air Hockey
- Poker Tables • Dart Sets • Bumper Pool Tables
- Monogrammed Poker Chips & Much More!

23622 S. Woodward at 9½ Mile
Pleasant Ridge
542-8429

1969

FINAL STANDINGS

EAST DIVISION	W	L	PCT
Baltimore	109	53	.673
DETROIT	90	72	.556
Boston	87	75	.537
Washington	86	76	.531
New York	80	81	.497
Cleveland	62	99	.385
WEST DIVISION			
Minnesota	97	65	.599
Oakland	88	74	.543
California	71	91	.438
Kansas City	69	93	.426
Chicago	68	94	.420
Seattle	64	98	.395

Manager: Mayo Smith

In sharp contrast to the previous spring, when the Tigers had entered the new season with well-founded confidence, there were many distractions to take their minds off of baseball as the 1969 campaign began.

For one thing, the American League had been realigned into two divisions, necessitating a playoff between division winners to determine which team would advance to the World Series. No longer would it be sufficient to simply finish first. Critics warned that it would be entirely possible for a weak first-place team from a weak division to eliminate a strong winner from a strong division in the short best-three-out-of-five playoff, thereby negating the importance of the 162-game season.

The defending world champion Tigers were in the Eastern Division of the AL, along with the New York Yankees, Baltimore Orioles, Boston Red Sox, Cleveland Indians and Washington Senators.

Further complicating matters was the fact that the major league players, in an effort to force the club owners to sweeten the players' pension fund, threatened to strike and refused to report for spring training until their differences could be resolved. Nearly two weeks of valuable training-camp time was lost before the two sides finally resolved their differences.

As reigning champs, the Tigers were, of course, considered "the team to beat" in 1969. It was a role they had earned and a role that they relished, but it did not come without its side effects.

Some of the players took their new-found success in stride, while others, perhaps inevitably, began to suffer from slightly swelled heads. After all, it isn't every day that a ballplayer can honestly say he is No. 1. And for the Tigers, that distinction had been a particularly long time in coming.

However, in the minds of the Tigers and most of their followers, there was no doubt the Tigers, with their championship team intact, could again overwhelm their American League rivals.

By the middle of April, however, it was already apparent it would not be all that easy for the Tigers to repeat. As their losses unexpectedly began to match their victories, some of the players began to press, trying too hard to carry too much of the load by themselves.

One player who was particularly troubled was young Willie Horton. As Horton struggled at the plate, his frustrations began to mount—and so did the boos and catcalls from the Tiger fans. Finally, thoroughly confused and distressed, Horton ripped off his uniform in the clubhouse and walked out on the team. He was immediately suspended without pay and dropped briefly out of sight before he returned and apologized and was reinstated.

Denny McLain also posed a problem because of his off-the-field activities. No Tiger savored the post-Series spotlight more than McLain and it often seemed to his teammates that baseball was of secondary importance to Denny as he jetted around the country in his own plane, playing the organ between pitching appearances.

Team rules meant little to McLain. He broke many of them with alarming regularity, sometimes with the approval of Tiger manager Mayo Smith.

Some teammates resented McLain's special privileges. Others felt whatever Denny did off the field was all right so long as he continued to win. There was a suspicion in the minds of some that if Smith did try to crack down on Denny, McLain might lose some of his desire to win.

The situation finally came to a head at the All-Star Game when Smith, who was managing the AL team, gave McLain permission to fly home for a dental appointment and Denny failed to return to Washington, D.C. in time for the game, even though he was scheduled to be the starting pitcher.

To make matters worse, McLain left in the middle of the game and flew to Florida, stranding Mickey Lolich and his wife, who had flown from Detroit to Washington with Denny, and were expecting to make the return trip with him as well.

Both developments became public knowledge and Tiger general manager Jim Campbell had no choice but to crack down, ordering McLain not to take off on his own unless the entire team was idle that day.

Injuries began to pile up and pitching coach Johnny Sain, who had been hailed as a genius the season before, was fired in an ongoing dispute with Mayo Smith.

Meanwhile, the Orioles were winning with the monotonous regularity that had been the Tigers' trademark in '68. Although the Tigers managed to finish second, they were nevertheless a demoralizing 19 games behind Baltimore.

Individually, several players excelled. In spite of everything, McLain won 24 games and lost nine while Mickey Lolich won 19 times. Newcomer Mike Kilkenny also impressed, tossing four shutouts in eight late-season wins.

Al Kaline, Norm Cash and Jim Northrup carried their share of the load but Bill Freehan, Mickey Stanley and Don Wert all trailed off.

By the end of the season, the Tigers were a beaten team, merely going through the motions.

As part of baseball's Centennial celebration, the all-time Tiger team was selected, and it included two players—Kaline and McLain—who were still in uniform.

The dream team featured Hank Greenberg at first base, Charlie Gehringer at second, shortstop Billy Rogell, third baseman George Kell, Kaline, Ty Cobb and Harry Heilmann in the outfield, Mickey Cochrane behind the plate, and lefthander Hal Newhouser along with the righthanded McLain.

Kaline received more votes in the outfield than Cobb did—16,115 to 14,211—but Cobb was voted The Greatest Tiger Ever, easily outdistancing runner-up Kaline in that balloting 9,193 to 3,928.

BATTING RECORDS

	B	G	AB	R	H	HR	SB	AVE	RBI
Northrup, Jim	L	148	543	79	160	25	4	.295	66
Cash, Norm	L	142	483	81	135	22	2	.280	74
Kaline, Al	R	131	456	74	124	21	1	.272	69
Horton, Willie	R	141	508	66	133	28	3	.262	91
Freehan, Bill	R	143	489	61	128	16	1	.262	49
McAuliffe, Dick	L	74	271	49	71	11	2	.262	00
Gutierrez, Cesar	R	17	49	5	12	0	1	.245	0
Matchick, Tom	L	94	298	25	72	0	3	.242	32
Stanley, Mickey	R	149	592	73	139	16	8	.235	70
Price, Jim	R	72	192	21	45	9	0	.234	28
Brown, Ike	R	70	170	24	39	5	2	.229	12
Wert, Don	R	132	423	46	95	14	3	.225	50
Tresh, Tom (45 NY, 94 Det.)	B	139	474	59	100	14	4	.211	46
Brown, Gates	L	60	93	13	19	1	0	.204	6
Woods, Ron (17 Det., 72 NY)	R	89	186	21	34	2	2	.183	10
Tracewski, Dick	R	66	79	10	11	0	3	.139	4
Campbell, Dave	R	32	39	4	4	0	0	.103	2

Less than 10 games: Wayne Redmond.

PITCHING RECORDS

	T	G	IP	W	L	PCT	ERA
Timmerman, Tom	R	31	56	4	3	.571	2.73
McLain, Denny	R	42	325	24	9	.727	2.80
Lolich, Mickey	L	37	281	19	11	.643	3.14
Kilkenny, Mike	L	39	128	8	6	.571	3.38
Wilson, Earl	R	35	215	12	10	.545	3.31
Dobson, Pat	R	49	105	5	10	.333	3.60
Hiller, John	L	40	99	4	4	.500	4.00
Sparma, Joe	R	23	93	6	8	.429	4.74

Less than 45 innings: Fred Scherman, Fred Lasher, Bob Reed, Norm McRae, Gary Taylor, Daryl Patterson, Don McMahon and Dick Radatz.

INSURANCE & ESTATE APPRAISALS	DIAMONDS WATCHES

Gerald H. Lane

Schaldenbrand Jewelers, Inc.

AMERICAN CENTER
27777 FRANKLIN RD.
SOUTHFIELD, MICHIGAN 48034   358-1430

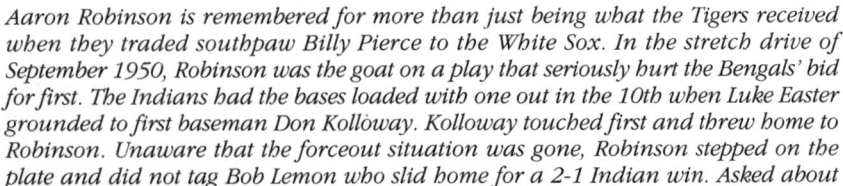

⚾ ⚾ ⚾

Aaron Robinson is remembered for more than just being what the Tigers received when they traded southpaw Billy Pierce to the White Sox. In the stretch drive of September 1950, Robinson was the goat on a play that seriously hurt the Bengals' bid for first. The Indians had the bases loaded with one out in the 10th when Luke Easter grounded to first baseman Don Kolloway. Kolloway touched first and threw home to Robinson. Unaware that the forceout situation was gone, Robinson stepped on the plate and did not tag Bob Lemon who slid home for a 2-1 Indian win. Asked about the play, Robinson explained that he never saw Kolloway step on first. The Tigers eventually finished three games in back of the league-leading Yankees.

1970

FINAL STANDINGS

EAST DIVISION	W	L	PCT
Baltimore	108	54	.667
New York	93	69	.574
Boston	87	75	.537
DETROIT	79	83	.488
Cleveland	76	86	.469
Washington	70	92	.432

WEST DIVISION			
Minnesota	98	64	.605
Oakland	89	73	.549
California	86	76	.531
Kansas City	65	97	.401
Milwaukee	65	97	.401
Chicago	56	106	.346

Manager: Mayo Smith

Just as everything went right for the Tigers in their mad dash to the world title two years earlier, everything went wrong for them in 1970.

First, there was the Denny McLain affair. In February, when the Tigers should have been eagerly looking forward to spring training, came charges in a prominent national magazine that McLain had put up money in 1967 to finance a bookmaking operation run by a gambler with Mafia connections. Also the magazine suggested that McLain's mysterious and costly foot injury at the height of the 1967 pennant race occurred as a result of a Mafia hoodlum stomping on Denny's foot.

On February 19, Baseball Commissioner Bowie Kuhn suspended McLain indefinitely while he continued his own investigation into the matter.

If that wasn't disturbing enough, it was learned that McLain, even though he was earning about $90,000 a year from the Tigers and an equal amount from his personal appearances, was teetering on the brink of bankruptcy.

The absence of McLain overshadowed the Tigers' spring training preparations. It was a source of constant distraction to the players, even though they insisted they could still win without their ace righthander. Then on March 31, with the start of the regular season just a few days away, Kuhn announced he was suspending McLain until July 1.

The Tigers were both depressed and encouraged by the length of the suspension. Many feared it might have been much longer. At least now, they reasoned, if they could stay near the top of the standings until midseason, they would have a good chance when McLain returned. Some suggested the suspension of McLain might make the rest of the Tigers more determined than ever as they sought to prove they could win without him.

The Tigers were hot and cold during the first half of the season. One of the brightest moments occurred in Cleveland on June 21 when shortstop

Cesar Gutierrez came off of the bench in the second game of a doubleheader against the Indians and collected seven hits in seven trips to the plate in a 12-inning game.

Nearly 54,000 jubilant fans showed up at Tiger Stadium July 1 to welcome McLain back into uniform. Obviously, despite all of the controversy and all of Denny's faults, the Tiger fans still adored him.

Unfortunately for the Tigers, McLain's performance on the mound did not match the reception he received from the fans as the New York Yankees knocked him out of the game in the sixth inning. McLain's long layoff had obviously diminished his effectiveness and although he won occasionally, he never regained the form that had made him so famous.

The Tigers' offense also suffered a severe blow when Willie Horton tore the ligaments in his ankle chasing a fly ball in late July and was lost for the rest of the season.

On August 2, the Tigers paid tribute to the great Al Kaline by honoring him with a day at Tiger Stadium. Kaline called it, "The greatest day of my life."

It was, however, one of the last happy occasions for Kaline or for the Tigers for the rest of the 1970 season.

The team soon began losing with alarming regularity. What was even worse was the pitiful way in which they performed, more often than not, in those defeats.

On August 28, McLain was suspended again, this time by the Tigers, for dumping buckets of water over two reporters' heads. A few days later, just as Tiger general manager Jim Campbell was about to lift his suspension, Commissioner Kuhn stepped in and suspended McLain for the rest of the season for allegedly carrying a gun.

The season was over for the Tigers—and they knew it—even though nearly a month remained on the schedule. Almost to a man, they quit caring—and it showed, as they stumbled home fourth in the AL East, 29 games behind Baltimore.

The loss of McLain, who compiled a lackluster 3-5 record, as well as that of Horton, was too much for the Tigers to overcome. Nearly every player suffered through an off-season at the plate as the Tigers slumped to dead last in the league in hitting with an anemic .238 average.

The pitchers had their problems, too, as Mickey Lolich lost 19 times while leading the team with only 14 victories. As a staff, the team's earned run average was an unsightly 4.09—the highest by any Tiger pitching corps in 20 years. Only the performance of reliever Tom Timmerman, who saved 27 games and won six others, as well as that of youngsters Les Cain and Daryl Patterson, gave the Tigers reason to be encouraged.

At season's end, Mayo Smith was fired as manager and replaced by fiery Billy Martin.

And, on the eve of the opening of the World Series, the Tigers rid themselves of McLain permanently, trading him, pitcher Norm McRae, infielder Don Wert and outfielder Elliott Maddox to the Washington Senators for infielders Eddie Brinkman and Aurelio Rodriguez and pitchers Joe Coleman and Jim Hannan.

It was a headline-making climax to what had been a headline-making season.

BATTING RECORDS

	B	G	AB	R	H	HR	SB	AVE	RBI
Horton, Willie	R	96	371	53	113	17	0	.305	69
Lamont, Gene	L	15	44	3	13	1	0	.295	4
Brown, Ike	R	56	94	17	27	4	0	.287	15
Kaline, Al	R	131	467	64	130	16	2	.278	71
Northrup, Jim	L	139	504	71	132	24	3	.262	80
Cash, Norm	L	130	370	58	96	15	0	.259	53
Stanley, Mickey	R	142	568	83	143	13	10	.252	47
Maddox, Elliott	R	109	258	30	64	3	2	.248	24
Gutierrez, Cesar	R	135	415	40	101	0	4	.243	22
Freehan, Bill	R	117	395	44	95	16	0	.241	52
McAuliffe, Dick	L	146	530	73	124	12	5	.234	50
Brown, Gates	L	81	124	18	28	3	0	.226	24
Jones, Dalton	L	89	191	29	42	6	1	.220	21
Wert, Don	R	128	363	34	79	6	1	.218	33
Collins, Kevin	L	25	24	2	5	1	0	.208	3
Price, Jim	R	52	132	12	24	6	0	.182	15
Nagelson, Russ (28 Det., 17 Clev.)	L	45	56	8	9	1	0	.161	4
Szotkiewicz, Ken	L	47	84	9	9	3	0	.107	9

Less than 10 games: Tim Holsey.

PITCHING RECORDS

	T	G	IP	W	L	PCT	ERA
Hiller, John	L	47	104	6	6	.500	3.03
Scherman, Fred	L	48	70	4	4	.500	3.21
Lolich, Mickey	L	40	273	14	19	.424	3.79
Cain, Les	L	29	181	12	7	.632	3.83
Niekro, Joe	R	38	213	12	13	.480	4.06
Timmerman, Tom	R	61	85	6	7	.462	4.13
Lasher, Fred (12 Det., 43 Clev.)	R	55	67	2	10	.167	4.16
Wilson, Earl	R	18	96	4	6	.400	4.41
McLain, Denny	R	14	91	3	5	.375	4.65
Patterson, Daryl	R	43	78	7	1	.875	4.85
Reed, Bob	R	16	46	2	4	.333	4.89
Kilkenny, Mike	L	36	129	7	6	.538	5.16

Less than 45 innings: Lerrin LaGrow, Norm McRae, Jerry Robertson and Dennis Saunders.

you can take it personally, at

National Bank of Royal Oak

215 South Center Street
4609 Crooks Road
4710 Rochester Road
1821 North Campbell

399-5200

MEMBER FDIC

Tigers with Eight or More Home Runs with Bases Loaded

There have been 62 players who have hit more than eight home runs with the bases loaded. Lou Gehrig stands out in the American League with 23. The Tiger leaders are Rudy York, 12 times and Hank Greenberg with 11. Al Simmons and Vic Wertz did it on ten occasions with Willie Horton and Rusty Staub doing it nine times. Ray Boone, Eddie Mathews, Jim Northrup, Norm Cash and Dick McAuliffe all hit homers with the bases loaded eight times.

1971

FINAL STANDINGS

EAST DIVISION	W	L	PCT
Baltimore	101	57	.639
DETROIT	91	71	.562
Boston	85	77	.525
New York	82	80	.506
Washington	63	96	.396
Cleveland	60	102	.370
WEST DIVISION			
Oakland	101	60	.627
Kansas City	85	76	.528
Chicago	79	83	.488
California	76	86	.469
Minnesota	74	86	.463
Milwaukee	69	92	.429

Manager: Billy Martin

The arrival of Billy Martin, plus the addition of Aurelio Rodriguez, Eddie Brinkman and Joe Coleman gave the Tigers good reason to be encouraged about their prospects in 1971.

The Tigers' decision to hire Martin was particularly surprising to many observers because brash Billy was not at all typical of the type of managers the conservative Tigers had turned to in the past. Always before they had favored sound baseball men whom they knew would adhere totally to company policy and never embarrass the ball club. But Martin was well-known for his outspoken tongue and his off-the-field antics, which had included punching the team's traveling secretary when he managed the Minnesota Twins and brawling with one of his own players, Twins' pitcher Dave Boswell.

However, the Tigers were desperate. The team had quit terribly under Mayo Smith and general manager Jim Campbell knew he needed someone who could light a fire under his club in a hurry.

The Tigers responded to Martin's prodding and began the 1970 season with a new-found enthusiasm and aggressive attitude that had been so sorely lacking the season before.

On the negative side, however, the Tigers were stunned by the sudden unexpected loss of pitcher John Hiller, who suffered a heart attack during the off-season, and Les Cain sidelined with a sore shoulder. Then, days before the team was to break camp and head north, Coleman was struck on the head by a line drive in an exhibition game and suffered a fractured skull.

In an effort to bolster their sadly depleted pitching staff, the Tigers picked up veterans Dean Chance and Dave Boswell, Martin's old brawling buddy.

Later, they acquired veteran infielder Tony Taylor to back Dick McAuliffe up at second base.

In July, the All-Star Game was played at Tiger Stadium for the first time since 1951, with the American League prevailing, 6-4.

As the second half of the regular season began, in spite of their many injuries, the Tigers did not quit as they had done the summer before. Billy Martin saw to that. Instead, they impressed many people as being perhaps the most improved team in the American League.

Mickey Lolich, who had labored so long in the shadow of the more controversial, more spectacularly successful Denny McLain, flourished as never before now that he was the No. 1 man on the pitching staff.

The pot-bellied lefthander with the rubber arm won 25 games and lost only 14, striking out 308 enemy batters in a Herculean 376 innings on the mound. It was a workhorse performance that had the experts recalling the long-ago iron man feats of pitchers like Ed Walsh and Grover Cleveland Alexander.

Coleman, who replaced McLain as the leading righthander in the starting rotation, recovered quickly from his near-tragic accident and went on to win 20 games. For relief, the Tigers turned to lefthander Fred Scherman, who displaced Tom Timmerman as the bullpen ace, winning 11 games and saving 20 others. However, three pitchers do not make a pennant winner and that trio got little help as the Tigers finished second behind Baltimore.

The Tigers' hitting improved dramatically under Martin. Two of the key cogs in the attack were veterans Al Kaline, who hit .294, and Norm Cash, who batted .283 with 32 home runs after many observers had written him off as over-the-hill.

Behind the plate, Bill Freehan bounced back from back surgery to bat .277 with 21 home runs. And Mickey Stanley's average soared to .292.

The Denny McLain deal did wonders for the Tigers' defense, too, as Rodriguez and Brinkman made the left side of the infield airtight. Brinkman shattered a major league record late in the season when he played 56 games in a row at shortstop without committing an error. Although the Tigers did finish second, boosting their win total from 79 to 91, they nevertheless still ended up a dozen games behind the Orioles. Obviously, there was still a lot of work to do before the Tigers could catch the Birds.

Following the season, Martin's contract as manager was extended for another season—through 1973—and Kaline, who had modestly turned down a six-figure contract the winter before because he didn't believe he deserved it, became the first $100,000-a-year player in Detroit Tiger history.

Statistics

BATTING RECORDS

	B	G	AB	R	H	HR	SB	AVE	RBI
Brown, Gates	L	82	195	37	66	11	4	.338	29
Kaline, Al	R	133	405	69	119	15	4	.294	54
Stanley, Mickey	R	139	401	43	117	7	1	.292	41
Horton, Willie	R	119	450	64	130	22	1	.289	72
Taylor, Tony	R	55	181	27	52	3	5	.287	19
Cash, Norm	L	135	452	72	128	32	1	.283	91
Freehan, Bill	R	148	516	57	143	21	2	.277	71
Northrup, Jim	L	136	459	72	124	16	7	.270	71
Collins, Kevin	L	35	41	6	11	1	0	.268	4
Brown, Ike	R	59	110	20	28	8	0	.255	19
Jones, Dalton	L	83	138	15	35	5	1	.254	11
Rodriguez, Aurelio	R	154	604	68	153	15	4	.253	39
Price, Jim	R	29	54	4	13	1	0	.241	7
Brinkman, Eddie	R	159	527	40	120	1	1	.228	37
McAuliffe, Dick	L	128	477	67	99	18	4	.208	57
Gutierrez, Cesar	R	38	37	8	7	0	0	.189	4

Less than 10 games: Tim Holsey, Gene Lamont, Marvin Lane and John Young.

PITCHING RECORDS

	T	G	IP	W	L	PCT	ERA
Scherman, Fred	L	69	113	11	6	.647	2.71
Lolich, Mickey	L	45	376	25	14	.641	2.92
Coleman, Joe	R	39	286	20	9	.690	3.15
Chance, Dean	R	31	90	4	6	.400	3.50
Timmerman, Tom	R	52	84	7	6	.538	3.86
Denehy, Bill	R	31	49	0	3	.000	4.22
Cain, Les	L	26	145	10	9	.526	4.34
Niekro, Joe	R	31	122	6	7	.462	4.50
Kilkenny, Mike	L	30	86	4	5	.444	5.02
Perranoski, Ron (36 Minn., 11 Det.)	L	47	61	1	5	.167	5.46

Less than 45 innings: Bill Gilbreth, Chuck Seelbach, Jack Whillock, Jim Foor, Bill Zepp, Dave Boswell (3 Det., 15 Balt.), Jim Hannon (7 Det., 21 Mil.) and Daryl Patterson (12 Det., 4 Oak.).

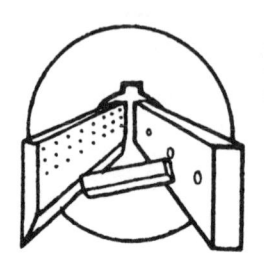

Detroit
EDGE TOOL COMPANY

MANUFACTURERS OF

MACHINE KNIVES & WAYS

6570 E. Nevada Ave.
Detroit, Mich. 48234
313/366-4120

Six Hits or More in One Game

Thirty-six times in the American League players have had six hits or more. One of the first to do it was Bill Nance of the Detroit Tigers on July 13, 1901, when he had five singles and a double. Bobby Veach also did it in 12 innings on September 17, 1920; his six hits included a double and a triple and home run. On May 5, 1925, Ty Cobb had six hits, one of which was a double. Doc Cramer, then playing with Philadelphia, had six hits, all singles on June 20, 1932. Doc also had six hits on July 13, 1935 while also playing with the Philadelphia Athletics. Bruce Campbell, who later became a Tiger, had six hits when he played for Cleveland on July 2, 1936—5 singles and a double. Rip Radcliff, then with the White Sox, on July 18, 1936 went to bat seven times and had two doubles and four singles. George Kell on September 20, 1946 with seven times at bat had five singles and a double.

1972

FINAL STANDINGS

EAST DIVISION	W	L	PCT
DETROIT	86	70	.551
Boston	85	70	.548
Baltimore	80	74	.519
New York	79	76	.510
Cleveland	72	84	.462
Milwaukee	65	91	.417

WEST DIVISION	W	L	PCT
Oakland	93	62	.600
Chicago	87	67	.565
Minnesota	77	77	.500
Kansas City	76	78	.494
California	75	80	.484
Texas	54	100	.351

Manager: Billy Martin

There was little doubt about the Tiger offense as they prepared for the 1972 campaign. After all, they had led both major leagues in home runs the previous season and featured that same formidable lineup of Al Kaline, Norm Cash, Willie Horton, Bill Freehan and Jim Northrup.

The problem was their pitching. Mickey Lolich and Joe Coleman had proven themselves to be winners, but no one could be sure about the rest of the staff. Guys like Tom Timmerman, Les Cain, Joe Niekro and Mike Kilkenny were all question marks for one reason or another.

To add to that uncertainty, one week before the 1972 season was to open, the major league players voted to go on strike in an effort to win increased pension benefits.

Billy Martin, for one, was convinced the strike would be particularly costly to the Tigers because they were a veteran club and veteran players usually need more time to get ready for a season than the kids do.

Plus, the Tigers had worked very hard in spring training preparing themselves for the season ahead, and a long strike would mean that much, if not all, of that effort had been wasted.

The strike was finally settled on April 14 and a decision was made to cancel all games that had been missed. That meant the Tigers would play a 156-game schedule while the other contending clubs in the American League East would play 154 or 155 games. It was an imbalance that was going to loom particularly large at the end of the year.

When play resumed, oddly enough, it was the Tigers' offense that was disappointing and inconsistent. And it was their questionable pitching staff that kept them in the thick of the pennant race.

In spite of their early-season slump and a couple of costly injuries to Kaline, the Tigers continued to battle Baltimore for the division lead. Both clubs had trouble winning and it often seemed like neither team wanted to take command of the race.

On August 13, in desperation after the Tigers had lost four in a row, Martin drew the names of his starting lineup out of a cap. The makeshift lineup prevailed, 3-2.

Down the stretch, the struggling Tigers and Orioles were joined in the pennant race by Boston and New York. Finally, it came down to the final three games of the season, between Detroit and the Boston Red Sox, at Tiger Stadium. Whichever team won two of those three games would be the Eastern Division champ.

The Tigers took the opener, 4-1, as Mickey Lolich struck out 15 batters and Kaline collected three hits in four trips. Then they clinched the crown by winning the second game, 3-1, as Kaline again came through, driving in one run and scoring another.

Because they played one more game than the runner-up Red Sox, the Tigers were able to win the division title by a mere half game.

Much of the credit went to Martin for molding the veteran Tigers into a pennant contender, then goading them to excel. The Tigers, who batted only .237 as a team, won with pitching and defense—and a few of Billy's brainstorms.

Meanwhile general manager Jim Campbell gave Martin the extra horses he needed by acquiring veterans Woody Fryman, Duke Sims and Frank Howard, all of whom figured prominently in the Tigers' late-season pennant push.

Kaline was another key contributor, finishing with a flurry to boost his average to .313, Al's best mark since 1961. Eddie Brinkman was named "Tiger of the Year" by Detroit's sportswriters for his nearly flawless performance in the field featuring one 72-game errorless span.

But it was the pitching staff that really made the difference. Mickey Lolich again reached the 20-victory plateau, this time with 22 wins. Coleman won 19, including five down the stretch in September. Fryman chipped in 10 clutch victories during the final two months, after he was obtained from Philadelphia. Fred Scherman and Chuck Seelbach joined forces in the bullpen to give the Tigers one of their most effective relief duos in many years.

And the fans responded. Nearly 1.9 million paid to see the Tigers play at home, giving Detroit the league lead in attendance and the third highest total in the history of the franchise.

BATTING RECORDS

	B	G	AB	R	H	HR	SB	AVE	RBI
Sims, Duke	L	38	98	11	31	4	0	.316	19
Kaline, Al	R	106	278	46	87	10	1	.313	32
Taylor, Tony	R	78	228	33	69	1	5	.303	20
Freehan, Bill	R	111	374	51	98	10	0	.262	56
Northrup, Jim	L	134	426	40	111	8	4	.261	42
Cash, Norm	L	137	440	51	114	22	0	.259	61
Brown, Ike	R	51	84	12	21	2	1	.250	10
Howard, Frank (95 Texas, 14 Det.)	R	109	320	29	78	10	1	.244	38
McAuliffe, Dick	L	122	408	47	98	8	0	.240	30
Rodriguez, Aurelio	R	153	601	65	142	13	2	.236	56
Stanley, Mickey	R	142	435	45	102	14	1	.234	55
Horton, Willie	R	108	333	44	77	11	0	.231	36
Brown, Gates	L	103	252	33	58	10	3	.230	31
Jata, Paul	R	32	74	8	17	0	0	.230	3
Haller, Tom	L	59	121	7	25	2	0	.207	13
Brinkman, Eddie	R	156	516	42	105	6	0	.203	49
Jones, Dalton (7 Det., 72 Texas)	L	79	158	14	24	4	1	.152	19
Comer, Wayne	R	27	9	1	1	0	0	.111	1
Knox, John	L	14	13	1	1	0	0	.077	0

Less than 10 games: Ike Blessitt, John Gamble, Marvin Lane, Gene Lamont and Joe Staton.

PITCHING RECORDS

	T	G	IP	W	L	PCT	ERA
Fryman, Woody	L	16	114	10	3	.769	2.05
Lolich, Mickey	L	41	327	22	14	.611	2.50
Coleman, Joe	R	40	280	19	14	.576	2.80
Timmerman, Tom	R	34	150	8	10	.444	2.88
Seelbach, Chuck	R	61	112	9	8	.529	2.89
Slayback, Bill	R	23	82	5	6	.455	3.18
Kilkenny, Mike (1 Det., 1 Oak., 22 Clev.)	L	24	60	4	1	.800	3.45
Scherman, Fred	L	57	94	7	3	.700	3.64
Niekro, Joe	R	18	47	3	2	.600	3.83

Less than 45 innings: Les Cain, Jim Foor, Bill Gilbreth, John Hiller, Fred Holdsworth, Lerrin LaGrow, Don Leshnock, Phil Meeler, Ron Perranoski, Bob Strampe and Chris Zachary.

1972 PLAYOFFS

Anyone who thought the 1972 American League Championship Playoff, pitting the Tigers against the Western Division champion Oakland A's would be anticlimactic after the Tigers' season-long struggle to win their own division, was in for a big surprise.

The opening game featured a duel of ace pitchers: Mickey Lolich of the Tigers against Oakland's Catfish Hunter.

And the two hurlers lived up to their reputations. Going into the 11th inning, the score was tied at 1-1. Then Al Kaline homered and with Lolich still going strong, the Tigers were three outs away from victory. It was not to be, however, as pinch-hitter Gonzalo Marquez singled with two A's on base and drove them both home as Kaline's throw to third struck the second runner and skipped away, allowing him to continue on across the plate.

"I went from hero to goat quicker than ever before," sighed Kaline.

Game two was no contest as Oakland's Blue Moon Odom shut the Tigers out 5-0, holding them to just three hits. A near-riot erupted in the seventh inning when A's shortstop Campy Campaneris flung his bat at Tiger pitcher Lerrin LaGrow after the hurler had struck him on the foot with a pitch.

Both Campaneris and LaGrow were ejected from the game and Campaneris was subsequently fined $500 and suspended for the duration of the playoff.

One game away from elimination, the Tigers turned to Joe Coleman when they returned home. And the righthander didn't let them down, striking out 14 A's while scattering seven hits en route to a 3-0 victory. Although it didn't count on his regular season record, it was Coleman's 20th triumph of the season.

The fourth game again pitted Lolich against Hunter, and again the two pitchers rose to the occasion. The score was tied at 1-1 when the A's suddenly came alive with two runs in the top of the 10th inning. The Tiger Stadium crowd grew quiet. They could sense that the end was near.

But the home town heroes loaded the bases before the A's could get anybody out in the bottom of the 10th. When second baseman Gene Tenace dropped the ball on a tailor-made double play, one Tiger crossed the plate. Then Oakland reliever Dave Hamilton walked Norm Cash with the bases filled to force home the tying run. Jim Northrup's single to right sent Kaline racing home with the winning run.

The following day, with the AL pennant squarely on the line, the Tigers fell just short as reliever Vida Blue edged Woody Fryman and his teammates 2-1.

It was hardly a convincing victory. Reggie Jackson pulled a hamstring scoring Oakland's initial run, and Tenace drove George Hendrick home with the winner with his only hit in 17 at bats in the playoff.

The frustrated Tiger fans, realizing their team had put up a gallant fight to come so close, stopped play several times during the final few innings

Statistics

when they littered the field with toilet paper, smoke bombs, fire crackers and other debris.

It was a sad ending to what had otherwise been a very satisfying season.

A.L.C.S. PLAYOFFS — INDIVIDUAL AVERAGES

	G	AB	R	H	HR	SB	PCT	RBI
I. Brown	1	2	0	1	0	0	.500	2
Coleman	1	2	0	1	0	0	.500	0
Northrup	5	14	0	5	0	0	.357	1
Stanley	4	6	0	2	0	0	.333	0
Cash	5	15	1	4	1	0	.267	2
Kaline	5	19	3	5	1	0	.263	1
Freehan	3	12	2	3	1	0	.250	3
Brinkman	1	4	0	1	0	0	.250	0
Sims	4	14	0	3	0	0	.214	0
McAuliffe	5	20	3	4	1	0	.200	1
Taylor	4	15	0	2	0	0	.133	0
Horton	5	10	0	1	0	0	.100	0
Knox	1	0	0	0	0	0	.000	0
LaGrow	1	0	0	0	0	0	.000	0
Niekro	1	0	0	0	0	0	.000	0
Scherman	1	0	0	0	0	0	.000	0
Zachary	1	0	0	0	0	0	.000	0
Seelbach	2	0	0	0	0	0	.000	0
Hiller	3	0	0	0	0	0	.000	0
Haller	1	1	0	0	0	0	.000	0
G. Brown	3	2	1	0	0	0	.000	0
Fryman	2	3	0	0	0	0	.000	0
Lolich	2	7	0	0	0	0	.000	0
Rodriguez	5	16	0	0	0	0	.000	0

PITCHING RECORDS

	G	IP	W	L	PCT	R	H	BB	SO
Coleman	1	9	1	0	1.000	0	7	3	14
Hiller	3	3⅓	1	0	1.000	0	1	1	1
LaGrow	1	1	0	0	.000	0	0	0	1
Scherman	1	⅔	0	0	.000	0	1	0	1
Lolich	2	19	0	1	.000	4	14	5	10
Fryman	2	12⅓	0	2	.000	6	11	2	8
Seelbach	2	1	0	0	.000	2	4	0	0
Zachary	1	0†	0	0	.000	1	0	1	0

†Pitched to one batter.

Just like the Pros wear. the AUTHENTIC RED WINGS Jersey by C.C.M. is available in white only. Adult sizes only: 44, 48, 52.

WINGS PRO WEIGHT JERSEY
$99.00

To place order by phone or to receive our NEW 1990-91 MERCHANDISE CATALOG call

SOUVENIRS (313) 567-7340

1973

FINAL STANDINGS

EAST DIVISION	W	L	PCT
Baltimore	97	65	.599
Boston	89	73	.549
DETROIT	85	77	.525
New York	80	82	.494
Milwaukee	74	88	.457
Cleveland	71	91	.438
WEST DIVISION			
Oakland	94	68	.580
Kansas City	88	74	.543
Minnesota	81	81	.500
California	79	83	.488
Chicago	77	85	.475
Texas	57	105	.352

Managers: Billy Martin and Joe Schultz

The memory of their division title and near-miss in the American League playoffs the season before sent the Tigers slipping into the 1973 campaign with high hopes.

After all, if Billy Martin's "Over-the-Hill" gang, as many folks had begun to call the Tigers, could come so close, why couldn't they go all the way?

The Tigers were a veteran club that knew how to win. They had playoff experience and many of the mainstays of the 1968 World Championship squad were still on the team.

And, of course, there was the presence of Martin. Martin's mystique as a manager who could work magic with a ball club, coaxing the most out of his players and transforming even mediocre athletes into pennant contenders, was at its zenith in the Motor City.

In the minds of many, including some members of the media, Billy Martin could do no wrong, at least not on the ball field. He was, they argued, simply the best manager in baseball.

But the Tigers were not the best team in baseball in 1973. They were not the best team in the American League. They were not even the best team in the AL Eastern Division any longer.

Although no one seemed to realize it at the time, the Tigers had begun a rapid downhill slide. But that great decline did not begin until after the Tigers had given their ever-optimistic followers sufficient reason to stay interested throughout much of 1973.

As they had done so successfully the season before, the Tigers again turned to veteran major leaguers, fading former stars who had played for Martin before, in an effort to bolster their weak spots.

To give Billy a fourth starting pitcher, they picked up Jim Perry from the Minnesota Twins. And, to beef up their bullpen, they added well-traveled reliever Bob Miller.

But it became obvious the Tigers were merely trying to apply Band-Aids, to temporarily plug their holes, in an effort to get one more championship out of a once-great nucleus. It was also obvious the Tigers did not believe their farm system had produced anyone who could help them at the present time.

Perry did the job he was hired to do, winning 14 times, but many of the Tigers' other key cogs let the team down. Joe Coleman, for example, enjoyed the winningest season of his career at 23-15. But, much to the dismay of the Tigers, their leading righthander lost seven games in a row at the time of the season when they needed his victories the most.

Mickey Lolich, who joined the $100,000 salary class in '73, making him the first six-figure pitcher in Tiger history, also disappointed, winning 16 while losing 15. In fairness to The Mick, however, it must be pointed out that seven of those setbacks were by one run.

The Tigers were again counting on the combination of righthander Chuck Seelbach and lefty Fred Scherman coming out of the bullpen to bail them out of many tight spots. But Seelbach hurt his arm almost before spring training had begun and made only five appearances on the mound all year. Scherman, meanwhile, faded to 2-2 with only one save, before he busted his hand in September when he slammed a clubhouse cabinet with his fist.

Fortunately for the Tigers, John Hiller bounced back from his heart attack in January of 1971 to become the ace of the relief corps, winning 10 games himself and compiling a major league record 38 saves. Hiller's was one of the most inspiring comeback sagas in the history of the national pastime.

But the big story of the 1973 season occurred off the field. Billy Martin got into enough trouble to convince Tiger owner John Fetzer and general manager Jim Campbell that it was time to fire him.

The Tigers' top brass had been considering that option ever since Martin quit the club for one day during spring training because he felt Campbell was meddling in his handling of the players. Martin's penchant for constantly popping off didn't sit well with the folks in the front office, either.

The friction and tension increased when Martin failed to accompany the team on a charter flight from Oakland to Chicago, traveling instead on his own to Kansas City to attend to personal business.

This was in direct violation of an order from Campbell that Martin travel with the team. To make matters worse, Billy didn't arrive at the ballpark in Chicago until 35 minutes before the start of the Tigers' series opener against the White Sox.

Later, Martin publicly attacked the Tigers' farm system, complaining that the front-running Baltimore Orioles seemed to have all of the good, young players. That did not please Campbell at all.

The situation reached a head when Martin announced he had ordered two of his pitchers, Joe Coleman and Fred Scherman, to throw spitballs at

Statistics ——————————————————————————— 161

the Cleveland Indians. Martin believed Cleveland pitcher Gaylord Perry had been throwing spitters at the Tigers.

Immediately, American League president Joe Cronin suspended Billy for three days. Before Martin could return, Campbell fired him, promoting third base coach Joe Schultz to manage the club for the remainder of the season.

In view of all that turmoil, it was perhaps surprising that the Tigers fared as well as they did in '73, finishing third in the division, 12 games behind Baltimore.

BATTING RECORDS

	B	G	AB	R	H	HR	SB	AVE	RBI
Cash, Ron	R	14	39	8	16	0	0	.410	6
Horton, Willie	R	111	411	42	130	17	1	.316	53
Northrup, Jim	L	110	404	55	124	12	4	.307	44
Veryzer, Tom	R	18	20	1	6	0	0	.300	2
Brown, Ike	R	42	76	12	22	1	0	.289	9
Knox, John	L	12	32	1	9	0	1	.281	3
McAuliffe, Dick	L	106	343	39	94	12	0	.274	47
Cash, Norm	L	121	363	51	95	19	1	.262	40
Howard, Frank	R	85	227	26	58	12	0	.256	29
Kaline, Al	R	91	310	40	79	10	4	.255	45
Sims, Duke (80 Det., 4 NY)	L	84	261	34	64	9	1	.245	31
Stanley, Mickey	R	157	602	81	147	17	0	.244	57
Sharon, Dick	R	91	178	20	43	7	2	.242	16
Brinkman, Eddie	R	162	515	55	122	7	0	.237	40
Brown, Gates	L	125	377	48	89	12	1	.236	50
Freehan, Bill	R	110	380	33	89	6	0	.234	29
Taylor, Tony	R	84	275	35	63	5	9	.229	24
Rodriguez, Aurelio	R	160	555	46	123	9	3	.222	58
Reese, Rick (59 Det., 22 Minn.)	L	81	125	17	18	3	0	.144	7

Less than 10 games: Joe Staton, Bob Didier, John Gamble and Marvin Lane.

PITCHING RECORDS

	T	G	IP	W	L	PCT	ERA
Hiller, John	L	65	125	10	5	.667	1.44
Coleman, Joe	R	40	288	23	15	.605	3.53
Lolich, Mickey	L	42	309	16	15	.516	3.82
Perry, Jim	R	35	203	14	13	.519	4.03
Scherman, Fred	L	34	62	2	2	.500	4.21
LaGrow, Lerrin	R	21	54	1	5	.167	4.33
Strahler, Mike	R	22	80	4	5	.444	4.39
Timmerman, Tom (17 Det., 29 Clev.)	R	46	163	9	8	.529	4.64
Farmer, Ed (16 Clev., 24 Det.)	R	40	62	3	2	.600	4.94
Fryman, Woody	L	34	170	6	13	.316	5.35

Less than 45 innings: Fred Holdsworth, Gary Ignasiak, Dave Lemanczyk, Bob Miller, Bill Slayback and Chuck Seelbach.

1974

FINAL STANDINGS

EAST DIVISION	W	L	PCT
Baltimore	91	71	.562
New York	89	73	.549
Boston	84	78	.519
Cleveland	77	85	.475
Milwaukee	76	86	.469
DETROIT	72	90	.444

WEST DIVISION			
Oakland	90	72	.556
Texas	84	76	.525
Minnesota	82	80	.506
Chicago	80	80	.500
Kansas City	77	85	.475
California	68	94	.420

Manager: Ralph Houk

The Great Debate over who would replace Billy Martin as Tiger manager in 1974 didn't last long. Jim Campbell named Ralph Houk to be the Tigers' new man on the field, less than two weeks after his resignation as manager of the New York Yankees. Even that change did not occur without controversy.

Soon after Houk quit the Yanks and signed with the Tigers, Oakland manager Dick Williams decided he had had his fill of A's owner Charley Finley, and announced his resignation. Immediately, there was speculation—encouraged by Williams—that Dick would replace Houk as manager of the New York Yankees.

But Finley wasn't about to give up his manager without a fight. He announced that if the Yankees tried to sign Williams, he would demand compensation. Yankee owner George Steinbrenner, in turn, informed the Tigers that since Finley wanted compensation for Williams, New York wanted compensation from Detroit for signing Houk.

After hearing arguments by all concerned, American League president Joe Cronin ruled that while the Yankees could not sign Williams without first satisfying Finley, they had no right to demand compensation from the Tigers for Houk since they had already accepted Ralph's resignation.

The Tigers had won their battle for Houk, but they soon discovered victory would not always be so easily attained.

The Tigers, who had stuck with the same cast of characters for so many years, now had a major rebuilding job to do. And they knew it. Meanwhile, it was obvious they were overmatched against the top contending clubs in the American League.

Game after game, the Tigers fell hopelessly far behind early, often in the very first inning.

The highlight of the season was Al Kaline's successful drive to reach the 3,000-hit plateau, making Al only the 12th player in major league history to achieve that goal. It was a fitting climax to what had been a brilliant career spanning two decades. And with the Tigers clearly going nowhere in the pennant race in the near future, Kaline was ready—indeed, even eager—to retire. An era had ended in Detroit, and the Tiger management realized it. The time had come for them to clean house.

Norm Cash, who had been such a stalwart at first base for so many seasons, was given his outright release in August. Jim Northrup, a key outfield performer on the world championship 1968 club, was sold to Montreal.

Individually, few Tigers had reason to be proud of their performance in '74 as the team nose-dived all the way to last place in the American League East—only the second cellar finish in the club's 74-year history.

Mickey Lolich, who was expected to lead the team in victories, slumped badly and lost 21 games—making him the first Tiger pitcher since Hooks Dauss in 1920 to lose that often.

Joe Coleman, the Tigers' No. 1 righthander, got off to a fast start, then suddenly lost the winning touch, while Lerrin LaGrow and Bill Slayback, never got going.

The lone exception on the pitching staff was relief ace John Hiller who won 17 games to break the league record for victories by a reliever.

The Tiger hitters also had their problems. Only Willie Horton, who missed half the season because of a knee injury, and Bill Freehan, who enjoyed a solid second half, provided punch at the plate.

It was painfully evident it would be a while before the Tigers would be bona fide pennant contenders again.

Fred Lynn, then playing with the Boston Red Sox, had one of the best days in major league history. It was on June 18, 1975 in Detroit when Fred hit three homers, a triple and a single. He drove in ten runs as the Red Sox clobbered the Tigers 15-1.

BATTING RECORDS

	B	G	AB	R	H	HR	SB	AVE	RBI
Knox, John	L	55	88	11	27	0	5	.307	6
Horton, Willie	R	72	238	32	71	15	0	.298	47
Freehan, Bill	R	130	445	58	132	18	2	.297	60
Sanders, Reggie	R	26	99	12	27	3	1	.273	10
Oglivie, Ben	L	92	252	28	68	4	12	.270	29
Roberts, Leon	R	17	63	5	17	0	0	.270	7
Kaline, Al	R	147	558	71	146	13	2	.262	64
LeFlore, Ron	R	59	254	37	66	2	23	.260	13
Sutherland, Gary	R	149	619	60	157	5	1	.254	49
Northrup, Jim (97 Det., 8 Balt.)	L	105	383	43	93	12	0	.243	45
Brown, Gates	L	73	99	7	24	4	0	.242	17
Moses, Gerry	R	74	198	19	47	4	0	.237	19
Veryzer, Tom	R	22	54	4	13	2	1	.236	9
Lane, Marvin	R	50	103	16	24	2	2	.233	9
Cash, Norm	L	53	149	17	34	7	1	.228	12
Nettles, Jim	L	43	141	20	32	6	3	.227	17
Cash, Ron	R	20	62	6	14	0	0	.226	5
Rodriguez, Aurelio	R	159	571	54	127	5	2	.222	49
Brinkman, Eddie	R	153	502	55	111	14	2	.221	54
Stanley, Mickey	R	99	394	40	87	8	5	.221	34
Lamont, Gene	L	60	92	9	20	3	0	.217	8
Sharon, Dick	R	60	129	12	28	2	4	.217	10
Meyer, Dan	L	13	50	5	10	2	1	.200	7
Wockenfuss, John	R	13	29	1	4	0	0	.138	2

Less than 10 games: Ike Brown.

PITCHING RECORDS

	T	G	IP	W	L	PCT	ERA
Hiller, John	L	59	150	17	14	.548	2.64
Lemanczyk, Dave	R	22	79	2	1	.667	4.00
Lolich, Mickey	L	41	308	16	21	.432	4.15
Coleman, Joe	R	41	286	14	12	.538	4.32
Fryman, Woody	L	27	142	6	9	.400	4.32
Ray, Jim	R	28	52	1	3	.250	4.47
LaGrow, Lerrin	R	37	216	8	19	.296	4.66
Slayback, Bill	R	16	55	1	3	.250	4.77
Walker, Luke	L	28	92	5	5	.500	4.99

Less than 45 innings: Fred Holdsworth, Vern Ruhle and Chuck Seelbach.

1975

FINAL STANDINGS

EAST DIVISION	W	L	PCT
Boston	95	65	.594
Baltimore	90	69	.566
New York	83	77	.519
Cleveland	79	80	.497
Milwaukee	68	94	.420
DETROIT	57	102	.358

WEST DIVISION	W	L	PCT
Oakland	98	64	.605
Kansas City	91	71	.562
Texas	79	83	.488
Minnesota	76	83	.478
Chicago	75	86	.466
California	72	89	.447

Manager: Ralph Houk

The Tigers were proudly pointing to all of their new faces as the 1975 season began. They had acquired slugger Nate Colbert from the San Diego Padres in exchange for shortstop Eddie Brinkman, and were predicting as many as 40 home runs from their new hard-hitting first baseman. They were also counting on a new nucleus of youngsters—pitcher Vern Ruhle, shortstop Tom Veryzer, and outfielders Ron LeFlore, Leon Roberts and Danny Meyer—to do what a group of guys named Horton, Freehan, Lolich, Stanley and Northrup had done for the team in the '60s.

Unfortunately, it was all talk. The Tigers were not a bad team in 1975. They were terrible.

For the second season in a row—and only the third time in history—they finished dead last. No other team in either league lost as often as the 1975 Tigers who failed 102 times. They might even have broken the all-time Tiger record of 104 losses had not three games been cancelled by inclement weather and never rescheduled.

All in all, it was a frustrating summer.

The lowlight came when the Tigers lost 19 games in a row to break the club record for futility, falling just one setback shy of the American League record.

After briefly leading the division for a few days in April, the Tigers could do little right.

Defensively, they committed more errors than any Tiger team since 1944. Offensively, they scored fewer runs, swiped fewer bases, and drew fewer bases on balls than any other team in the AL. And, on the mound, the pitchers allowed more earned runs than any Tiger staff since 1953.

They won only six times during all of August, and only five times in September. In their final 58 games, the Tigers lost 47 times.

Colbert, of whom the Tigers expected so much, failed to produce at all and was gone by midseason. John Hiller, the ace of the bullpen whom the Tigers depended on in the late innings, missed the final two months of the season because of injury.

Mickey Lolich and Joe Coleman, the two mainstays on the Tigers' pitching staff, also continued to have their problems. Lolich, who passed Warren Spahn to become baseball's all-time left-handed strikeout king, compiled a 12-18 record, while Coleman was 10-18 with a 5.55 e.r.a.

The Tigers did find reason to be encouraged in the performances of youngsters LeFlore, Roberts, Ruhle, Veryzer and Meyer. Even so, they obviously were not ready to carry the club into contention. LeFlore, for example, stole only 28 bases—even though he went into the season expecting to take 50 or 60.

Willie Horton finally stayed healthy and happy for the whole season, putting together the kind of campaign he had always been capable of. As the Tigers' everyday designated hitter, Horton appeared in every game, smacking 25 homers and driving in 92 runs.

After the season ended, the Tigers did some more house cleaning, this time trading their long-time left-handed ace, Mickey Lolich, to the New York Mets for outfielder Rusty Staub.

BATTING RECORDS

	B	G	AB	R	H	HR	SB	AVE	RBI
Oglivie, Ben	L	100	332	45	95	9	11	.286	36
Horton, Willie	R	159	615	62	169	25	1	.275	92
Knox, John	L	43	86	8	23	0	1	.267	2
LeFlore, Ron	R	136	550	66	142	8	28	.258	37
Sutherland, Gary	R	129	503	51	130	6	0	.258	39
Roberts, Leon	R	129	447	51	115	10	3	.257	38
Stanley, Mickey	R	52	164	26	42	3	1	.256	19
Veryzer, Tom	R	128	404	37	102	5	2	.252	48
Freehan, Bill	R	120	427	42	105	14	2	.246	47
Rodriguez, Aurelio	R	151	507	47	124	13	1	.245	60
Humphrey, Terry	R	18	41	0	10	0	0	.244	1
Meyer, Dan	L	122	470	56	111	8	8	.236	47
Pierce, Jack	L	53	170	19	40	8	0	.235	22
Wockenfuss, John	R	35	118	15	27	4	0	.229	13
James, Art	L	11	40	2	9	0	1	.225	1
Baldwin, Billy	L	30	95	8	21	4	2	.221	8
Michael, Gene	B	56	145	15	31	3	0	.214	13
Brown, Gates	L	47	35	1	6	1	0	.171	3
Colbert, Nate	R	45	156	16	23	4	0	.147	18

Less than 10 games: Gene Lamont, Jerry Manuel, Bob Molinaro and Chuck Scrivener.

PITCHING RECORDS

	T	G	IP	W	L	PCT	ERA
Hiller, John	L	36	70	2	3	.400	2.17
Lolich, Mickey	L	32	24	12	18	.400	3.78
Ruhle, Vern	R	32	190	11	12	.478	4.03
LaGrow, Lerrin	R	32	164	7	14	.333	4.38
Walker, Tom	R	36	115	3	8	.273	4.45
Lemanczyk, Dave	R	26	109	7	7	.500	4.46
Bare, Ray	R	29	150	8	13	.381	4.48
Arroyo, Fernando	R	14	53	2	1	.667	4.56
Reynolds, Bob (7 Balt., 21 Det., 5 Clev.)	R	33	50	0	5	.000	5.19
Coleman, Joe	R	31	201	10	18	.357	5.55

Less than 45 innings: Ike Brookens, Steve Grilli, Tom Makowski, Gene Pentz and Ed Glynn.

Matt Brady's

TAVERN

still the same great food atmosphere & cocktails*

31231 Southfield Road
Birmingham, MI 48009
(313) 642-6422
*you supply the conversation

Tiger Players with More Than 150 Triples

Sam Crawford has the most three-base hits in major league history. He had 312 triples during his 19 years in the major leagues. Ty Cobb has the second highest total with 298 in his 24 seasons. Hans Wagner had 252 triples during his career with the Pittsburgh Pirates. There are 50 ballplayers who have had more than 150 triples; among them are Goose Goslin, Heinie Manush and Harry Heilmann.

1976

FINAL STANDINGS

EAST DIVISION	W	L	PCT
New York	97	62	.610
Baltimore	88	74	.543
Boston	83	79	.512
Cleveland	81	78	.509
DETROIT	74	87	.460
Milwaukee	66	95	.410

WEST DIVISION	W	L	PCT
Kansas City	90	72	.556
Oakland	87	74	.540
Minnesota	85	77	.525
California	76	86	.469
Texas	76	86	.469
Chicago	64	97	.398

Manager: Ralph Houk

In addition to Rusty Staub, the Tigers also strengthened themselves for 1976 by acquiring veteran pitcher Dave Roberts to replace Mickey Lolich in the starting rotation and catcher Milt May to assist aging Bill Freehan. But the biggest difference in the '76 Tigers was made by a player who wasn't even on the major league roster when spring training began.

For the record, the Tigers improved more in 1976 than any other team in either major league, adding 17 victories to their win total to inch up to fifth place in the American League East. But few people noticed. Everyone was too busy watching Mark Fidrych, The Bird.

No doubt about it: 1976 was The Year of The Bird.

Not even on the roster when spring training began, not sure he would be able to make the team, not allowed to make his first big league start until May 15, Fidrych nevertheless attracted more attention in his first season in the big leagues than most players do in their entire careers.

Fidrych became a national phenomenon, especially in the American League cities where he and the Tigers performed.

They called him flakey. They called him free-spirited. And folks loved the curly haired 22-year-old righthander wherever he went. The record books shall forever show that Fidrych won 19 games and lost only nine in his rookie season, compiling a fine 2.34 e.r.a. What those numbers don't show is that The Bird attracted crowds totaling 899,969 to the 29 games which he started, including 605,677 at home in Tiger Stadium.

Many teams go through an entire season without drawing the crowds that The Bird drew all by himself.

He was fresh. He was funny. He was fantastic.

Fidrych talked to the ball on the mound, telling it where to go and what to do. And more often than not—as his winning record attests—the ball obeyed. Fidrych's boyish enthusiasm and charm made him a favorite of teammates and rivals alike, as well as members of the media, eager for an interesting new story angle.

While Fidrych was attracting most of the attention and getting most of the headlines, other Tigers were doing their jobs with improved efficiency, too.

Ron LeFlore, the speedster who signed with the Tigers as soon as he was paroled from prison, rebounded from a shaky season in 1975 to rank as one of the premier players in the league. LeFlore, who had never played organized baseball at any level until he signed with the Tigers and was sent to the minor leagues, started the season with a 30-game hitting streak, was named to the AL All-Star team, and finished the season with a fine .316 batting average. In addition, he stole 58 bases, giving the Tigers a legitimate threat on the base paths for the first time in many years.

Rusty Staub, along with LeFlore and Fidrych, also made the All-Star team, and with good reason. Staub, who came to the Tigers from the New York Mets in exchange for Mickey Lolich, proved himself to be one of the most consistently dependable hitters in the league, driving in 96 runs while batting .299.

Another newcomer, first baseman Jason Thompson, also gave the Tigers good cause to grin and eagerly look forward to the future as he belted 17 homers, the most by any Tiger rookie since Rudy York hit 35 in 1937.

As improved as they were, the Tigers might have fared far better had they not been beset by a series of crippling injuries to key players that seriously hampered their efforts to climb higher in the standings. Milt May, who had earned the job of No. 1 catcher, ran into a wall in Oakland in April and fractured his foot, ending his season after only 15 at bats. Willie Horton, who had been the Tigers' big gun the season before, was also hobbled by a foot injury that reduced his contribution greatly. Third baseman Aurelio Rodriguez and shortstop Tom Veryzer were also lost to injuries. And in September, the Tigers lost LeFlore, the man who made their offense go, when he tore up his knee.

Still, the Tigers seemed to have turned the corner. Only on the mound were they still lacking the stuff that contenders are made of.

In addition to Fidrych, Dave Roberts was a reliable starter, winning 16 while losing 17. And John Hiller flashed his old familiar form out of the bullpen, winning 12 games and saving 13 others.

After two years of gloom, the Tigers could hold their heads high again.

Ron LeFlore is the only player in the majors to lead both leagues in stolen bases. Ron topped the American League with 68 stolen bases in 1978 when he played for the Tigers. He stole 97 for the Montreal Expos in 1980 to lead the National League.

Statistics

BATTING RECORDS

	B	G	AB	R	H	HR	SB	AVE	RBI
LeFlore, Ron	R	135	544	93	172	4	58	.316	39
Staub, Rusty	L	161	589	73	176	15	3	.299	96
Oglivie, Ben	L	115	305	36	87	15	9	.285	47
Mankowski, Phil	L	24	85	9	23	1	0	.271	4
Freehan, Bill	R	71	237	22	64	5	0	.270	27
Johnson, Alex	R	125	429	41	115	6	14	.268	45
Kimm, Bruce	R	63	152	13	40	1	4	.263	6
Horton, Willie	R	114	401	40	105	14	0	.262	56
Wagner, Mark	R	39	115	9	30	0	0	.261	12
Stanley, Mickey	R	84	214	34	55	4	2	.257	29
Meyer, Dan	L	105	294	37	74	2	10	.252	16
Rodriguez, Aurelio	R	128	480	40	115	8	0	.240	50
Veryzer, Tom	R	97	354	31	83	1	1	.234	25
Wockenfuss, John	R	60	144	18	32	3	0	.222	10
Scrivener, Chuck	R	80	222	28	49	2	1	.221	16
Thompson, Jason	L	123	412	45	90	17	2	.218	54
Sutherland, Gary (42 Det., 59 Mil.)	R	101	232	19	49	1	0	.211	15
Garcia, Pedro (41 Mil., 77 Det.)	R	118	333	33	68	4	4	.204	29
Lane, Marvin	R	18	48	3	9	0	0	.188	5
Manuel, Jerry	B	54	43	4	6	0	1	.140	2

Less than 10 games: Milt May.

PITCHING RECORDS

	T	G	IP	W	L	PCT	ERA
Fidrych, Mark	R	31	250	19	9	.679	2.34
Hiller, John	L	56	121	12	8	.600	2.38
Ruhle, Vern	R	32	200	9	12	.429	3.92
Roberts, Dave	L	36	252	16	17	.485	4.00
Laxton, Bill	L	26	95	0	5	.000	4.09
Crawford, Jim	L	32	109	1	8	.111	4.53
Bare, Ray	R	30	134	7	8	.467	4.63
Grilli, Steve	R	36	66	3	1	.750	4.64
Coleman, Joe	R	12	67	2	5	.286	4.86
Lemanczyk, Dave	R	20	81	4	6	.400	5.09

Less than 45 innings: Ed Glynn and Frank MacCormack.

1977

FINAL STANDINGS

EAST DIVISION	W	L	PCT
New York	100	62	.617
Baltimore	97	64	.602
Boston	97	64	.602
DETROIT	74	88	.457
Cleveland	71	90	.441
Milwaukee	67	95	.414
Toronto	54	107	.335
WEST DIVISION			
Kansas City	102	60	.630
Texas	94	68	.580
Chicago	90	72	.556
Minnesota	84	77	.522
California	74	88	.457
Seattle	64	98	.395
Oakland	63	98	.391

Manager: Ralph Houk

Based on what had transpired the previous season, the Tigers did not think they were at all out of line in predicting they might be bona fide contenders in 1977.

After all, there seemed to be no limit to what Mark Fidrych might accomplish. Ron LeFlore had become a full-fledged star. Jason Thompson appeared capable of great slugging feats. And Milt May, Steve Kemp, Willie Horton, Tom Veryzer, Aurelio Rodriguez and Dave Roberts could not possibly all be injured again. However, it was again injury that proved the Tigers' undoing in 1977. This time, the injury was to the one player the Tigers could least afford to lose: Mark Fidrych.

The Tigers simply assumed The Bird would win at least 20 games the second time around. And, of course, he would do wonders for their attendance, not to mention the morale of the rest of the team.

Instead, Fidrych tore the cartilage in his right knee while leaping for a fly ball during batting practice and had to undergo surgery that forced him to miss the first two months of the season. Then, after only 11 starts, Fidrych developed what was diagnosed as tendonitis in his right arm and was sent home to rest for the remainder of the season.

It was a bitter blow, not only because the Tigers were counting on The Bird to be the ace of their pitching staff, but also because of what his presence meant in terms of enthusiasm and confidence to the rest of the team.

With Fidrych's contribution reduced to six wins and four losses, much of the burden fell on the shoulders of rookie righthander Dave Rozema, the "new Bird" who was supposed to follow in Fidrych's footsteps.

Rozema didn't disappoint, winning 15 games and losing only seven before he, too, was sidelined by stiffness in his pitching arm. With Rozema and Fidrych together in the starting rotation all season, the Tigers might indeed have been a factor in the American League East.

Desperate for starting pitching, the Tigers traded Dave Roberts, who was a disappointing 4-10, and turned to another rookie, Jack Morris. But he, too, was soon sidelined because of stiffness in his arm, meaning the Tigers had three starting pitchers on the staff.

In an effort to fill the gap, manager Ralph Houk called on John Hiller to start from time to time, and as a result Hiller's effectiveness as a reliever was diminished. Hiller finished the season with a disappointing 8-14 record, a 3.56 e.r.a., and only seven saves.

With Hiller struggling, Steve Foucault, who had been obtained from the Texas Rangers in April in exchange for an unhappy Willie Horton, emerged as the bullpen ace with seven wins and 13 saves.

All of the problems the Tigers had with their pitching staff detracted from the efforts made by several of the other players.

Ron LeFlore, whose remarkable prison-to-the-big-leagues life story was soon to be the subject of a book and made-for-TV movie, had his second outstanding season in a row. LeFlore became the first Tiger since Al Kaline in 1955 to collect at least 200 hits and score at least 100 runs in the same season. Furthermore, he stole 39 bases and socked 16 home runs, batting a healthy .325, the top mark by any righthanded hitter in the league.

Jason Thompson led the team with 31 homers, two of which cleared the rightfield roof at Tiger Stadium. Thompson also topped the team with 105 rbi, while Rusty Staub smacked 22 home runs and knocked in 101 runs.

Rookie Steve Kemp, whose performance in left field made it possible for the Tigers to trade long-time hero Willie Horton, drove in 88 runs and socked 18 homers to establish himself along with LeFlore and Thompson as a star of the future.

The Tigers also were successful with their first free agent investment, too, as Tito Fuentes hit .309, the best by any Tiger second baseman since the great Charlie Gehringer hit .313 in 1940.

Who was on base when Hank Aaron hit his 715th home run surpassing Babe Ruth's record of 714? It was Darrell Evans, then playing with the Atlanta Braves. He had reached first base on Bill Russell's error and then scored ahead of Aaron.

BATTING RECORDS

	B	G	AB	R	H	HR	SB	AVE	RBI
LeFlore, Ron................................	R	154	652	100	212	16	39	.325	57
Fuentes, Tito	B	151	615	83	190	5	4	.309	51
Horton, Willie (1 Det., 139 Texas)	R	140	523	55	151	15	2	.289	75
Corcoran, Tim	L	55	103	13	29	3	0	.282	15
Staub, Rusty	L	158	623	84	173	22	1	.278	101
Mankowski, Phil............................	L	94	286	21	79	3	1	.276	27
Wockenfuss, John	R	53	164	26	45	9	0	.274	25
Thompson, Jason	L	158	585	87	158	31	0	.270	105
Oglivie, Ben.................................	L	132	450	63	118	21	9	.262	61
Kemp, Steve................................	L	151	552	75	142	18	3	.257	88
Whitaker, Lou...............................	L	11	332	5	8	0	2	.250	2
Adams, Bob	R	15	24	2	6	2	0	.250	2
May, Milt	L	115	397	32	99	12	0	.249	46
Stanley, Mickey	R	75	222	30	51	8	0	.230	23
Rodriguez, Aurelio	R	96	306	30	67	10	1	.219	32
Veryzer, Tom	R	125	350	31	69	2	0	.197	28
Parrish, Lance..............................	R	12	46	10	9	3	0	.196	7
Trammell, Alan	R	19	43	6	8	0	0	.186	0
Wagner, Mark...............................	R	22	48	4	7	1	0	.146	3
Scrivener, Chuck	R	61	72	10	6	0	0	.083	2
Kimm, Bruce	R	14	25	2	2	0	0	.080	1

Less than 10 games: Louis Alvarado and Bob Molinaro.

PITCHING RECORDS

	T	G	IP	W	L	PCT	ERA
Fidrych, Mark...............................	R	11	81	6	4	.600	2.89
Rozema, Dave..............................	R	28	218	15	7	.682	3.09
Foucault, Steve.............................	R	44	74	7	7	.500	3.15
Hiller, John..................................	L	45	124	8	14	.364	3.56
Wilcox, Milt..................................	R	20	106	6	2	.750	3.64
Morris, Jack	R	7	46	1	1	.500	3.74
Arroyo, Fernando	R	38	209	8	18	.308	4.17
Sykes, Bob	L	32	133	5	7	.417	4.41
Crawford, Jim	L	37	126	7	8	.467	4.79
Grilli, Steve..................................	R	30	73	1	2	.333	4.83
Roberts, Dave	L	22	129	4	10	.286	5.15
Ruhle, Vern	R	14	66	3	5	.375	5.70

Less than 45 innings: Ray Bare, Ed Glynn and Bruce Taylor.

1978
FINAL STANDINGS

EAST DIVISION	W	L	PCT
New York	100	63	.613
Boston	99	64	.607
Milwaukee	93	69	.574
Baltimore	90	71	.559
DETROIT	86	76	.531
Cleveland	69	90	.434
Toronto	59	102	.366 |//
WEST DIVISION			
Kansas City	92	70	.568
California	87	75	.537
Texas	87	75	.537
Minnesota	73	89	.451
Chicago	71	90	.441
Oakland	69	93	.426
Seattle	56	104	.350

Manager: Ralph Houk

For the second spring in a row, the Tigers found themselves counting on a strong comeback by Mark Fidrych as the 1978 season began. They seemed to have everything else, all the ingredients that they needed to make a serious run at the pennant again.

Ron LeFlore and Steve Kemp were fixtures in the outfield, Jason Thompson could supply the power at first base, Rusty Staub was one of the most dependable runs batted in men in the game, Lance Parrish appeared ready to realize the stardom that people had always predicted for him, and rookies Lou Whitaker and Alan Trammell gave the Tigers stability and efficiency in the middle of the infield.

All that the Tigers needed was a season from Fidrych comparable to his rookie year. Instead, what they got was three starts. Period. Total. The mysterious pain in The Bird's right arm simply refused to disappear. Gradually, reluctantly, the Tigers came to realize it was time they stopped counting on anything at all from the once-exciting Fidrych.

Dave Rozema, in his second season in the big leagues, also struggled most of the year, compounding the Tigers' pitching problems. And Steve Foucault, coming out of the bullpen, could no longer consistently get enemy hitters out.

The Tigers did strengthen their pitching by the springtime acquisition of veteran righthander Jack Billingham, who turned in a surprisingly fine 15-8 performance in his first season in the American League.

Milt Wilcox, another former Cincinnati Red, also helped make up for Fidrych and Rozema's ineffectiveness, leading the staff in strikeouts with 132 and complete games with 16 while winning 13.

Offensively, the Tigers had their disappointments, too. Jason Thompson tailed off badly during the second half of the season when he was slowed by injuries and managed to hit only one home run during August. Lance Parrish failed to live up to his billing as the Tigers' star catcher of the future, especially at the plate; Tim Corcoran simply couldn't hit during the regular season with the same regularity he displayed during spring training.

Centerfielder Ron LeFlore again found it difficult to get rolling early in the season. Even so, he finished the year with an All-Star rush, ending with a .297 batting average that included 198 hits, stealing 68 bases, and scoring 126 runs. LeFlore was first in the American League in both runs scored and bases stolen and finished second behind Boston slugger Jim Rice in base hits.

Rusty Staub also ranked among the league leaders and finished second to Rice in runs batted in with 121.

Although they won 12 more games in 1978 than they did the season before, the Tigers dropped a notch in the standings, falling from fourth to fifth. Their 86-76 record was the Tigers' best effort since 1972, when they dominated the American League East and won the divisional title. They could point to that, and to the fact that only two teams in the AL—Milwaukee and California—improved their won-lost records more than the Tigers did in 1978.

But they could not erase the fact that they finished fifth, even though it was in what many experts considered to be the best division in baseball.

Ralph Houk, who had been thinking seriously all season about retiring, made it official in September and stepped down, announcing, "It's time for me to go fishing." To take Houk's place, the Tigers immediately promoted former major league catcher Les Moss, who had been extremely successful managing in the Tigers' farm system and who had been instrumental in developing many of the club's most promising young players.

Clearly, they believed they were on the brink of becoming winners again.

BATTING RECORDS

	B	G	AB	R	H	HR	SB	AVE	RBI
LeFlore, Ron	R	155	666	126	198	12	68	.297	62
Thompson, Jason	L	153	589	79	169	26	0	.287	96
Whitaker, Lou	L	139	484	71	138	3	7	.285	58
Wockenfuss, John	R	71	187	23	53	7	0	.283	22
Kemp, Steve	L	159	582	75	161	15	2	.277	79
Mankowski, Phil	L	88	222	28	61	4	2	.275	20
Staub, Rusty	L	162	642	75	175	24	3	.273	121
Trammell, Alan	R	139	448	49	120	2	3	.268	34
Corcoran, Tim	L	116	324	37	86	1	3	.265	27
Rodriguez, Aurelio	R	134	385	40	102	7	0	.265	43
Stanley, Mickey	R	53	151	15	40	3	0	.265	8
May, Milt	L	105	352	24	88	10	0	.250	37
Spikes, Charlie	R	10	28	1	7	0	0	.250	2
Wagner, Mark	R	39	109	10	26	0	1	.239	6
Dillard, Steve	R	56	130	21	29	0	1	.223	7
Parrish, Lance	R	85	288	37	63	14	0	.219	41

Less than 10 games: Dave Stegman.

PITCHING RECORDS

	T	G	IP	W	L	PCT	ERA
Hiller, John	L	51	92	9	4	.692	2.34
Young, Kip	R	14	106	6	7	.462	2.81
Rozema, Dave	R	28	209	9	12	.429	3.14
Wilcox, Milt	R	29	215	13	12	.520	3.76
Billingham, Jack	R	30	201	15	8	.652	3.88
Sykes, Bob	L	22	94	6	6	.500	3.94
Slayton, Jim	R	35	234	17	11	.607	4.12
Morris, Jack	R	28	106	3	5	.375	4.33
Baker, Steve	R	15	63	2	4	.333	4.55

Less than 45 innings: Fernando Arroyo, Sheldon Burnside, Jim Crawford, Mark Fidrych, Steve Foucault, Ed Glynn, Bruce Taylor and Dave Tobik.

First Edition Lounge

Great Hamburgers

Satellite Dish T.V. Reception
Giant 7 Ft. T.V. Screen

featuring ALL
MAJOR SPORTING EVENTS
NO CARRY-OUTS

18334 W. Warren Ave.
2 Blocks West of Southfield Fwy. 271-7528

"The West Side's Best Sports Spot."
Your Host, Tom Osman   ESTABLISHED DEC. 6, 1971

Runs Batted In Leaders

Hank Aaron is the all-time leader with runs batted in with 2,297, followed closely by Babe Ruth with 2,204. Ty Cobb had 1,960 rbi in his 24-year career. Al Simmons, who played with the Tigers in 1936, had 1,827 rbi during his career. Goose Goslin had 1,609, Al Kaline had 1,583, Harry Heilmann, 1,551, Rusty Staub 1,474, Eddie Mathews 1,453, Charlie Gehringer 1,427, and Hank Greenberg 1,276.

1979

FINAL STANDINGS

EAST DIVISION	W	L	PCT
Baltimore	102	57	.642
Milwaukee	95	66	.590
Boston	91	69	.569
New York	89	71	.556
DETROIT	85	76	.528
Cleveland	81	80	.503
Toronto	53	109	.327
WEST DIVISION			
California	88	74	.543
Kansas City	85	77	.525
Texas	83	79	.512
Minnesota	82	80	.506
Chicago	73	87	.456
Seattle	67	95	.414
Oakland	54	108	.333

Managers: Les Moss and Sparky Anderson

As the Tigers began spring training for the 1979 campaign, they had every reason to feel confident. The long rebuilding process, which had begun at the end of the 1973 season when Billy Martin was fired, finally appeared over.

The Tigers had a new, no-nonsense manager in Les Moss and the players—many of whom knew Moss from their developing days in the minor leagues—saw him as the ideal man to lead them to victory.

Unfortunately, they were in for a lot of surprises.

First, Rusty Staub, the Tigers' designated hitter deluxe demanded to renegotiate his existing contract and refused to report for spring training, threatening to quit baseball and go into the restaurant business full-time unless the Tigers met his demands. The Tigers, who had earlier extended Staub's contract—at his request—refused to give in this time, even though Rusty had driven in 121 runs the season before, making him the most productive DH in the American League.

It became a matter of principle with the Tiger management, and a matter of pride with Staub. Neither side would budge.

Back and forth, they bickered all spring: Rusty Staub against Tiger general manager Jim Campbell. Before long, their squabble detracted from the Tigers' spring training efforts and divided the players. Many felt Staub was much too valuable to lose; that the front office had no choice but to make Rusty happy. Others insisted the Tigers could win without Staub; that Rusty was thinking only of himself, not his teammates.

Staub held out through the first month of the regular season before finally agreeing to report on May 1. By then the Tigers had encountered some other unpleasant surprises, too.

Mark Fidrych again proved a major disappointment in his effort to bounce back, eventually losing all three of his decisions. Dave Rozema, who had followed Fidrych as the Tigers' rookie pitching phenom, continued to experience arm and shoulder problems, too.

Meanwhile, Jim Campbell had another move on his mind. Down in Cincinnati, Sparky Anderson, the long-time highly successful manager of the Reds, was sitting idle, having been unceremoniously fired the year before. Campbell admired Anderson and believed he would be the perfect man to manage the Tigers. The Tiger GM was not necessarily unhappy with the job Les Moss was doing, but he felt the chance to hire a manager with Anderson's credentials might never come along again. And Campbell was afraid if he waited, Sparky would sign with someone else.

So, in mid-June, with the Tigers one game over .500 and playing reasonably well, Campbell stunned everyone by firing Moss and hiring Anderson.

Sparky, exuberant and outspoken as always, bounced into town and talked about "catching lightning in a bottle." He boasted about putting the Tigers into the pennant playoffs in the near future. He compared their talent to the team he had inherited in 1970 in Cincinnati.

But turning the Tigers around was easier said than done. They lost three in a row as soon as Anderson took charge of the team, and nine of Sparky's first 11 games at the helm. Suddenly instead of being only seven games out of the lead, the Tigers were 14 1/2 back. And Sparky, after issuing his ultimatum that the Tigers would "do things my way or hit the highway," began cleaning house.

First to go was Staub, who batted only .236 in 68 games after he finally joined the team in May. One by one, others who didn't fit into Sparky's plans disappeared.

Not all of the surprises in 1979 were bad. With speedster Ron LeFlore leading the way with 78 steals, the new-look Tigers swiped 176 bases—their best effort on the base paths since the immortal Ty Cobb was running at will.

Another outfielder, Steve Kemp, came into his own, batting .318 with 26 homers and 105 rbi, while Champ Summers, who had spent time in Anderson's doghouse in Cincinnati before joining the Tigers in May, hit a surprising .313 with 20 home runs.

Jack Morris, from whom the Tigers had been expecting big things, lived up to those expectations by going 17-7 after he was summoned from Evansville in May.

The Tigers got some unexpected good news in the bullpen, too. Aurelio Lopez, who had been acquired from St. Louis before the season began, along with outfielder Jerry Morales, suddenly blossomed under Anderson, recording a 10-5 record with 21 saves after Sparky arrived and began pitching him regularly.

Still the Tigers could finish no better than fifth in the American League East. They had reason to be disappointed, but they had ample reason to be encouraged, too.

BATTING RECORDS

	B	G	AB	R	H	HR	SB	AVE	RBI
Kemp, Steve	L	134	490	88	156	26	5	.318	105
Summers, Champ	L	90	246	47	77	20	7	.313	51
LeFlore, Ron	R	148	600	110	180	9	78	.300	57
Jones, Lynn	R	95	213	33	63	4	9	.296	26
Whitaker, Lou	L	127	423	75	121	3	20	.286	42
Trammell, Alan	R	142	460	68	127	6	17	.276	50
Parrish, Lance	R	143	493	65	136	19	6	.276	65
Wagner, Mark	R	75	146	16	40	1	3	.274	13
Wockenfuss, John	R	87	231	27	61	15	2	.264	46
Brookens, Tom	R	68	190	23	50	4	10	.263	21
Peters, Rick	B	12	19	3	5	0	0	.263	2
May, Milt (6 Det., 65 Chi.)	L	71	213	24	54	7	0	.254	31
Rodriguez, Aurelio	R	106	343	27	87	5	0	.254	36
Thompson, Jason	L	145	492	58	121	20	2	.246	79
Gibson, Kirk	L	12	38	3	9	1	3	.237	4
Staub, Rusty	L	68	246	32	58	9	1	.236	40
Putnam, Ed	R	21	39	4	9	2	0	.231	4
Corcoran, Tim	L	18	22	4	5	0	1	.227	6
Mankowski, Phil	L	42	99	11	22	0	0	.222	8
Morales, Jerry	R	129	440	50	93	14	10	.211	56
Stegman, David	R	12	31	6	6	3	1	.194	5
Machemer, Dave	R	19	26	8	5	0	0	.192	2
Greene, Altar	L	29	59	9	8	3	0	.136	6

Less than 10 games: Dan Gonzales.

PITCHING RECORDS

	T	G	IP	W	L	PCT	ERA
Lopez, Aurelio	R	61	127	10	5	.667	2.41
Morris, Jack	R	27	198	17	7	.708	3.28
Billingham, Jack	R	35	158	10	7	.588	3.30
Rozema, Dave	R	16	97	4	4	.500	3.51
Robbins, Bruce	L	10	46	3	3	.500	3.91
Petry, Dan	R	15	98	6	5	.545	3.95
Tobik, Dave	R	37	69	3	5	.375	4.33
Wilcox, Milt	R	33	196	12	10	.545	4.35
Underwood, Pat	L	27	122	6	4	.600	4.59
Hiller, John	L	43	79	4	7	.364	5.22
Baker, Steve	R	21	84	1	7	.125	6.64

Less than 45 innings: Fernando Arroyo, Sheldon Burnside, Mike Chris, Mark Fidrych, Bruce Taylor and Kip Young.

McVee's Pub & Grub

23380 Telegraph
Just North of 9 Mile Rd.
Southfield

Phone: 352-8243

*Where All Good People
Get Together
For Fun - Food - Drinks*

Tiger Nickname

Many persons, even Detroiters, wrongly associate the nickname "Tigers" with Ty Cobb's early connection with the present American League team, but they were Tigers long before the coming of Ty. George Stallings, an early manager of the Tigers, took the credit. He said when he was first manager in Detroit he changed a lot of things. Among other things, he thought maybe the change of uniform would change their luck. He put striped stockings on the players—black and a sort of yellowish-brown. He didn't think of their resemblance to a tiger's stripes at the time, but the fans and some early writers noticed it and soon started calling the club the Tigers. And they've been the Tigers ever since.

1980

FINAL STANDINGS

EAST DIVISION	W	L	PCT
New York	103	59	.636
Baltimore	100	62	.617
Milwaukee	86	76	.531
Boston	83	77	.519
DETROIT	84	78	.519
Cleveland	79	81	.494
Toronto	67	95	.414

WEST DIVISION	W	L	PCT
Kansas City	97	65	.599
Oakland	83	79	.512
Minnesota	77	84	.478
Texas	76	85	.472
Chicago	70	90	.438
California	65	95	.406
Seattle	59	103	.364

Manager: Sparky Anderson

Sparky Anderson, never at a loss for words, was unusually outspoken, even for him, as the Tigers embarked on the 1980 season, Sparky's first full year at the helm.

"I don't see why we can't win 90 games," the Tiger manager boldly predicted.

Immediately the media, and then the fans, jumped all over his words. Most of them wanted to believe him. After all, the Tigers had not played well enough to participate in post-season playoffs since 1972. Besides, the silver-haired skipper made his prediction sound so convincing.

"We'll score runs," he promised. "If our pitching comes through, we'll contend."

Well, the Tiger manager was right about his team scoring runs anyway. The Tigers scored 830 runs during the 1980 season. No team in either major league scored more.

The problem was that the Tiger pitchers permitted the opposition to score almost as often and almost as easily as the Tigers themselves scored. In the end, the Tigers' earned run average was an unsightly 4.25.

As Anderson himself observed, "We scored more than five runs a game on the average. We just have to find a way to keep the other team from scoring six."

In spite of the inability of their pitchers to get the other side out, the Tigers did manage to win 84 games, while losing 78. Nevertheless, they again ran fifth, which was hardly what Anderson and the Tigers had in mind when the summer began.

The Tigers thought they had solved part of their pitching problem before the season even opened, when they traded Ron LeFlore to Montreal for left-hander Dan Schatzeder. Many observers felt that Anderson was merely getting rid of LeFlore, who had made a habit of breaking Sparky's team rules. But Anderson insisted the chance to add a quality pitcher such as Schatzeder was what motivated the Tigers to make the trade.

Schatzeder, however, was a disappointing 11-13 and hardly the dominant force in the starting rotation that the Tigers had hoped for.

Jack Morris didn't have the type of season the Tigers expected from him, either, posting a 16-15 mark when most everyone had considered him a cinch to win 20 games.

Veteran Milt Wilcox, who injured his shoulder in an on-the-field brawl with the Kansas City Royals after he had brushed back George Brett, struggled during the final two months and finished at 13-11.

Among the starting pitchers, only promising young Dan Petry (10-9) had an earned run average under 4.00, coming in at 3.92. In the bullpen, Aurelio Lopez was again the man, saving 21 games while compiling a 13-6 record.

Offensively, the Tigers featured several players who enjoyed fine seasons. Although Kirk Gibson, the "next Mickey Mantle" and high-priced Tiger bonus baby out of Michigan State University, was sidelined for much of the season after wrist surgery, Ricky Peters filled the gap in centerfield by batting .291 and impressing people as a player who could make things happen.

Champ Summers had another stellar summer, batting .297 with 60 rbi. Alan Trammell put together his best year in the big leagues, hitting .300 and scoring 107 runs, Richie Hebner, acquired from the New York Mets during the winter, batted .290 with 82 rbi, and Steve Kemp knocked in 101 runs.

It had been a difficult season. Anderson admitted it was the most disappointing year of his managerial career. But the Tigers—and Sparky—were determined to prove their preseason predictions had not been as far-fetched as the critics claimed. The only way they could do that would be by winning next year.

Jack Billingham, who pitched for the Tigers from 1978 until 1980, pitched for the Cincinnati Reds in 1974. On April 4 pitching in Cincinnati, he gave up a home run to Hank Aaron. It was Aaron's 714th career homer and tied Babe Ruth's lifetime mark.

BATTING RECORDS

	B	G	AB	R	H	HR	SB	AVE	RBI
Trammell, Alan	R	146	560	107	168	9	12	.300	65
Summers, Champ	L	120	347	61	103	17	4	.297	60
Kemp, Steve	L	135	508	88	149	21	5	.293	101
Peters, Ricky	B	133	477	79	139	2	13	.291	42
Hebner, Richie	L	104	341	48	99	12	0	.290	82
Thompson, Jason (36 Det., 102 Calif.)	L	138	438	69	126	21	2	.288	90
Corcoran, Tim	L	84	153	20	44	3	0	.288	18
Parrish, Lance	R	144	553	79	158	24	6	.286	82
Brookens, Tom	R	151	509	64	140	10	13	.275	66
Wockenfuss, John	R	126	372	56	102	16	1	.274	65
Cowens, Al (34 Calif., 108 Det.)	R	142	522	69	140	6	6	.268	59
Gibson, Kirk	L	51	175	23	46	9	4	.263	16
Lentine, Jim	R	67	161	19	42	1	2	.261	17
Jones, Lynn	R	29	55	9	14	0	1	.255	6
Papi, Stan (1 Bos., 46 Det.)	R	47	114	12	27	3	0	.237	17
Wagner, Mark	R	45	72	5	17	0	0	.236	3
Whitaker, Lou	L	145	477	68	111	1	8	.233	45
Dyer, Duffy	R	48	108	11	20	4	0	.185	11
Stegman, Dave	R	65	130	12	23	2	1	.177	9

Less than 10 games: Dan Gonzales.

PITCHING RECORDS

	T	G	IP	W	L	PCT	ERA
Underwood, Pat	L	49	113	3	6	.333	3.59
Lopez, Aurelio	R	67	124	13	6	.684	3.77
Rozema, Dave	R	42	145	6	9	.400	3.92
Petry, Dan	R	27	165	10	9	.526	3.92
Tobik, Dave	R	17	61	1	0	1.000	3.98
Schatzeder, Dan	L	32	193	11	13	.458	4.02
Weaver, Roger	R	19	64	3	4	.429	4.10
Morris, Jack	R	36	250	16	15	.516	4.18
Wilcox, Milt	R	32	199	13	11	.542	4.48
Robbins, Bruce	L	15	52	4	2	.667	6.62

Less than 45 innings: Mark Fidrych, Jerry Ujdur and John Hiller. Jack Billingham appeared in 8 games with Detroit and 7 with Boston.

Freehan-Bocci & Co.
MANUFACTURERS REPRESENTATIVES

BILL FREEHAN

999 Haynes Street
Suite 305
Birmingham, Michigan 48009
(313) 647-9600
FAX: (313) 645-9650

MEXICAN INDUSTRIES IN MICHIGAN, INC.

HANK AGUIRRE

13500 ROTUNDA DR.
DEARBORN, MI 48120
313-581-0077

•

1616 HOWARD ST.
DETROIT, MI 48216
313-963-6114

Stealing Home

There are 31 men who played in the major leagues who stole home 10 or more times. As would be expected, Ty Cobb leads with 35 steals of home. George Moriarty is the only other man who ever wore a Tiger uniform to steal home more than ten times. George did it eleven times. George's son is a prominent physician, Dr. George Moriarty, in Detroit, and his grandson is Michael Moriarty, the famous stage and screen actor who attended the University of Detroit High School.

1981
FINAL STANDINGS

EAST DIVISION - 1st Half	W	L	PCT
New York	34	22	.607
Baltimore	31	23	.574
Milwaukee	31	25	.554
DETROIT	31	26	.544
Boston	30	26	.536
Cleveland	26	24	.520
Toronto	16	42	.276

WEST DIVISION - 1st Half	W	L	PCT
Oakland	37	23	.617
Texas	33	22	.600
Chicago	31	22	.585
California	31	29	.517
Kansas City	20	30	.400
Seattle	21	36	.368
Minnesota	17	39	.304

EAST DIVISION - 2nd Half	W	L	PCT
Milwaukee	31	22	.585
DETROIT	29	23	.558
Boston	29	23	.558
Baltimore	28	23	.549
Cleveland	26	27	.491
New York	25	26	.490
Toronto	21	27	.438

WEST DIVISION - 2nd Half	W	L	PCT
Kansas City	30	23	.566
Oakland	27	22	.551
Texas	24	26	.480
Minnesota	24	29	.453
Seattle	23	29	.442
Chicago	23	30	.434
California	20	30	.400

Manager: Sparky Anderson

In 1972, when the Tigers won the Eastern half of the American League pennant, they did so with the help of a brief early-season strike, which reduced the season and enabled them to prevail by a half game. In 1981, a labor strike nearly catapulted the Tigers into post-season play again.

After haggling with the owners for more than a year, major league players walked out on strike on June 12, putting the national pastime out of business for 50 days.

Part of the strike settlement was a decision to let the teams start from scratch when play resumed. The four teams that had been in first place when the strike was called—the New York Yankees, Oakland A's, Philadelphia Phillies and Los Angeles Dodgers—would qualify to a playoff against the second-half title winner in their division before the regular playoffs began.

The Tigers, who lost 53 games because of the strike, were in fourth place when the strike came, 3 1/2 games behind the Yankees. They certainly were still in the race, even though they had Milwaukee, Baltimore and New York to pass.

As well as they played during the first half of the season, winning 31 and losing 26, the Tigers were even better during the second half.

Kirk Gibson, whose rare blend of speed and power made him the target of great expectations, led the Tigers' charge after the strike.

Gibson, who batted only .234 before the interruption, striking out 13 times in his last 20 at bats before the strike, hit like a terror when play resumed, batting .375 the second half to finish at .328 for the year.

Going into the final series of the regular season, a three-game weekend showdown against the Brewers in Milwaukee, the Tigers still had a chance for the second-half title. All they had to do was win two out of three against Milwaukee and the Tigers would meet New york in the mini-playoff.

It was the closest the Tigers had come since 1972. Unfortunately they could get no closer, losing the first two games to the Brewers to finish the second half tied with Boston for second place. Still, the Tigers won 29 and lost 23 after the strike. Overall, they were 60-49 which, under the regular full-season format, without a strike, would have been good enough for a close fourth-place finish.

The Tigers were, of course, disappointed. But they also had reason to feel pleased. They had, after all, finally experienced the pressures and tensions of a major league pennant race, which for most of them was a first. And they had battled to stay in the race in spite of a number of obvious shortcomings.

The Tigers had managed to win with only three dependable starters, when most other contenders were able to count on four.

Jack Morris, selected as the starting pitcher in the All-Star Game, finished the abbreviated season at 14-7 with a 3.05 e.r.a. Milt Wilcox continued to be a consistent winner, compiling a 12-9 mark with a 3.04 e.r.a. And Dan Petry posted a 10-9 mark and 3.00 e.r.a.

In the bullpen, the Tigers got some unexpected help from Kevin Saucier, a free-spirited lefthander, acquired from the Texas Rangers in an off-season trade. Saucier, whose animated dances and antics on the field as well as his pitching earned him the nickname "Hot Sauce," saved 13 games and had a 4-2 record with a glittering 1.65 e.r.a.

Gibson, of course, was the Tigers' hitting star, at least during the second half. Lou Whitaker was also a steady performer at second base and at the plate, where he batted .263. But Lance Parrish batted only .244 with 10 homers and 46 rbi while Steve Kemp hit .277 with 9 home runs and 49 rbi.

Clearly the Tigers had improved in some categories and declined in others. They had come close, but under unusual circumstances. To be a bona fide contender over the course of a full season, they obviously needed help, both on the mound and at bat.

BATTING RECORDS

	B	G	AB	R	H	HR	SB	AVE	RBI
Gibson, Kirk	L	83	290	41	95	9	17	.328	40
Kemp, Steve	L	105	372	52	103	9	9	.277	49
Jackson, Ron (54 Minn., 31 Det.)	R	85	270	29	73	5	6	.270	40
Whitaker, Lou	L	109	335	48	88	5	5	.263	36
Cowens, Al	R	85	253	27	66	1	3	.261	18
Jones, Lynn	R	71	174	19	45	2	1	.259	19
Trammell, Alan	R	105	392	52	101	2	10	.258	31
Peters, Rick	B	63	207	26	53	0	1	.256	15
Summers, Champ	L	64	165	16	42	3	1	.255	21
Fahey, Bill	L	27	67	5	17	1	0	.254	9
Brown, Darrell	R	16	4	4	1	0	1	.250	0
Parrish, Lance	R	96	348	39	85	10	2	.244	46
Brookens, Tom	R	71	239	19	58	4	5	.243	25
Hebner, Richie	L	78	226	19	51	5	1	.226	28
Kelleher, Mickey	R	61	77	10	17	0	0	.221	6
Wockenfuss, John	R	70	172	20	37	9	0	.215	25
Papi, Stan	R	40	93	8	19	3	1	.204	12
Leach, Rick	L	54	83	9	16	1	0	.193	11

Less than 10 games: Duffy Dyer and Marty Castillo.

PITCHING RECORDS

	T	G	IP	W	L	PCT	ERA
Saucier, Kevin	L	38	49	4	2	.667	1.65
Tobik, Dave	R	27	60	2	2	.500	2.69
Petry, Dan	R	23	141	10	9	.526	3.00
Wilcox, Milt	R	24	166	12	9	.545	3.03
Morris, Jack	R	25	198	14	7	.667	3.05
Rozema, Dave	R	28	104	5	5	.500	3.63
Lopez, Aurelio	R	29	82	5	2	.714	3.64
Schatzeder, Dan	L	17	71	6	8	.429	6.06

Less than 45 innings: Dennis Kinney, Larry Rothschild, Dave Rucker, Jerry Ujdur, Howard Bailey and George Cappuzzello.

Everything you want in a luxurious Hotel without the high, high price!

RATES - $67.00 - $87.00
Suites - $150.00

★ Spacious King and Queen rooms
★ Luxurious King Bed with Jacuzzi
★ Indoor 25 yard lap heated pool
★ Chardai's Restaurant
★ Shadows Nightclub
★ Meeting/Banquet Rooms
★ Rose Shores Fitness & Racquet Club
★ Rose Shores Travel

DAYS
INNS • HOTELS • SUITES
ROSEVILLE, MICHIGAN

Days Inn of Roseville
31960 Little Mack
Roseville, MI 48066
(313) 296-6700

For Reservations Call: 1 (800) 437-2747

The Bambino

Babe Ruth was born in Baltimore, Maryland on the sixth of February, 1895. He broke into the majors in 1914 with the Boston Red Sox as a pitcher. He was a great pitcher, but even better as a hitter, and in 1919, he switched full time to the outfield. He went to the New York Yankees in a deal in 1920 and played there for 15 years. In 1927 he hit 60 home runs. Lou Gehrig, also of the Yankees, hit 47 that season, and the third man in the League was Tony Lazzeri who hit 18. No other team in the American League hit as many homers as the Babe. Philadelphia had 56 and the St. Louis Browns had 55. Boston, Washington and Cleveland all had less than 30 home runs as a team. He was elected to Baseball's Hall of Fame in 1936. Babe passed away in New York on August 16, 1948.

1982

FINAL STANDINGS

EAST DIVISION	W	L	PCT
Milwaukee	95	67	.586
Baltimore	94	68	.580
Boston	89	73	.549
DETROIT	83	79	.512
New York	79	83	.488
Cleveland	78	84	.481
Toronto	78	84	.481

WEST DIVISION			
California	93	69	.574
Kansas City	90	72	.556
Chicago	87	75	.537
Seattle	76	86	.469
Oakland	68	94	.420
Texas	64	98	.395
Minnesota	60	102	.370

Manager: Sparky Anderson

The Tigers' near-miss in the strike-shortened campaign the year before sent them into the 1982 season believing they were ready to battle the best.

Kirk Gibson seemed to have finally found himself; Kevin Saucier looked untouchable coming out of the bullpen; Larry Herndon and Chet Lemon had been obtained in off-season trades; and, of course, the Tigers still had their nucleus of starting pitchers in Jack Morris, Dan Petry and Milt Wilcox.

The Tigers saw no reason why they shouldn't be right in the thick of things again, and this time emerge on top.

But suddenly Saucier couldn't seem to get anybody out. And the highstrung lefty had a difficult time adjusting to his unexpected failures. The harder he was hammered, the harder he pressed. And the harder he pressed, the harder he was hammered. To compound the Tigers' relief woes, Aurelio Lopez came down with a sore arm and had to be sent to Evansville, which sent Sparky Anderson scrambling in search of relief help.

Then Dave Rozema, who had won three games without a loss and compiled an outstanding 1.63 e.r.a., severely tore up his knee in May when he foolishly tried to execute a karate kick during a field brawl with the Minnesota Twins. That sent him to the sidelines for the remainder of the season and jeopardized his future.

Other relievers such as Elias Sosa and Pat Underwood proved they couldn't solve the Tigers' predicament. Only Dave Tobik, with nine saves, did a decent job in what was undeniably the best year of his career.

In spite of their problems in the bullpen, the Tigers nevertheless compiled the lowest earned run average in the league, with a mark of 3.80. They managed that mainly because of the efforts of Jack Morris (17 wins), Dan

Petry (15 victories), Milt Wilcox (12 wins) and rookie Jerry Ujdur (10 wins). Even those performances were somewhat disappointing because Petry and Wilcox were both sidelined by injuries that reduced their effectiveness and cut down on their wins.

Had they been healthy all season, and had they had a bullpen to back them up, the Tigers might not have finished fourth again in the AL East. One span in particular pointed up the weakness of the Tigers' pitching. They lost 15 out of 17 games during one stretch in June to tumble all the way from first place to fourth. Good teams, with solid pitching staffs, usually don't experience streaks like that.

Another reason the Tigers finished a distant 12 games behind Milwaukee was the fact that the Tigers lost the staggering total of 28 games from the seventh inning on, often because of a late-inning home run.

In the spring of the year, Sparky Anderson had called the 1982 Tigers the best team he had managed since his World Championship teams in Cincinnati. And several of the players showed why with their performances on the field.

Lance Parrish finally did the things people had long been predicting of him as he belted 32 homers to break the all-time American League record for home runs by a catcher.

Larry Herndon, acquired from San Francisco during the off-season when the Tigers gave up on pitcher Dave Schatzeder, also had a banner year, batting .292 with 23 homers and 88 rbi.

At the top of the batting order, second baseman Lou Whitaker hit .286 and gave the Tigers the dependable leadoff hitter they had been looking for since Ron LeFlore was traded away.

Kirk Gibson, who along with Parrish was supposed to be the Tigers' big gun, continued to be plagued by injuries, but rookies Glenn Wilson (.292 in 84 games) and Howard Johnson (.316) served notice that they were ready to play every day in the big leagues.

Once again, the Tigers went into the winter wondering what might have happened if everybody had stayed healthy, if everybody had enjoyed the sort of seasons expected of them. Once again, they were disappointed by their finish yet, once again, they could not help but be encouraged about the future.

⚾ ⚾ ⚾

Sam Jones was a Tiger in 1962 and won two games and lost four. On May 12, 1955, Sam was pitching for the Chicago Cubs and defeated the Pittsburgh Pirates 4-0 and did not give up a hit. He was the first black pitcher in major league history to pitch a no-hitter.

BATTING RECORDS

	B	G	AB	R	H	HR	SB	AVE	RBI
Johnson, Howard	B	54	155	23	49	4	7	.316	14
Wockenfuss, John	R	70	193	28	58	8	0	.301	32
Herndon, Larry	R	157	614	92	179	23	12	.292	88
Wilson, Glenn	R	84	322	39	94	12	2	.292	34
Whitaker, Lou	L	152	560	76	160	15	11	.286	65
Parrish, Lance	R	133	486	75	138	32	3	.284	87
Gibson, Kirk	L	69	266	34	74	8	9	.278	35
Hebner, Richie	L	68	179	25	49	8	1	.274	18
Lemon, Chet	R	125	436	75	116	19	1	.266	52
Cabell, Enos	R	125	464	45	121	2	15	.261	37
Laga, Mike	L	27	88	6	23	3	1	.261	11
Trammell, Alan	R	157	489	66	126	9	19	.258	57
Turner, Jerry	L	85	210	21	52	8	1	.248	27
Leach, Rick	L	82	218	23	52	3	4	.239	12
Ivie, Mike	R	80	259	35	60	14	0	.232	38
Brookens, Tom	R	140	398	40	92	9	5	.231	58
Jones, Lynn	R	58	139	15	31	0	0	.223	14
DeJohn, Mark	B	24	21	1	4	0	1	.190	1
Fahey, Bill	L	28	67	7	10	0	1	.149	4
Miller, Eddie	B	14	25	3	1	0	0	.040	0

Less than 10 games: Marty Castillo and Mick Kelleher.

PITCHING RECORDS

	T	G	IP	W	L	PCT	ERA
Petry, Dan	R	35	246	15	9	.625	3.22
Rucker, Dave	L	27	64	5	6	.455	3.38
Tobik, Dave	R	51	99	4	9	.308	3.56
Wilcox, Milt	R	29	194	12	10	.545	3.62
Ujdur, Jerry	R	25	178	10	10	.500	3.69
Pashnick, Larry	R	28	94	4	4	.500	4.01
Morris, Jack	R	37	266	17	16	.515	4.06
Sosa, Elias	R	38	61	3	3	.500	4.43
Underwood, Pat	L	33	99	4	8	.333	4.73

Less than 45 innings: Howard Bailey, Juan Berenguer, Dave Gumpert, Bill James, Dave Rozema, Aurelio Lopez, Larry Rothschild and Kevin Saucier.

Ginopolis'

ON THE GRILL
Family Casual Dining
Child's Menu Available

Featuring: Fresh Fish Selections
Chargrilling Specialties
B.B.Q. Ribs
Pastas

2273 Crooks Rd.
Rochester Hills
853-7333

27815 Middlebelt
at 12 Mile Road
Farmington Hills
851-8222

When he defeated the Oakland A's on September 14, 1968, Denny McLain became the first major league pitcher to win 30 games since 1934. Reggie Jackson had hit two homers for the A's and the Tigers trailed by a run as they came to bat in the ninth inning. Al Kaline walked and later scored on Danny Cater's error. Willie Horton's hit drove in Mickey Stanley and gave Denny his 30th win.

1983

FINAL STANDINGS

EAST DIVISION	W	L	PCT
Baltimore	98	64	.605
DETROIT	92	70	.568
New York	91	71	.562
Toronto	89	73	.549
Milwaukee	87	75	.537
Boston	78	84	.481
Cleveland	70	92	.432

WEST DIVISION			
Chicago	99	63	.611
Kansas City	79	83	.488
Texas	77	85	.475
Oakland	74	88	.457
California	70	92	.432
Minnesota	70	92	.432
Seattle	60	102	.370

Manager: Sparky Anderson

It was a year of success for the Tigers, a season not of potential but of performance.

The kids of yesterday became the stars of today, with tomorrow just around the corner. Fourth and fifth place belonged to someone else for once. The future was finally here.

The Tigers didn't finish first, but they were close enough for a glimpse of it. Second place was their best showing in 11 years, and not since their World Championship season of 1968 had the Tigers won as many games as they did in 1983. It wasn't a season which ended with confetti and champagne, but the confidence instilled by such improvement was almost as bubbly.

"It was a learning year," said Enos Cabell. "A lot of the younger players didn't know what it was like to stay close all season. Now they do. They'll be the wiser for it."

The pennant race came down to a September showdown with Baltimore and the hope against hope Detroit could win seven straight games from Baltimore. "It was a longshot," said Manager Sparky Anderson, "but at least we had a chance. It came down to us and them."

Eventually the Tigers fell short by six games, but again it was their clearest view of the top in a full season since they won the American League East in 1972.

On the field, it was a season of immense progress. Upstairs in the offices, it was a season of change. For one thing, the Tigers were sold. John E. Fetzer, sole owner of the team since 1961, stepped down reluctantly but gracefully, selling the club for close to $50 million to pizza baron Thomas Monaghan of Ann Arbor.

"It's a sad day for me," said Fetzer, one of the game's most respected owners. "But in Tom Monaghan, I feel we've found the man best suited to carry on the best interests of the Tigers."

Monaghan, who grew up in orphanages and foster homes in Michigan before establishing Domino's Pizza, said he would not make any major decisions about the club for at least two years. Fetzer would remain as chairman of the board for two years, tutoring Monaghan about major league ownership.

The name on the checkbook wasn't the only one that changed, however. Jim Campbell, the team's general manager since 1962, relinquished that post to Bill Lajoie while staying on as president and chief operating officer. "I've never felt better," said Campbell, who underwent open heart surgery in 1981, "but doctors have advised me to slow down a bit. I'm not retiring, though."

The team which became Lajoie's to mold and shape for 1984 contained one of the strongest lineups in the majors. Four Tigers hit .300 or better in 1983. Lou Whitaker led the way at .320, followed by Alan Trammell at .319, Enos Cabell at .311 and Larry Herndon at .302.

For the first time ever, three Tigers won a Gold Glove for defensive excellence. Again it was Whitaker and Trammell in the spotlight, joined by catcher Lance Parrish, who also became only the second Tiger since 1962 to drive in more than 110 runs. Parrish belted 27 home runs to go along with his 114 rbi. Herndon added 20 home runs and 92 rbi while Chet Lemon complemented an outstanding year in centerfield with 24 home runs and 69 rbi.

On the mound, Jack Morris took giant strides toward the heights always projected for him. A 20-13 record made Morris the Tigers' first 20-game winner in 10 years and he also led the league with 232 strikeouts.

Dan Petry almost made it a twosome in the elite circle, but fell short of 20 victories by losing his last start. Even so, Petry's 19-11 record brought him a lucrative four-year contract following the season. There were other encouraging events on the mound: the surprise of Juan Berenguer, the comeback of Aurelio Lopez, and the unexpected contributions of Dave Rozema.

All told, it was an entertaining season. But the Tigers had entertained before without success in the standings. It was different in 1983, though. The Tigers finally made some noise.

BATTING RECORDS

	B	G	AB	R	H	HR	SB	AVE	RBI
Whitaker, Lou	L	161	643	94	206	12	17	.320	72
Trammell, Alan	R	142	505	83	161	14	30	.319	66
Cabell, Enos	R	121	392	62	122	5	4	.311	46
Herndon, Larry	R	153	603	88	182	20	9	.302	92
Krenchicki, Wayne	L	59	133	18	37	1	0	.278	16
Fahey, Bill	L	19	22	4	6	0	0	.273	2
Wockenfuss, John	R	92	245	32	66	9	1	.269	44
Parrish, Lance	R	155	605	80	163	27	1	.269	114
Wilson, Glenn	R	144	503	55	135	11	1	.268	65
Jones, Lynn	R	49	64	9	17	0	1	.266	6
Lemon, Chet	R	145	491	78	125	24	0	.255	69
Grubb, John	L	57	134	20	34	4	0	.254	22
Leach, Rick	L	99	242	22	60	3	2	.248	26
Gibson, Kirk	L	128	401	60	91	15	14	.227	51
Brookens, Tom	R	138	332	50	71	6	10	.214	32
Ivie, Mike	R	12	42	4	9	0	0	.214	7
Johnson, Howard	B	27	66	11	14	3	0	.212	5
Castillo, Marty	R	67	119	10	23	2	2	.193	10
Laga, Mike	L	12	21	2	4	0	0	.190	2
Gonzales, Julio	R	12	21	0	3	0	0	.143	2

Less than 10 games: Sal Butera, Bob Molinaro and Bill Nahorodny.

PITCHING RECORDS

	T	G	IP	W	L	PCT	ERA
Lopez, Aurelio	R	57	115	9	8	.529	2.81
Berenguer, Juan	R	37	158	9	5	.643	3.14
Morris, Jack	R	37	294	20	13	.606	3.34
Rozema, Dave	R	29	105	8	3	.727	3.43
Abbott, Glenn (7 Seattle, 14 Det.)	R	21	129	7	4	.636	3.63
Bair, Doug	R	27	56	7	3	.700	3.88
Petry, Dan	R	38	266	19	11	.633	3.92
Wilcox, Milt	R	26	186	11	10	.524	3.97
Bailey, Howard	L	33	72	5	5	.500	4.88

Less than 45 innings: Dave Gumpert, Bill James, John Martin, Larry Pashnick, Dave Rucker, Jerry Ujder and Pat Underwood.

Dunleavy's Pub & Grub

34505 Grand River
Farmington, Michigan 48024
(313) 478-8866

Jack Dunleavy
Marty Burke

Lunches-Dinners

1984

FINAL STANDINGS

EAST DIVISION	W	L	PCT
DETROIT	104	58	.642
Toronto	89	73	.549
New York	87	75	.537
Boston	86	76	.531
Baltimore	85	77	.525
Cleveland	75	87	.463
Milwaukee	67	94	.416
WEST DIVISION			
Kansas City	84	78	.519
California	81	81	.500
Minnesota	81	81	.500
Oakland	77	85	.475
Chicago	74	88	.457
Seattle	74	88	.457
Texas	69	92	.429

Manager: Sparky Anderson

The Tigers won their first nine games of the 1984 season and then went on to post a 35-5 record for their first 40 games. They won 104 games during the entire season and finished 15 games ahead of the second place Toronto Blue Jays. They were in first place the entire season from opening day to the end of the year, the first club in the American League to lead from wire to wire since the New York Yankees in 1927.

The Tigers acquired Willie Hernandez and Dave Bergman in a trade with the Philadelphia Phillies for Glen Wilson and John Wockenfuss two weeks before the season opened.

Hernandez set a Tiger record with 80 appearances and 68 games finished. He saved 32 games in 33 game-saving situations. He was almost perfect for the entire season. Hernandez won the Most Valuable Player award as well as the Cy Young award.

Dave Bergman also proved invaluable for his clutch-hitting superb defensive work. Twice he delivered three-run homers to defeat the Toronto Blue Jays.

One of the nine wins to start the season for the Tigers was a no-hitter by Jack Morris, the fifth no-hitter by a Tiger pitcher and the first since Jim Bunning had held the Boston Red Sox hitless in 1958.

The Detroit starting pitchers were also outstanding. Morris was 19-11, Dan Petry 18-8 and Milt Wilcox 17-8.

The Tigers had power on offense. They hit 187 home runs, the most in both leagues. Lance Parrish had 98 rbi and 33 homers. Kirk Gibson hit .282 with 91 rbi and 27 home runs.

Alan Trammell hit .314 and was the fourth leading hitter in the league. Lou Whitaker hit .289 and Chet Lemon .287. And the Tigers were the strongest team in the majors down the middle with Lou, Alan, Chet and Lance.

Aurelio Lopez had a good year, at 10-1, with earned run average of 2.94. Doug Bair, Bill Scherrer, Juan Berenguer, and Dave Rozema also contributed. Detroit also got aid from Marty Castillo, Darrell Evans, Ruppert Jones, Johnny Grubb, Howard Johnson, Tom Brookens and Rusty Kuntz.

It was a great year for Detroit and more than 2.7 million fans attended the games at Tiger Stadium, only the second time Detroit had drawn over two million.

BATTING RECORDS

	B	G	AB	R	H	HR	SB	AVE	RBI
Trammell, Alan	R	139	555	85	174	14	19	.314	69
Allen, Rod	R	15	27	6	8	0	1	.296	3
Whitaker, Lou	L	143	558	90	161	13	6	.289	56
Lemon, Chet	R	141	509	77	146	20	5	.287	76
Garbey, Barbaro	R	110	327	45	94	5	6	.287	52
Kuntz, Rusty	R	84	140	32	40	2	2	.286	22
Jones, Ruppert	L	79	215	26	61	12	2	.286	37
Gibson, Kirk	L	149	531	92	150	27	29	.282	91
Herndon, Larry	R	125	407	52	114	7	6	.280	43
Bergman, Dave	L	120	271	42	74	7	3	.273	44
Grubb, Johnny	L	86	176	25	47	8	1	.267	17
Johnson, Howard	B	116	355	43	88	12	10	.248	50
Brookens, Tom	R	113	224	32	55	5	6	.246	26
Lowry, Dwight	L	32	45	8	11	2	0	.244	7
Parrish, Lance	R	147	578	75	137	33	2	.237	98
Castillo, Marty	R	70	141	16	33	4	1	.234	17
Evans, Darrell	L	131	401	60	93	16	2	.232	63
Baker, Doug	B	43	108	15	20	0	3	.185	12
Earl, Scotty	R	14	35	3	4	0	1	.114	1

Less than 10 games: Mike Laga and Nelson Simmons.

PITCHING RECORDS

	T	G	IP	W	L	PCT	ERA
Hernandez, Willie	L	80	140	9	3	.750	1.92
Lopez, Aurelio	R	71	138	10	1	.909	2.94
Petry, Dan	R	35	233	18	8	.692	3.24
Berenguer, Juan	R	31	168	11	10	.524	3.48
Morris, Jack	R	35	240	19	11	.633	3.60
Rozema, Dave	R	29	101	7	6	.538	3.74
Bair, Doug	R	47	94	5	3	.625	3.75
Wilcox, Milt	R	33	194	17	8	.680	4.00

Less than 45 innings: Roger Mason, Randy O'Neal, Glenn Abbott, Sid Monge, Bill Scherrer and Carl Willis.

1984 American League Championship Series

The Detroit Tigers finished the regular season 20 games better than the Western Division champs, the Kansas City Royals. In fact, there were four other teams in the Eastern Division of the American League to have a better record than the Royals. But with the two-division system, the Royals finished first in the West and qualified to play in the American League Championship Series (A.L.C.S.).

The Tigers defeated the Royals with three straight victories to sweep into the World Series.

The Tigers won the first game as Jack Morris and Willie Hernandez held the Royals to five hits and one run. The Tigers scored twice in the first inning on Lou Whitaker's single, Alan Trammell's triple and Lance Parrish's sacrifice fly. Homers by Larry Herndon and Trammell in the fourth and fifth inning made the score 4-0. They added four runs in the seventh, eighth and ninth innings, the last coming on a home run by Parrish. The Royals scored a harmless run in the seventh. The final score was 8-1.

The Tigers won the second game of the playoffs, but this time it took 11 innings. Detroit scored two in the first inning. Lou Whitaker was safe on an error and with one out Kirk Gibson and Lance Parrish had back-to-back doubles. Gibson made it 3-0 in the third inning when he homered. The Royals got a run off Dan Petry in the fourth and another in the seventh. They scored their third run off Willie Hernandez in the eighth and the game went into extra innings with the score tied at three apiece. Aurelio Lopez was pitching for Detroit and Dan Quisenberry for Kansas City.

In the eleventh inning, Parrish opened the Tiger half with a single. Darrell Evans sacrificed and both runners were safe when Don Slaught, the Kansas City catcher, fumbled the ball. Ruppert Jones forced Parrish at third. Then Johnny Grubb singled into right center, scoring Evans and Jones and putting the Tigers one game away from the American League pennant.

The third and final game was a pitchers duel between Milt Wilcox and Charlie Liebrandt. Detroit scored the only run of the game in the second inning. Barbaro Garbey singled to center, Chet Lemon forced Garbey to second, Darrell Evans singled sending Lemon to third, Marty Castillo grounded to Onix Concepcion who threw to Frank White at second, forcing Evans, but the relay to first was too late to catch Castillo, and Lemon scored the one and only run of the game as the Tigers clinched the championship and the right to play in the World Series for the first time since 1968. Liebrandt gave up only one more hit, a single to Kirk Gibson, while Wilcox allowed the Royals only two hits before giving way to Willie Hernandez in the ninth.

The Tigers were ready for the World Series.

A.L.C.S. PLAYOFFS — INDIVIDUAL AVERAGES

	G	AB	R	H	HR	SB	PCT	RBI
Baker	1	0	0	0	0	0	.000	0
Bergman	2	1	1	1	0	1	1.000	0
Brookens	2	2	0	0	0	0	.000	0
Castillo	3	8	0	2	0	1	.250	2
Evans	3	10	1	3	0	1	.300	1
Garbey	3	9	1	3	0	0	.333	0
Gibson	3	12	2	5	1	1	.417	2
Grubb	1	4	0	1	0	0	.250	2
Herndon	2	5	1	1	1	0	.200	1
Jones	2	5	1	0	0	0	.000	0
Kuntz	1	1	0	0	0	0	.000	0
Lemon	3	13	1	0	0	0	.000	0
Parrish	3	12	1	3	1	0	.250	3
Trammell	3	11	2	4	1	0	.364	3
Whitaker	3	14	3	2	0	0	.143	0
DH Hitters		12	1	4	0	0	.333	2
PH Hitters		3	0	0	0	0	.000	0
Totals		**107**	**14**	**25**	**4**	**4**	**.234**	**14**

PITCHING RECORDS

	G	IP	W	L	PCT	R	H	BB	SO
Hernandez	3	4.0	0	0	.000	1	3	1	3
Lopez	1	3.0	1	0	1.000	0	4	1	2
Morris	1	7.0	1	0	1.000	1	5	1	4
Petry	1	7.0	0	0	.000	2	4	1	4
Wilcox	1	8.0	1	0	1.000	0	2	2	8
Totals	**3**	**29.0**	**3**	**0**	**1.000**	**4**	**18**	**6**	**21**

Statistics — 207

1984 WORLD SERIES

First Game

The Tigers won the first game of the World Series in San Diego behind the pitching of Jack Morris. Jack held the Padres to two earned runs on eight hits.

Detroit scored in the first inning when Lou Whitaker doubled and came home on Alan Trammell's single to left. The Padres came back with two runs in their half of the first when, with two outs, Steve Garvey and Graig Nettles singled. Both scored when Terry Kennedy doubled. Detroit took the lead with two runs in the fifth when Lance Parrish doubled with two out and scored when Larry Herndon homered into the right field bleachers for a 3-2 win.

Second Game

Detroit opened the game with three runs in the first. Lou Whitaker started it off with a single and went to third on Alan Trammell's single. Kirk Gibson singled to right center, scoring Whitaker and sending Trammell to third. Gibson then stole second. Lance Parrish fouled out to Carmelo Martinez in the left field bullpen and Trammell scored after the catch and Gibson went to third. Darrell Evans then singled, scoring Gibson.

The Padres got one run back in the first inning when Alan Wiggins beat out a drag bunt. Tony Gwynn walked and Steve Garvey sacrificed. Graig Nettles flied to Ruppert Jones and Wiggins scored after the catch. The Padres got another run in the last of the fourth. Kurt Bevacqua singled to left and went to third on Garry Templeton's single. He then scored on an infield out.

In the San Diego fifth, Steve Garvey flied deep to Chet Lemon, Nettles walked, and Terry Kennedy got an infield hit, Nettles going to second. Then Bevacqua slammed a pitch into the left field bleachers for a home run, scoring Nettles and Kennedy ahead of him. That was all the scoring for the ball game giving San Diego a 5-3 victory. Dan Petry was the losing pitcher and Andy Hawkins was credited with the win.

Third Game

With one out in the Tigers second, Chet Lemon singled to right. He advanced to second on Tim Lollar's wild pitch, Darrell Evans flied to deep centerfield, and Lemon took third after the catch. Marty Castillo drilled a one-two pitch into the upper deck in leftfield, scoring Lemon ahead of him and giving the Tigers a 2-0 lead. Detroit added two more to lead, 4-0.

Each team added another run in the third inning and San Diego scored the game's final run in the seventh. Milt Wilcox was credited with a 5-2 win as Tom Loller was charged with the loss and the Tigers now had a two to one lead in the World Series.

Fourth Game

The fourth game belonged to Alan Trammell. Alan hit a home run in the first inning, scoring Lou Whitaker ahead of him and hit another home run in the third inning, also scoring Whitaker ahead of him, giving the Tigers a total of four runs. And that was all they needed.

Jack Morris allowed five hits and held the San Diego Padres to two runs. The Padres got one run in the second inning when Terry Kennedy hit a home run into the right field upper deck. They got another run in the ninth inning when with one out, Steve Garvey doubled off the left field fence, went to third when Graig Nettles bounced out to Whitaker, and scored on Jack Morris' second wild pitch of the 4-2 victory. Morris was credited with his second win of the series and Eric Show was charged with the loss.

Fifth Game

The Detroit Tigers claimed their first World Championship since 1968, defeating the San Diego Padres 8-4.

Dan Petry started for the Tigers, went to the fourth inning, then came Bill Scherrer, Aurelio Lopez and Willie Hernandez. Lopez was the winning pitcher.

The Tigers got off to a three-run lead in the first inning as Lou Whitaker opened the inning with a single to right and Kirk Gibson clouted a tremendous home run into the right field stands, scoring Alan Trammel ahead of him.

San Diego tied it at 3-3, but in the Detroit fifth, the Tigers got another run when Gibson singled off Nettle's glove. Martinez caught Parrish's long fly just in front of the left field fence, Gibson tagged up and advanced to second afterwards. Larry Herndon and Chet Lemon walked, loading the bases. Rusty Kuntz batted for John Grubb and got credit for a sacrifice fly when Wiggins caught his pop fly in short right after Gwynn appeared to lose the ball in the lights. Gibson tagged up and beat Wiggins' off-balance throw to the plate.

The Tigers made it 5-3 in the seventh when Lance Parrish hit a home run into the left field stands.

Then, in the eighth, after Marty Castillo walked, Whitaker laid down a sacrifice bunt and was safe when Templeton failed to cover second. Kirk Gibson then smashed his second tremendous home run of the day into the upper deck in right field, giving the Tigers an 8-4 lead. Hernandez closed the door in the ninth and the Series was over.

Alan Trammell was chosen as the outstanding player of the series and the Tigers were World Champions once more—for the first time since 1968 and the fourth time in their history.

WORLD SERIES INDIVIDUAL AVERAGES

	G	AB	R	H	HR	SB	PCT	RBI
Bergman	5	5	0	0	0	0	.000	0
Brookens	3	3	0	0	0	0	.000	0
Castillo	3	9	2	3	1	0	.333	2
Evans	5	15	1	1	0	0	.067	1
Garbey	4	12	0	0	0	0	.000	0
Gibson	5	18	4	6	2	3	.333	7
Grubb	4	3	0	1	0	0	.333	0
Herndon	5	15	1	5	1	0	.333	3
Johnson	1	1	0	0	0	0	.000	0
Jones	2	3	0	0	0	0	.000	0
Kuntz	2	1	0	0	0	0	.000	1
Lemon	5	17	1	5	0	2	.294	1
Parrish	5	18	3	5	1	1	.278	2
Trammell	5	20	5	9	2	1	.450	6
Whitaker	5	18	6	5	0	0	.278	0
DH Hitters		15	0	1	0	0	.067	1
PH Hitters		7	0	0	0	0	.000	1
Totals		**158**	**23**	**40**	**7**	**9**	**.253**	**23**

PITCHING RECORDS

	G	IP	W	L	PCT	R	H	BB	SO
Bair	1	.2	0	0	.000	0	0	0	1
Hernandez	3	5.1	0	0	.000	1	4	0	0
Lopez	2	3.0	1	0	1.000	0	1	1	4
Morris	2	18.0	2	0	1.000	4	13	3	13
Petry	2	8.0	0	1	.000	8	14	5	4
Scherrer	3	3.0	0	0	.000	1	5	0	0
Wilcox	1	6.0	1	0	1.000	1	7	2	4

Tiger STATS

DEPEND ON US...

J.P. McCarthy	 Jimmy Launce	 Paul Harvey	 Warren Pierce	 Joel Alexander		 Kevin Joyce
 Bob Hynes	 Oscar Frenette	Jetcopter 76	 Jimmy Barrett	 Mike Whorf		 Mike Deja
 Dick Haefner	 Dan Streeter	 Gene Healy	 Joan Siefert	 Rod Hansen		 Gene Fogel
 Tom Campbell	Sparky Anderson	 Ernie Harwell and Paul Carey		 Larry Henry		 Isiah Thomas
 Frank Beckmann	 Bob Thornbladh	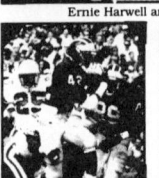 U of M Football	 Gary Moeller	 U of M Basketball		 Steve Fisher
 Paul Woods and Bruce Martyn		 Bryan Murray	 Detroit Red Wings	 Judy Coy		 John McMurray

"There's Only One."

WJR
AM RADIO 76

Copyright ©1990 WJR RADIO

1985

FINAL STANDINGS

EAST DIVISION	W	L	PCT
Toronto	99	62	.615
New York	97	64	.602
DETROIT	84	77	.522
Baltimore	83	78	.516
Boston	81	81	.500
Milwaukee	71	90	.441
Cleveland	60	102	.370

WEST DIVISION	W	L	PCT
Kansas City	91	71	.562
California	90	72	.556
Chicago	85	77	.525
Oakland	77	85	.475
Minnesota	77	85	.475
Seattle	74	88	.457
Texas	62	99	.385

Manager: Sparky Anderson

The Tigers' 1985 season began with promise and ended with a promise.

Following the 1984 World Championship season, fans, players and management saw no reason Detroit couldn't look forward to more of the same.

Manager Sparky Anderson said during the winter, "We'll be a better team, but that doesn't mean we'll win again. Everyone else in the division is better, too."

He was right on part of the prediction. Several of the Tigers' division rivals had improved, but Detroit wasn't a better team than it was the year before.

No one became alarmed when the Tigers played at a .500 pace in spring training. After all, the year before Detroit had one of the worst exhibition records in all baseball, then got off to the best start in major league history.

The big news from Lakeland was a bombshell dropped by Anderson. One day he announced he was moving All-Star second baseman Lou Whitaker to third base and replacing him at second with rookie phenom Chris Pittaro, who was trying to make the jump from Double-A to the majors. Whitaker balked at the switch and returned to second, but Anderson said Pittaro would open the season as his third baseman.

Pittaro collected three hits as the Tigers opened with a 5-4 victory over the Cleveland Indians. Detroit won its first six games and there was some talk that the Tigers might not only duplicate '84's 35-5 start, but they might improve on it.

Then the Tigers lost some of the magic. They stopped getting off to the early leads that carried them to victories the year before. They no longer enjoyed the late-inning heroics that thrilled the fans in '84.

Pittaro went the route of most spring sensations and it wasn't long before veteran Tom Brookens was once again the everyday third baseman.

One of the games that typified the '85 season occurred on April 21. The Tigers had loaded the bases in the 10th inning of a 2-2 tie with the Kansas City Royals. It was the perfect moment for the suicide squeeze and Anderson sent one of '84's heroes, Rusty Kuntz, to the plate to execute it.

A year ago Kuntz would have bunted the ball perfectly, allowing Kirk Gibson to score from third. This time Kuntz popped the ball into foul territory, catcher Jim Sundberg caught it, and Gibson was an easy double play victim. The Tigers lost 3-2 in the 13th inning.

From that moment, it seemed like the Tigers—and their fans—realized this was a new year, and not necessarily a better one.

Toronto, which had chased the Tigers in '84, was playing the best baseball in either league. The Blue Jays threatened to make a shambles of the American League East race when they won the first two games of an early June series with the Tigers to open an 8 1/2-game bulge, but Detroit won the last two games of the series. The Tigers stayed in contention the rest of the month and trailed Toronto by only 2 1/2 games when newcomer Walt Terrell blanked the Jays on a two-hitter on June 29.

But when the Tigers lost three of four games to the Minnesota Twins before the All-Star break and dropped three of four to the lowly Texas Rangers after the recess, it was time to think about next year.

Still, there were some highlights in 1985. Veteran Darrell Evans, who was on the trading block in May when many were writing him off as washed up, had one of the finest seasons in a major league career that began in 1969. Evans led both leagues with 40 homers. At 38, he became the oldest player to win an AL homer crown and the oldest player to hit 40 homers. He also became the first player to hit 40 homers in each league.

Rightfielder Kirk Gibson was one homer short of becoming the first Tiger to hit 30 home runs and steal 30 bases in the same season.

Gibson batted .287 and knocked in 97 runs.

Whitaker was putting together a brilliant season until he tailed off in the final month. The slender second baseman opened a lot of eyes when one of his homers cleared the right field roof. He also deposited several baseballs in the upper deck as he set a club record for homers by a second baseman with 21.

Catcher Lance Parrish hit 28 homers and led the team with 98 rbi, but was troubled much of the season by back spasms. Chet Lemon played his usual brand of centerfield, but didn't start stinging the ball at the plate until August.

Terrell, obtained from the New York Mets in the Howard Johnson deal, posted a 15-10 record, but said he could be more consistent.

Jack Morris and Dan Petry won 16 and 15 games, respectively, and left-hander Frank Tanana pitched well after his June acquisition. Willie Hernandez, although not as invincible as he was in '84, remained one of baseball's top relievers with 31 saves.

There were many individual disappointments.

One of the biggest was Milt Wilcox's failure to come back from off-season shoulder surgery. He won only one game after recording 17 victories the year before.

Aurelio Lopez slipped from 10-1 to 3-7, while many other members of the team's 1984 supporting cast—John Grubb, Dave Bergman, Barbaro Garbey, Marty Castillo and Kuntz—failed to duplicate their championship seasons.

The Tigers also missed Ruppert Jones. The outfielder couldn't reach contract terms with the Tigers and signed with California. His absence was often lamented as Anderson tried to find a platoon partner for left fielder Larry Herndon.

Shortstop Alan Trammell slipped to a .258 batting average and the punch he and Whitaker had provided at the top of the order in '84 was sorely lacking.

The Tigers made some moves during the off-season. The starting pitching was bolstered with the addition of lefthander Dave LaPoint and the team added speed when Garbey was traded to Oakland for outfielder Dave Collins.

Talk of a Tiger dynasty quieted in 1985 and a revamped team would take the field at Michigan and Trumbull in 1986.

BATTING RECORDS

	B	G	AB	R	H	HR	SB	AVE	RBI
Gibson, Kirk	L	154	581	96	167	29	30	.287	97
Whitaker, Lou	L	152	609	102	170	21	6	.279	73
Parrish, Lance	R	140	549	64	150	28	2	.273	98
Lemon, Chet	R	145	517	69	137	18	0	.265	68
Trammell, Alan	R	149	605	79	156	13	14	.258	57
Garbey, Barbaro	R	86	237	27	61	6	3	.257	29
Flynn, Doug	R	32	51	2	13	0	0	.255	2
Sanchez, Alejandro	R	71	133	19	33	6	2	.248	12
Evans, Darrell	L	151	505	81	125	40	0	.248	94
Grubb, Johnny	L	78	155	19	38	5	0	.245	25
Herndon, Larry	R	137	442	45	108	12	2	.244	37
Pittaro, Chris	B	28	62	10	15	0	1	.242	7
Simmons, Nellie	B	75	251	31	60	10	1	.239	33
Brookens, Tommy	R	156	485	54	115	7	14	.237	47
Melvin, Bob	R	41	82	10	18	0	0	.220	4
Baker, Doug	B	15	27	4	5	0	0	.185	1
Bergman, Dave	L	69	140	8	25	3	0	.179	7
Weaver, Jim	L	12	7	2	1	0	0	.143	0
Castillo, Marty	R	57	84	4	10	2	0	.119	5

Less than 10 games: Mike Laga, Scotti Madison and Rusty Kuntz.

PITCHING RECORDS

	T	G	IP	W	L	PCT	ERA
Hernandez, Willie	L	74	107	8	10	.444	2.70
O'Neal, Randy	R	28	94	5	5	.500	3.24
Morris, Jack	R	35	257	16	11	.593	3.33
Petry, Dan	R	34	239	15	13	.536	3.36
Terrell, Walt	R	34	229	15	10	.600	3.85
Tanana, Frank (20 Det., 13 Texas)	L	33	215	12	14	.462	4.27
Scherrer, Bill	L	48	66	3	2	.600	4.36
Lopez, Aurelio	R	51	86	3	7	.300	4.80
Berenguer, Juan	R	31	95	5	6	.455	5.59
Bair, Doug	R	21	49	2	0	1.000	6.24

Less than 45 innings: Mickey Mahler, Chuck Cary, Milt Wilcox and Bob Stoddard.

Frankenmuth Bavarian Inn

offers the finest food and facilities for

MEETINGS • PRIVATE PARTIES
BANQUETS • SEMINARS

Our Restaurant and Lodge combination offers tremendous flexibility for groups of 20 to 400. Our WORLD-FAMOUS FOOD & HOSPITALITY plus UNIQUE SHOPPING OPPORTUNITIES Guarantee increased attendance for YOU!

Restaurant

Seven unique German-Themed Dining Rooms plus Gift Shop, Bake Shop, Wine Shop, Candy Corner and Doll & Toy Factory

713 South Main Street
(Located on the West end of the Covered Bridge)
Frankenmuth, Michigan 48734
(517) 652-9941

Minutes off I-75 between Flint & Saginaw, Michigan

Lodge

Two indoor pools, Family Fun Center, 198 rooms, Lounge with live entertainment, Restaurant and Gift Shop.

One Covered Bridge Lane
(Located on the East end of the Covered Bridge)
Frankenmuth, Michigan 48734
(517) 652-2651

Easy access to both locations via our historic wooden covered bridge

1986

FINAL STANDINGS

EAST DIVISION	W	L	PCT
Boston	95	66	.590
New York	90	72	.556
DETROIT	87	75	.537
Toronto	86	76	.531
Cleveland	84	78	.519
Milwaukee	77	84	.478
Baltimore	73	89	.451
WEST DIVISION			
California	92	70	.568
Texas	87	75	.537
Kansas City	76	86	.469
Oakland	76	86	.469
Chicago	72	90	.444
Minnesota	71	91	.438
Seattle	67	95	.414

Manager: Sparky Anderson

Hank Greenberg would have loved it. Baseballs were flying out of American League ball parks in 1986 in record number, 2,290 times to be exact (a league record that was eclipsed the following season.)

And the Tigers were at the head of the home run parade. Surprisingly, Detroit's major league-leading total of 198 dingers were produced without any one player reaching 30. Darrell Evans, at age 47, led the team for the second consecutive year with 29. Six players, however, did hit 20 or more home runs including: Evans with 29; Kirk Gibson with 28; Lance Parrish with 22; Alan Trammell with 21; and Lou Whitaker and Darnell Coles with 20 apiece. This was the first time an entire infield had all players with 20 or more home runs.

Third baseman Darnell Coles, who was acquired from Seattle during the winter, capped off the feat by hitting his 20th as the season drew to a close. "I was starting to think about it," said Coles. "I didn't want to be the only one who didn't do it." The 24-year-old Coles tied Gibson for the team lead with 86 rbi while playing impressive (if at times erratic) defense at the hot corner.

Whitaker committed only 11 errors at second base, but saw his string of three straight Gold Glove Awards snapped by Kansas City's Frank White. Offensively, Sweet Lou scored 95 runs and drove in 73 from his lead-off position. Trammell posted similar numbers—105 runs scored and 75 rbi—while hitting behind Whitaker.

Gibson started the season with a 4-for-4 5-rbi opening day against the Red Sox at Tiger Stadium. On April 22, Gibson was hitting .359 when he severely twisted his ankle avoiding a pickoff at first base. It was June 3 before Gibson got his next hit. By that time, the Tigers trailed the Red Sox by 10 games.

Although the Tigers turned in the best record in the American League East after the All-Star break (44-31), it wasn't enough to catch the front-running Red Sox.

Starter Jack Morris earned "Tiger of the Year" honors as voted by the Detroit baseball writers after he notched career highs in wins (21), winning percentage (.724) and strikeouts per nine innings (7.5). The Tiger hurler finished fifth in the Cy Young Award voting, behind award-winner Roger Clemens of Boston.

Number two starter Walt Terrell won 15 games for the second consecutive season, featuring a 10-3 record at Tiger Stadium. And Willie Hernandez became the player the fans loved to hate despite recording 24 saves and being selected to the All-Star team. Allowing 13 home runs and being charged with 7 losses (17 over two seasons) made Hernandez a target for Tiger Stadium hecklers. "Why? Why me? I don't think I deserve this stuff," said Hernandez after the season. "What good is being rich and famous if you're unhappy, if you don't feel good about yourself."

BATTING RECORDS

	B	G	AB	R	H	HR	SB	AVE	RBI
Baker, Doug	B	13	21	1	3	0	0	.125	0
Bergman, Dave	L	95	130	14	30	1	0	.231	9
Brookens, Tommy	R	98	281	42	76	3	11	.270	25
Coles, Darnell	R	142	521	67	142	20	6	.273	86
Collins, Dave	B	124	419	44	113	1	27	.270	27
Engle, Dave	R	35	86	6	22	0	0	.256	4
Evans, Darrell	L	151	507	78	122	29	3	.241	85
Fields, Bruce	R	16	43	4	12	0	1	.279	6
Gibson, Kirk	L	119	441	84	118	28	34	.268	86
Grubb, Johnny	L	81	210	32	70	13	51	.333	0
Harper, Brian	R	19	36	2	5	0	0	.139	3
Heath, Mike	R	30	96	11	26	4	11	.265	4
Herndon, Larry	R	106	283	33	70	8	2	.247	37
Laga, Mike	L	15	45	6	9	3	8	.200	0
Lemon, Chet	R	126	403	45	101	12	53	.251	2
Lowry, Dwight	L	56	150	21	46	3	18	.307	0
Parrish, Lance	R	91	327	53	84	22	62	.276	0
Sheridan, Pat	L	98	236	41	56	6	19	.237	9
Spilman, Harry	L	24	49	6	12	3	8	.245	0
Tolman, Tim	R	15	34	4	6	0	2	.176	1
Trammell, Alan	R	151	524	107	159	21	75	.277	25
Whitaker, Lou	L	144	584	95	157	20	73	.269	13

Less than 10 games: Scotti Madison and Matt Nokes.

Statistics

PITCHING RECORDS

	T	G	IP	W	L	PCT	ERA
Campbell, Bill	R	34	56	3	6	.333	3.88
Hernandez, Willie	L	64	89	8	7	.533	3.55
King, Eric	R	33	138	11	4	.733	3.51
Lapoint, Dave	L	16	68	3	6	.333	5.72
Morris, Jack	R	35	267	21	8	.724	3.27
Petry, Dan	R	20	116	5	10	.333	4.66
Tanana, Frank	L	34	217	12	9	.571	4.56
Thurmond, Mark	L	25	52	4	1	.800	1.92

Less than 45 innings: Chuck Cary, Jack Lazorko, Randy O'Neal, John Pacella, Bill Scherer and Bryan Kelly.

Consecutive Pinch Hits

The record for the most consecutive pinch hits during a season is eight. It is a record shared by two former Tigers: National Leaguers Dave Philley playing with the Philadelphia Phillies in 1958 and Rusty Staub with the New York Mets in 1983.

1987

FINAL STANDINGS

EAST DIVISION	W	L	PCT
DETROIT	98	64	.605
Toronto	96	66	.593
Milwaukee	91	71	.562
New York	89	73	.549
Boston	78	84	.481
Baltimore	67	95	.414
Cleveland	61	101	.377
WEST DIVISION			
Minnesota	85	77	.525
Kansas City	83	79	.512
Oakland	81	81	.500
Seattle	78	85	.475
California	75	87	.463
Texas	75	87	.463

Manager: Sparky Anderson

If one picture is worth a thousand words, then the two contrasting photos that ran in the Monday October 5th edition of most Detroit area newspapers spoke volumes. One showed Tigers' pitcher Frank Tanana leaping into the arms of Darrell Evans. The other photo was of George Bell in the visiting dugout at Tiger Stadium. His face was buried in his hands. Guess which team had just clinched the American League East championship.

Tanana had just out-dueled Jimmy Key on a Sunday afternoon for a 1-0 victory. The game gave the Tigers a final two-game margin over Toronto. The only run of the game came when Larry Herndon's fly ball barely eluded Bell and landed in the seats in the lower deck. "This is the greatest feeling I've ever had," said Sparky Anderson after that game. "Nobody understands how hard a road this was, but these guys are true professionals. I'm so proud to take them into Minnesota on Wednesday."

The regular season ended on an incredible high. That was in sharp contrast to the way it all began. The 1987 season had all the prospects of a long and dismal campaign. Going 9-20 in Lakeland is hardly cause for optimism. Especially when you're heading into the season without the team's No. 2 catcher, a guy who'd been an All Star six times. Lance Parrish departed the team through free agency. He wound up in the National League with Philadelphia. That left the position in the hands of journeymen and rookies.

The Tigers stumbled out of the gate. They lost 19 of their first 30 games and by Memorial Day were already 11 games out of first place. Almost miraculously, a transformation was made. The ugly duckling turned into a swan. Alan Trammell became a clean-up hitter capable of a .340 batting average, 28 homers and 105 rbi.

Jack Morris put his contract problems behind him and fashioned his usual 18 victories. Journeyman veteran Mike Heath and rookie Matt Nokes gave the Tigers more offensive production than Lance Parrish ever had at the catching position. First baseman Darrell Evans proved that if life doesn't begin at 40, it certainly continues. He hit 34 homers. Mike Henneman went from a minor leaguer with a mediocre record to a division champ's bullpen stopper.

Sparky Anderson manipulated his talent in such an incredible way that he got the most out of a team that couldn't win against left-handers and with a bullpen that seemed to be put together with baling wire and chewing gum. General Manager Bill LaJoie was busy filling in the missing pieces with key acquisitions like veteran slugger Bill Madlock and right-hander Doyle Alexander.

Few gave the Tigers a chance in the regular season. The Tigers proved them wrong. Many gave the Tigers a thumbs up in their American League Championship Series with the Twins. The Tigers proved them wrong again.

The first two games of the A.L.C.S. were played at the Metrodome in Minneapolis. Alexander got the start for the Tigers. He hadn't lost a game since joining the team and had racked up nine wins. The Twins rattled Alexander and the Tigers, winning 8-5.

Gary Gaetti blasted homers in his first two trips to the plate. Frank Viola got the win and Alexander lost his aura. "When Gary Gaetti hit the first one there was a big sign of relief on the bench," said Minnesota's Tom Brunansky.

Things didn't get any better in the second game. To make matters worse for Detroit, it was former Tiger Juan Berenguer who came on in the second game to preserve a 6-3 victory for the Twins. Big Juan struck out four of the five batters he faced. With every strikeout, he thrust his glove into the air. "I don't go for that arm-waving stuff," said Anderson. "When you have a sleeping dog, you don't embarrass him. When that dog wakes up, he's liable to bite you."

But there wasn't much bite to the Tigers in October 1987. They seemed emotionally spent after their seven games against Toronto in the final two weekends of the regular season. They won four of those games. Toronto ended the season by losing its last seven.

"It's getting real close to Thousand Oaks," said Anderson after his team fell again to the Twins at Tiger Stadium in the fourth game. The Tiger manager didn't know how close. They lost, 9-5, the next night at Tiger Stadium and the Twins had won the series, four games to one. Sparky's gang was done for the season and he was heading home to California.

BATTING RECORDS

	B	G	AB	R	H	HR	SB	AVE	RBI
Bean, Billy	L	26	66	6	17	0	1	.258	4
Bergman, Dave	L	91	172	25	47	6	0	.273	22
Brookens, Tommy	R	143	444	59	107	13	7	.241	59
Coles, Darnell	R	53	140	14	27	4	0	.181	15
Evans, Darrell	L	150	499	90	128	34	6	.257	99
Gibson, Kirk	L	128	487	95	135	24	26	.277	79
Grubb, Johnny	L	59	114	9	23	2	0	.202	13
Harper, Terry	R	31	64	4	13	3	1	.203	10
Heath, Mike	R	93	270	34	76	8	1	.281	33
Herndon, Larry	R	89	324	32	73	9	1	.324	47
Lemon, Chet	R	146	470	75	130	20	0	.277	75
Lowry, Dwight	R	13	25	0	5	0	0	.200	1
Lusader, Scott	L	23	47	8	15	1	1	.319	8
Madlock, Bill	R	87	326	56	91	14	4	.279	50
Mercado, Orlando	R	10	22	2	3	0	0	.136	1
Morrison, Jim	R	34	117	15	24	4	2	.205	19
Nokes, Matt	L	135	461	69	133	32	2	.289	87
Sheridan, Pat	L	141	421	57	109	6	18	.259	49
Trammell, Alan	R	151	597	109	205	28	21	.343	105
Whitaker, Lou	L	149	604	110	160	16	13	.265	59
Walewander, Jim	B	53	54	24	13	1	2	.250	4

Less than 10 games: Tim Tolman and Doug Baker.

PITCHING RECORDS

	T	G	IP	W	L	PCT	ERA
Alexander, Doyle	R	11	88	9	0	1.000	1.53
Henneman, Mike	R	55	97	11	3	.786	2.98
Hernandez, Willie	L	45	49	3	4	.429	3.67
King, Eric	R	55	116	6	9	.400	4.89
Morris, Jack	R	34	266	18	11	.621	3.38
Petry, Dan	R	30	135	9	7	.563	5.61
Robinson, Jeff	R	29	127	9	6	.600	5.37
Tanana, Frank	L	34	219	15	10	.600	3.91
Terrell, Walt	R	35	245	17	10	.630	4.05
Thurmond, Mark	L	48	62	0	1	.000	4.23

Less than 45 innings: Brian Kelly, Morris Madden, Dickie Noles and Nate Snell.

SPORTLAND USA

Headquarters for Sports Souvenirs

**Carrying souvenirs from
all major college football teams in the county
(caps, T-shirts, sweatshirts, etc.)**

- **OPEN YEAR ROUND**
- **MONDAY-SATURDAY 10 a.m. to 5 p.m.**
- **ALSO OPEN BEFORE, DURING AND AFTER TIGER HOME GAMES**
- **SPORTS SOUVENIRS FOR ALL PRO TEAMS**
- **MAIL AND PHONE ORDERS ACCEPTED**
- **MASTERCARD AND VISA ACCEPTED**

Located just a pop fly east of Tiger Stadium is the great store for the sports enthusiast. You'll find shelves to the ceiling, all filled with spots paraphernalia. Whether it's baseball, basketball, football or hockey, you'll find major league or pro favorites at Sportsland USA. You'll find many college teams. Hats, pro caps, T-shirts, uniforms, pennants, jackets, mugs, souvenirs, baseball cards, buttons and many more items are available. You'll find thousands to choose from, so make it a point to visit Sportsland USA.

1444 Michigan at Trumbull in Detroit
PHONE (313) 962-7452

VISIT OUR NEW LOCATIONS:

- FAIRLANE MEADOWS — Ford Rd. at Greenfield
- FRANKENMUTH — Frankemuth Exit Off I-75
- MONROE — LaPlaisance Rd. Exit Off I-75 (In the Mall)

Statistics

1988

FINAL STANDINGS

EAST DIVISION	W	L	PCT
Boston	89	73	.549
DETROIT	88	74	.543
Toronto	87	75	.537
Milwaukee	87	75	.537
New York	85	76	.528
Cleveland	78	84	.481
Baltimore	54	107	.335

WEST DIVISION			
Oakland	104	58	.642
Minnesota	91	71	.562
Kansas City	84	77	.522
California	75	87	.463
Chicago	71	90	.441
Texas	70	91	.435
Seattle	68	93	.422

Manager: Sparky Anderson

There weren't any championships for the Tigers in 1988. There was just a near miss—but Manager Sparky Anderson had no complaints. "There are teams with more talent that should hang their heads when they see what we accomplished," Anderson said after the Tigers finished second, one game behind the Boston Red Sox. "This team came to play every day, no matter what. It never gave you one excuse and there were plenty of excuses because of the injuries we had . . . I've never been prouder of any team, even my championship teams," Anderson said. Still, it was a season of frustration for the Tigers, who wound up with a 88-74 mark.

"I think we can all look back and see where we could have won two more games," said veteran first baseman Darrell Evans, who led the team with 22 homers, including his 400th on September 20 against Cleveland. But Evans batted only .208 and was released after the season.

The Tigers led the American League East longer than any other team. They took over first place on June 20, in the midst of a thrilling three-game sweep of the New York Yankees, and stayed there—except for three days in July—until September 5 when the Red Sox went in front to stay. The slump that killed the Tigers was a 4-19 tailspin that began with a three-game sweep by the Minnesota Twins from August 22-24.

Injuries played a major role in the skid. Right-hander Jeff Robinson had been Detroit's most consistent starter, winning 12 of 14 decisions from the end of April until mid-August. He didn't make a start after August 23 because of a circulatory problem in his pitching hand.

Although Trammell hit .311 and paced the team with 145 hits and 69 rbi, he missed a career high 34 games with various ailments. Whitaker missed

47 games, including the last 27 after injuring his knee dancing at his wife's birthday party.

The Tigers knew before the season started that scoring runs might be difficult. Left fielder Kirk Gibson was declared a free agent in a collusion ruling during the off-season and signed with the Los Angeles Dodgers. The Tigers missed his bat. Luis Salazar and Pat Sheridan did a good job of replacing Gibson for the first half of the season, but they tailed off after the midway point. Sheridan didn't hit a home run after July 4, and finished with 11 homers and a .254 average. Salazar, who batted .305 with 10 homers and 45 rbi before the All-Star break, hit only two homers and drove in 17 runs the rest of the year and slipped to a .270 average.

Anderson was wary even when the Tigers were leading the division. "We've got too many proven .240 hitters who are batting between .280 and .300. If they all start leveling off at the same time, we're going to have trouble scoring," Anderson predicted.

Catcher Matt Nokes, who hit 32 homers and knocked in 87 runs as a rookie in 1987, dropped to 16 homers and 53 rbi. Newcomers Ray Knight and Gary Pettis didn't provide much offense, hitting .217 and .210, respectively; although Pettis won a third Gold Glove and ranked second in the American League with 44 stolen bases.

The lack of hitting made it a struggle for the pitchers too. Jack Morris was 15-13, his career low as a starter. Doyle Alexander, who was 23-4 in September and October from 1983-87, was only 6-7 after the All-Star break and finished 14-11. Frank Tanana was 14-11 and made eight unsuccessful starts in quest of victory number 15. Walt Terrell was supported with only 23 runs in his last 11 starts, finished 7-16 and was traded to San Diego during the off-season.

The bullpen was a bright spot as Mike Henneman recorded 22 saves and a 1.87 e.r.a. Rookie Paul Gibson had a 2.93 e.r.a. as a strong middle reliever and Guillermo Hernandez recorded 10 saves.

The Tigers rebounded from their 4-19 skid to win 9 of their last 12 games, including a sweep of the Yankees on the final weekend of the season, but by then the damage had been done. Second place was all they could salvage.

Tiger Players with 400 or More Stolen Bases

Ty Cobb leads the Tigers in lifetime stolen bases with 892. Ron LeFlore is the second highest with 455. Donie Bush had 405. They are the only three men who played for the Tigers who had 400 or more stolen bases.

BATTING RECORDS

	B	G	AB	R	H	HR	SB	AVE	RBI
Bean, Billy	L	10	11	2	2	0	0	.182	0
Bergman, Dave	L	116	289	37	85	5	0	.294	35
Brookens, Tommy	R	136	441	62	107	5	4	.243	38
Evans, Darrell	L	144	437	48	91	22	1	.208	64
Heath, Mike	R	86	219	24	57	5	1	.208	18
Herndon, Larry	R	76	174	16	39	4	20	.224	20
Knight, Ray	R	105	299	34	65	3	1	.217	33
Lemon, Chet	R	144	512	67	135	17	1	.264	64
Lovullo, Torey	B	12	21	2	8	1	0	.381	2
Lusader, Scott	L	16	16	3	1	1	0	.063	3
Lynn, Fred	L	27	90	9	20	7	0	.222	19
Morrison, Jim	R	24	74	7	16	0	0	.216	6
Murphy, Dwayne	L	49	144	14	36	4	1	.250	19
Nokes, Matt	L	122	382	53	96	16	0	.251	53
Pettis, Gary	B	129	458	65	96	3	36	.210	44
Salazar, Luis	R	130	452	61	122	12	6	.270	62
Sheridan, Pat	L	127	347	47	88	11	8	.254	47
Trammell, Alan	R	128	466	73	145	15	7	.311	62
Walewander, Jim	B	88	175	23	37	0	11	.211	6
Whitaker, Lou	L	115	403	54	111	12	2	.275	55

Less than 10 games: Ivan DeJesus and Chris Bando.

PITCHING RECORDS

	T	G	IP	W	L	PCT	ERA
Alexander, Doyle	R	34	229	14	11	.560	4.32
Gibson, Paul	L	40	92	4	2	.667	2.93
Henneman, Mike	R	65	91	9	6	.600	1.87
Hernandez, Willie	L	63	68	6	5	.545	3.06
King, Eric	R	23	69	4	1	.800	3.41
Morris, Jack	R	34	235	15	13	.536	3.94
Robinson, Jeff	R	24	172	13	6	.684	2.98
Tanana, Frank	L	32	203	14	11	.560	4.21
Terrell, Walt	R	29	206	7	16	.304	3.97

Less than 45 innings: Don Heinkel, Mark Huismann, Ted Power and Mike Trujillo.

IT'S A WHOLE NEW BALLGAME!

*Mystery Prizes,
Pre-Game Contests,
Picnics & Pizza Parties*

Call For Information: 419-893-9483
Ned Skeldon Stadium
AAA Affialiate Of The Detroit Tigers

The first night baseball game in the American League was played on May 16, 1939 in Philadelphia. The Cleveland Indians won the game with five runs in the tenth inning. The losing pitcher for Philadelphia was LeRoy Parmelee, a lifetime resident of the Monroe area in Michigan. Roy had pitched in the National League with the old New York Giants for nearly 10 years. Upon his retirement he came back to Monroe and sold for the Automobile Club of Michigan for many years and later managed the Monroe office. He passed away on August 31, 1981.

1989

FINAL STANDINGS

EAST DIVISION	W	L	PCT
Toronto	89	73	.549
Baltimore	87	75	.537
Boston	83	79	.512
Milwaukee	81	81	.500
New York	74	87	.460
Cleveland	73	89	.451
DETROIT	59	103	.364

WEST DIVISION	W	L	PCT
Oakland	99	63	.611
Kansas City	92	70	.568
California	91	71	.562
Texas	83	79	.512
Minnesota	80	82	.494
Seattle	73	89	.451
Chicago	69	92	.429

Manager: Sparky Anderson

Bottom. Rock bottom. That's where the Tigers landed two seasons after claiming the 1987 American League East crown.

Like many other seasons, this one began with springtime hopes of a pennant race. Eight losses in their first 10 games, however, put the Tigers at the bottom of the standings in early April.

By the All-Star break, the Tigers were 17 games out of first place in the American League East. They were nine games off the pace of their nearest competitor. The pennant race had turned from a preseason dream into a midseason nightmare.

"I won't make any excuses for 1989," said Manager Sparky Anderson. "But in all my years in baseball, I've never seen a team so devastated by key injuries as we had last year." Even the iron man of the pitching staff, Jack Morris, fell to the injury bug. Morris, who had averaged more than 35 starts per season from 1982-88, found his name on the disabled list for the first time in his career and started only 24 games. For the first time since 1978, Morris didn't lead the team in innings pitched and wins.

With number two starter Jeff Robinson limited to 12 games, the Tigers had significant holes to fill. A revolving door was set up on the pitcher's mound which opened for 22 different Tiger pitchers during the season. Of those, 15 different hurlers were handed at least one starting assignment.

The net result was a Tiger team that allowed 816 runs, the highest total in the league. Couple that with an offense that produced only 617 runs (the second lowest figure in the league) and the bottom line is a team with the worst record in the American League.

Injuries limited Alan Trammell's season to 121 games, his shortest season since the strike year of 1981. Trammell, who had 43 rbi, was moved from the fourth position in the batting order to the second spot midway through 1989. "Alan played hurt all season and never really had the chance to get untracked," said Anderson; "Just a normal Alan Trammell season gives us a big boost at the plate and in the field."

The Tiger batting order was riddled with disappointments. Chris Brown wasn't the answer at third base after hitting just .193 in 17 games. Brown was released early in the season. Acquired from Baltimore in September of 1988, 37-year-old Fred Lynn finished with 11 home runs and 46 rbi, his lowest totals since 1981. Ken Williams, acquired from the White Sox before the start of the season, batted just .205 and Matt Nokes failed to duplicate the kind of year he had as a rookie in 1987.

The highlight of the season was the play of Lou Whitaker. Sweet Lou, voted "Tiger of the Year", set career highs in home runs (28), RBI (85), and slugging percentage (.462). No other Tiger hit more than 11 homers or drove in more than 47 runs.

Gary Pettis, who won his second consecutive Gold Glove as a Tiger, emerged as one of the League's top lead-off hitters. His .375 on-base percentage topped the team and only Whitaker could match his total of 77 runs scored.

The lows, however, far outnumbered the highs as the Tigers finished one loss shy of tying the 1952 club record of 104.

BATTING RECORDS

	B	G	AB	R	H	HR	SB	AVE	RBI
Bergman, Dave	L	137	385	38	103	7	1	.268	37
Brown, Chris	R	17	57	3	11	0	0	.193	4
Brumley, Mike	B	92	212	33	42	1	8	.198	11
Heath, Mike	R	122	396	38	104	10	7	.263	43
Jones, Tracy	R	46	158	17	41	3	1	.259	26
Lemon, Chet	R	127	414	45	98	7	1	.237	47
Lovullo, Torey	B	29	87	8	10	1	0	.115	4
Lusader, Scott	L	40	103	15	26	1	3	.252	8
Lynn, Fred	L	117	353	44	85	11	1	.241	46
Nokes, Matt	R	87	268	15	67	9	1	.250	39
Pettis, Gary	B	119	444	77	114	1	43	.257	18
Pedrique, Al	R	31	69	1	14	0	0	.203	5
Richie, Rob	L	19	49	6	13	1	0	.265	10
Schu, Rich	R	99	266	25	57	7	1	.214	21
Sheridan, Pat	L	50	120	16	29	3	4	.242	15
Sinatro, Matt	R	13	25	2	3	0	0	.120	1
Strange, Doug	B	64	196	16	42	1	3	.214	14
Trammell, Alan	R	121	449	54	109	5	10	.243	43
Ward, Gary	R	113	292	27	74	9	1	.253	30
Whitaker, Lou	L	148	509	77	128	28	6	.251	85
Williams, Ken	R	94	258	29	53	6	9	.205	23

Less than 10 games: Billy Bean and Jeff Datz.

PITCHING RECORDS

	T	G	IP	W	L	PCT	ERA
Alexander, Doyle	R	33	223	6	18	.250	4.44
Gibson, Paul	L	45	129	4	8	.333	4.64
Henneman, Mike	R	90	90	11	4	.733	3.70
Hudson, Charles	R	18	67	1	5	.167	6.35
Morris, Jack	R	24	170	6	14	.300	4.86
Nunez, Ed	R	49	54	3	4	.429	4.17
Ritz, Kevin	R	74	74	4	6	.400	4.38
Robinson, Jeff	R	16	78	4	5	.444	4.73
Schwabe, Mike	R	13	58	2	4	.333	6.04
Tanana, Frank	L	33	224	10	14	.417	3.58
Williams, Frank	R	42	72	3	3	.500	3.64

Less than 45 innings: Brian DuBois, Shawn Holman, Brad Havens, Dave Beard, Randy Bockus, Willie Hernandez, Mike Trujillo, Ramon Pena, Steve Searcy, David Palmer and Randy Nosek.

The first broadcast of a Detroit Tigers game was on April 19, 1937 with the Tigers defeating the Cleveland Indians 8-5 at Navin Field. Ty Tyson was the first announcer and continued through 1942. Ty also broadcast the games on TV along with Harry Heilmann and Paul Williams from 1947 through 1952.

1990
FINAL STANDINGS

EAST DIVISION	W	L	PCT
Boston	88	74	.543
Toronto	86	76	.531
DETROIT	79	83	.488
Cleveland	77	85	.475
Baltimore	76	85	.472
Milwaukee	73	88	.453
New York	67	95	.414
WEST DIVISION			
Oakland	103	59	.636
Chicago	94	68	.580
Texas	83	78	.516
California	80	82	.494
Seattle	77	85	.475
Kansas City	75	86	.466
Minnesota	74	88	.457

Manager: Sparky Anderson

For much of 1990, the Detroit Tigers had a chance to finish with a .500 record. They fell short of that goal with a 79-83 slate. That left them nine games behind division leader Boston at season's end. As one of baseball's winningest clubs through the decade of the '80s, that might not seem a successful season, but coming off their dismal 1989 season, it represented 20 wins more than the previous year.

The improvement was due mainly to the acquisition of Cecil Fielder. There were other reasons. Alan Trammell, who had a bad year in 1989 because of injuries, was the Trammell of old. He played shortstop as well as it could be played and for a while he contended for the league lead in batting.

Starting pitching proved a problem for Detroit. Jack Morris, Frank Tanana and Jeff Robinson did not have the seasons that were expected of them. Dan Petry pitched well for a while and then came down with an arm problem. The relief pitching, however, was outstanding. Statistics do not tell the full story of how well the bullpen delivered. Won and lost records are inconclusive and save records can be misleading. But to those who followed the Tigers closely in 1989, the work of Ed Nunez, Paul Gibson, Mike Henneman, Jerry Don Gleaton, Lance McCullers, and Clay Parker was most memorable. They all had lower earned run average records than any of the starting pitchers and the final figures do not do justice to their performances.

Travis Fryman came up from Toledo in the middle of the year and batted .297. He had been a shortstop, but because Sparky Anderson had Trammell at short, he switched Fryman to third base where he is expected to play for the next four or five years. Not only did Fryman hit well, batting with power and hitting nine home runs, but he also showed great ability in the field and a great throwing arm. The versatile Tony Phillips was a pleasant surprise, playing with enthusiasm at third, short, second, and even in the outfield. Toward the end of the season the Tigers came up with Milt Cuyler, and stationed him in centerfield where he showed speed and great range, although his hitting ability remains to be seen.

The real story of the 1990 season, however, was Cecil Fielder. Cecil started his professional career with Butte in the Pioneer League in 1982. He went to Florence in the South Carolina League in 1983 and was traded by his parent club, the Kansas City Royals, to Toronto for former Tiger Leon Roberts. He played briefly with Toronto in 1985, 1986, 1987 and 1988 with limited success. In 1989 he played in Japan and was signed in 1990 by the Tigers as a free agent.

From the beginning of the year until the end Fielder was outstanding. He saved his best for the last, however on the last day of the season he hit his 50th and 51st home runs. Thus, Cecil Fielder became only the 11th man in major league history to hit 50 homers or more in a year. He drove in 132 runs, leading both leagues. And his home run total of 51 also led both leagues by a wide margin. After batting near .300 much of the year, his average suffered during his drive to reach the 50 home run plateau and he finished at .277. He fielded his position very capably and was a tremendous asset to the team in every way.

The 1990 season marked a great improvement over 1989 for the Tigers. With better starting pitching in 1991, they could again become a threat in their division.

Statistics

BATTING RECORDS

	B	G	AB	R	H	HR	SB	AVE	RBI
Bergman, Dave	L	100	205	21	57	2	3	.278	26
Coles, Darnell*	R	89	215	22	45	3	0	.209	20
Cuyler, Milt	B	19	51	8	13	0	1	.255	8
Fielder, Cecil	R	159	573	104	159	51	0	.277	132
Fryman, Travis	R	66	232	32	69	9	3	.297	27
Heath, Mike	R	122	370	46	100	7	7	.270	38
Jones, Tracy	R	50	118	15	27	4	1	.229	9
Lemon, Chet	R	104	322	39	83	5	3	.258	32
Lindeman, Jim	R	12	32	5	7	2	0	.219	8
Lusader, Scott	L	45	87	17	21	2	0	.241	16
Moseby, Lloyd	L	122	431	64	107	14	17	.248	51
Nokes, Matt	L	44	111	12	30	3	0	.270	8
Phillips, Tony	B	152	573	97	144	8	19	.251	54
Romero, Ed	R	32	70	8	16	0	0	.229	4
Salas, Mark	L	73	164	18	38	9	0	.232	24
Sheets, Larry	L	131	160	40	94	10	1	.261	52
Shelby, John	B	78	222	22	55	4	3	.248	20
Trammell, Alan	R	146	559	71	170	14	12	.304	89
Ward, Gary	R	106	309	32	79	9	2	.256	46
Whitaker, Lou	L	132	472	75	112	18	8	.237	60
Williams, Ken	R	57	83	10	11	0	2	.133	5

Less than 10 games: Rich Rowland and Johnny Paredes.

* Detroit record only

PITCHING RECORDS

	T	G	IP	W	L	PCT	ERA
DuBois, Brian	L	12	58	3	5	.375	5.09
Gleaton, Jerry Don	L	57	83	1	3	.250	2.94
Gibson, Paul	L	61	97	5	4	.556	3.05
Henneman, Mike	R	69	94	8	6	.571	3.05
McCullers, Lance*	R	20	45	2	0	1.000	3.02
Morris, Jack	R	36	250	15	18	.455	4.51
Nunez, Ed	R	42	80	3	1	.750	2.24
Parker, Clay*	R	29	73	3	3	.500	3.58
Petry, Dan	R	32	150	10	9	.526	4.45
Robinson, Jeff	R	27	145	10	9	.526	5.96
Searcy, Steve	L	16	75	2	7	.222	4.66
Tanana, Frank	L	34	176	9	8	.529	5.31
Terrell, Walt*	R	13	75	6	4	.600	4.54

Less than 45 innings: Scott Aldred, Randy Nosek, Mike Schwabe, Steve Warnick, Urbano Lugo, Kevin Ritz, and Matt Kinzer.

* Detroit record only

TRIVIA

The questions in this section will test your knowledge of baseball trivia. Except for the three questions below, the answers are right after the questions so you don't need a hunting license to find them.

Q 1. Nine men and only nine men have been named the most valuable player in their leagues for two consecutive years. Who are they? (Hint: All nine positions are covered.)

Q 2. What Tiger pitcher won a game in the World Series but never posted a victory during that regular season?

Q 3. When Bob Gibson struck out 17 Tigers in the 1968 World Series, whose record did he break?

(Answers on page 257)

Trivia

Q What was Phil Regan's nickname?

A *"The Vulture."*

Q Who won the All-Star games played in Detroit?

A *The American League won in 1941 and 1971, while the National League won in 1951.*

Q What is the best single-season attendance in Detroit Tiger history?

A *In 1984, the Tigers drew 2,704,794 at home.*

Q How many times has Alan Trammell been selected to the All-Star team?

A *Six times.*

Q Who holds the Tiger record for most triples in one season?

A *Sam Crawford had 26 in 1914.*

Q What is the record for most triples in one season in the major leagues?

A *Owen Wilson of the Pittsburgh Pirates had 36 triples during the 1912 season. In the American League Joe Jackson, then with Cleveland in 1912, and Sam Crawford had 26 in 1914.*

Q What was Harry Heilmann's lifetime batting average?

A *Harry hit .342 for his 17 years in the major leagues, which was the same average as Babe Ruth.*

Q Who was the last Tiger to lead the American league in triples?

A *Jake Wood led the league in triples in 1961 with 14 triples.*

Q What is the record for most triples lifetime in the major leagues?

A *Sam Crawford, Hall of Fame ballplayer, playing for Detroit and Cincinnati, had 312 triples during his career.*

Q Who was the last Tiger to lead the American League in doubles?

A *Al Kaline in 1961 had forty doubles to lead the American League.*

Q What player has the most stolen bases in a single World Series?

A *Lou Brock stole 7 bases in both the 1967 and 1968 World Series.*

Q What was the nickname of Dick Bartell who played shortstop for Detroit in 1940 and part of 1941?
A *Rowdy Richard.*

Q The Tigers had a double play combination composed of two brothers. Who were they?
A *Milt and Frank Bolling. Frank played with the Tigers from 1954 through 1960. Brother Milt came along in 1958 and played 24 games at shortstop and third base.*

Q When did Aurelio Rodriguez leave the Tigers and where did he go?
A *He was the regular third baseman from 1971 through 1979. He left after 1979, went to San Diego, New York Yankees, Chicago White Sox, then to Baltimore, and then again to the White Sox.*

Q Name the only three ballplayers to hit home runs over the left field stands at Tiger Stadium.
A *Harmon Killebrew in 1962 and Frank Howard in 1968, and Cecil Fielder in 1990.*

Q Who was "Hot Sauce?"
A *Kevin Saucier who pitched for Detroit in 1981 and 1982.*

Q What Tiger announcer was killed in an automobile crash in 1958?
A *Mel Ott.*

Q Who took Lou Gehrig's place the day he retired?
A *Babe Dahlgren.*

Q What former Tiger in the 1954 World Series made a hero out of Willie Mays when Mays made a tremendous catch of his fly ball?
A *Vic Wertz.*

Q Where were George Zuverink, Dave Philley and Frank Carswell born?
A *Zuverink in Holland, Michigan; Philley in Paris, Texas; and Carswell in Palestine, Texas.*

Trivia

Q   What are the two highest team batting averages?

A   *The New York Giants had a team average of .319 in 1930 and the Tigers had a team batting average of .316 in 1921.*

Q   What is the best record the Tigers have ever had?

A   *In 1984 they won 104 games and lost 58 for a .642 percentage. In 1968 they won 103 games and lost 59 games for a .636 percentage. On three other occasions they won 100 games or more.*

Q   When did the Tigers finish in last place?

A   *1952 was the first year that the Tigers finished in the cellar. They also finished last in the East Division in 1975 and 1989.*

Q   What former Tiger had a brother who was an umpire in the American League?

A   *Tom Haller who caught for the Tigers in 1972 was a brother of Bill Haller, long-time American League umpire.*

Q   What Tiger played in the most games for the Tigers?

A   *Al Kaline played in 2,834 games, topping Ty Cobb by 29.*

Q   Who was known as "The Monster"?

A   *Dick Radatz from Berkley, Michigan.*

Q   Who replaced Norm Cash as first baseman for the Tigers?

A   *Cash played first for the Tigers from 1960 until 1974. Bill Freehan played 65 games at first in 1974 and Cash played 44. Dan Meyer was the regular first baseman in 1975.*

Q   What is the record for most consecutive hits by a pinch hitter?

A   *Dave Philley, playing for the Philadelphia Phillies, hit safely eight consecutive times in September 1958. Rusty Staub, playing for the Mets, equaled the record in 1983. Staub and Philley each later played for the Tigers.*

Q   What was the first year that Ernie Harwell broadcast Tiger games?

A   *1960, after he came here from Baltimore.*

Q What Tiger uniform numbers have been retired?

A *Al Kaline - 6, Charlie Gehringer - 3, and Hank Greenberg - 5.*

Q Who was the youngest player to ever appear in a major league game?

A *Joe Nuxhall, pitching for Cincinnati, was 15 years, 10 months, and 11 days old when he pitched on June 10, 1944. Carl Scheib was 16 years, 8 months, and 5 days old when he pitched for the Philadelphia Athletics on September 6, 1943.*

Q When Babe Ruth hit his 60th home run against the Washington Senators in 1927, what future Hall of Fame pitcher made his last appearance pitch-hitting?

A *Walter Johnson.*

Q Ty Cobb is generally considered the greatest Tiger of them all. Why haven't the Tigers retired his number?

A *Cobb played with the Tigers from 1905 through 1926. There were no numbers on the uniforms in those days.*

Q What is the most home runs ever hit in one month by a major leaguer?

A *Rudy York hit 18 homers in the month of August in 1937.*

Q Who led the American League in batting in 1987 and who was the leading Tiger?

A *Wade Boggs led the league with a .363 mark, Paul Molitor was second with .353. Alan Trammell led the Tigers and was third in the league with .343.*

Q How many times has Alan Trammell led Tiger regulars in batting average?

A *Five times: in 1980, 1984, 1986, 1987, and 1990.*

Q What is the highest batting average that Alan Trammell has had since joining the Tigers?

A *Trammell hit .343 in 1987.*

Q Did Mickey Cochrane win the MVP when playing for the Tigers?

A *Yes, in 1934.*

Trivia

Q   Whom did Sparky Anderson replace as manager of the Tigers?

A   *Les Moss.*

Q   Who was the leading hitter for the Tigers in the 1984 playoffs?

A   *Kirk Gibson, at .417.*

Q   Who was the first Tiger to lead the A.L. in runs batted in?

A   *Ty Cobb in 1907 drove in 116 runs—and led the league four of the next five years.*

Q   Who was named the most valuable player in the playoffs in 1984?

A   *Kirk Gibson.*

Q   How many times have the Detroit Tigers been in the divisional playoffs?

A   *In 1972 they lost to Oakland; in 1984 they defeated Kansas City; and in 1987 they lost to the Minnesota Twins.*

Q   How many times was Al Kaline on an All-Star team?

A   *Eighteen times. Bill Freehan was on an All-Star team 11 times and Harvey Kuenn 8 times.*

Q   Was Denny McLain ever named MVP in the American League?

A   *Yes, in 1968.*

Q   What former Tiger pitcher gave up Hank Aaron's 714th home run?

A   *Jack Billingham, while with the Cincinnati Reds on April 4, 1974.*

Q   Who was the last Tiger pitcher to lead the American League in shutouts?

A   *Mickey Lolich tied four others with six shutouts in 1967.*

Q   When did Jack Morris last pitch in relief?

A   *September 23, 1978, at Baltimore.*

Q   Was Frank Tanana ever chosen as Rookie of the Year?

A   *Yes, by The Sporting News in 1974.*

Q   Off what Detroit pitcher did Babe Ruth get his 700th home run?

A   *Tommy Bridges.*

Q   What Tiger pitcher was nicknamed "Hot Sauce"?
A   *Kevin Saucier.*

Q   What pitcher with the Tigers in 1930 and 1931 later became the broadcaster for the Cincinnati Reds and is in the Hall of Fame?
A   *Waite Hoyt.*

Q   What Tiger pitcher had the most losses during his career?
A   *George "Hookie" Dauss was the loser 182 times.*

Q   Was Guillermo "Willie" Hernandez ever picked as a Rookie of the Year?
A   *Yes, as the Chicago Cubs best rookie in 1977.*

Q   Who holds the record for most shutouts lifetime by a Tiger hurler?
A   *Mickey Lolich shut out the opposition 39 times during his Tiger career.*

Q   Who holds the Tiger record for most shutouts in a season?
A   *Denny McLain shut out the opposition on nine occasions in 1969.*

Q   Was John Hiller ever named Fireman of the Year?
A   *Hiller was named Fireman of the Year in 1973 by The Sporting News.*

Q   How long did Mark Fidrych pitch for the Tigers?
A   *Mark was with the Tigers 5 years and won 29 and lost 19.*

Q   How close did Walt Terrell come to pitching a no-hitter?
A   *Terrell went to two outs in the ninth inning before allowing a hit in a game against California on August 20, 1986. Wally Joyner broke it up with a double to right field.*

Q   Which former Tiger pitcher had the most complete games in a career?
A   *George Mullin pitched 353 complete games.*

Q   In the championship series of 1984 with Kansas City, who were the winning pitchers for the Tigers?
A   *Milt Wilcox, Aurelio Lopez and Jack Morris as the Tigers won three straight.*

Trivia —————————————————————————————— **243**

Q Who were the last 30-game winners before Denny McLain?

A *Lefty Grove in the American League in 1931 and Dizzy Dean in the National League in 1934. Grove pitched for the Philadelphia Athletics and Dean for the St. Louis Cardinals.*

Q Who was the "designated" catcher for Mark Fydrich in his great season of 1976?

A *Bruce Kimm.*

Q What former Tiger ruined Bob Lemon's bid for a perfect game in 1951?

A *Vic Wertz hit a home run in the eighth inning and was the only man to reach first base that day.*

Q What former Tiger pitcher and manager had his numbers retired by a National League team?

A *Freddy Hutchinson managed Detroit in 1952, 1953 and 1954. He later went to the National League and managed the Cardinals and Reds had his number retired by the Reds. Hutch passed away from cancer in Seattle, Washington, in 1964.*

Q What is the major league longevity record for pitching for one club?

A *Walter Johnson pitched for the Washington Senators for 21 years. Ted Lyons pitched 21 years for Chicago White Sox from 1923 through 1946 except for three war years.*

Q Which pitcher lost the most World Series games in his career?

A *Whitey Ford lost eight games.*

Q What former Tiger pitcher came from Ney, Ohio?

A *Ned Garver, who won 20 games for the St. Louis Browns when they finished in the basement in 1951.*

Q What player hit the most home runs in World Series history?

A *Mickey Mantle, with 18 home runs in his 12 World Series.*

Q What former Tiger once hit two grand-slam home runs in one game?

A *Jim Northrup hit two grand-slammers on his son's birthday, June 24, 1968.*

Q In 1965 the Detroit Baseball Writers Association began an annual selection of the Tiger of the Year. How many Tigers have won that award more than once?

A *Denny McLain won it three times, Ron LeFlore won it twice, and Alan Trammell won it twice.*

Q How many games did Guillermo Hernandez appear in during the A.L.C.S. playoffs in 1984.

A *He pitched in all three games.*

Q Frank Lary was known as the Yankee Killer when he pitched for the Tigers from 1954 through 1964. What was his record against the Yankees?

A *He won 28 games and lost 13 to the Yankees; Taters won 7 straight games from New York in 1958 and 1959.*

Q What Tiger pitcher has won the most games lifetime for Detroit?

A *George "Hookie" Dauss won 222 games during his career.*

Q What pitcher appeared in the most games for the Tigers?

A *John Hiller pitched in 545 games as a Tiger.*

Q Who pitched the first night game no-hitter in the American League?

A *Bob Lemon of the Cleveland Indians held the Tigers hitless on June 30, 1948 at Briggs Stadium.*

Q Who is the only pitcher to pitch against Babe Ruth and Mickey Mantle?

A *Al Benton.*

Q What pitchers of the Tigers have had the most 20-win seasons?

A *George Mullin won 20 games five times.*

Q Who were the Tiger coaches in 1968?

A *Johnny Sain, Tony Cuccinello, Hal Naragon and Wally Moses.*

Q What Tiger pitchers were named American League Rookie Pitcher of the Year?

A *Mark Fidrych in 1976, Dave Rozema in 1977 and Mike Henneman in 1987.*

Trivia

Q Who was the Tiger's first Most Valuable Player in the American League?

A *The Baseball Writers Association of America named Ty Cobb the MVP in 1911.*

Q Was Harvey Kuenn ever named Rookie of the Year?

A *Yes, in 1953.*

Q What major league team has had the most individual batting championships?

A *Ty Cobb led 12 times; Harry Heilmann four times; and Heinie Manush, Charlie Gehringer, Harvey Kuenn, Norm Cash, George Kell and Al Kaline once each for a grand total of 22 times.*

Q Before Cecil Fielder in 1990, who was the last Tiger batter to lead the American League in strikeouts?

A *Jake Wood fanned 141 times in 1961.*

Q Did Maury Wills ever play for the Tigers?

A *No, he tried out for the team but never made it.*

Q Who replaced Billy Martin as manager of the Tigers in 1973?

A *Joe Schultz finished the 1973 season as the skipper of the Tigers after Martin was fired. (They went 14-14 while he was at the helm.)*

Q How many home runs did Hank Greenberg hit with Detroit?

A *306; he hit 25 more for Pittsburgh to close out his career in 1947.*

Q Who was the last major leaguer to hit four homers in one game?

A *Rocky Colavito.*

Q What is the most home runs hit by a pinch hitter?

A *Cliff Johnson had 19 pinch hit home runs, Jerry Lynch had 18, and Gates Brown had 16.*

Q What did Mike Heath do the first game he played with the Tigers?

A *He hit a home run off Steve Carlton.*

Q   What is the most home runs that Darrell Evans ever hit in the big leagues?

A   He hit 41 with Atlanta in 1973.

Q   Who was the last Tiger to lead the American League in home runs?

A   Darrell Evans led the American League in 1985 with 40 at the age of 38.

Q   Who hit the most home runs in a season for the Tigers?

A   Hank Greenberg hit 58 homers in the 1938 season.

Q   What was Mark Fidrych's record during his first season with the Tigers?

A   He was 19-9.

Q   Who was the first black pitcher to pitch a no-hitter in the major leagues?

A   Sam Jones of the Chicago Cubs in 1955. Sam, whose nickname was "Toothpick", later pitched for the Tigers in 1962.

Q   What former Tiger shares the record for consecutive hits in a World Series?

A   Goose Goslin had six consecutive hits in the 1924 World Series, a feat tied by Thurman Munson of the Yankees in 1976. Goslin was playing for Washington.

Q   Who played third base for the Tigers in the 1984 World Series?

A   Marty Castillo played most of the time with Tommy Brookens and Darrell Evans also playing at third.

Q   When was the first World Series played?

A   1903 between Boston Red Sox and Pittsburgh Pirates with the Red Sox winning in eight games 5 to 3.

Q   Who had the best batting average in the 1984 World Series?

A   Alan Trammell hit .450.

Q   Who hit the most home runs in the 1984 World Series?

A   Kirk Gibson and Alan Trammell each hit two for Detroit. Kurt Bevacqua hit two for San Diego.

Trivia

Q What former Tiger was the starting pitcher in the first game played at night in a World Series?

A Pat Dobson pitched in the fourth game of the 1971 Series against the Pittsburgh Pirates. Pat was pitching for the Orioles.

Q What player appeared in the most games in World Series?

A Yogi Berra was in 75 games in 14 Series.

Q How many games did Jack Morris win in the 1984 World Series?

A Two games, with a 2.00 ERA.

Q Who won the other two games for the Tigers?

A Aurelio Lopez and Milt Wilcox.

Q Name the Detroit outfield for the World Series of 1984.

A Kirk Gibson in right, Larry Herndon in left, and Chet Lemon in center.

Q Claude Passeau of the Chicago Cubs pitched a one-hitter against the Tigers in the 1945 World Series. Who got the hit?

A Rudy York singled in the third inning for the lone hit; Bob Swift got the only walk off Passeau.

Q Who hit Tiger home runs in the 1984 playoffs?

A Kirk Gibson, Alan Trammell, Lance Parrish and Larry Herndon.

Q How many home runs did the Kansas City Royals get off Tiger pitching in the 1984 playoffs?

A None.

Q What is the highest batting average for one World Series?

A Babe Ruth, in a four-game Series in 1928, hit .625.

Q In the 1987 playoffs Minnesota defeated the Tigers four games to one. Who was the winning pitcher for the Tigers in their lone victory?

A The third game was won by the Tigers at Tiger Stadium and the winning pitcher was Mike Henneman in relief of Walt Terrell.

Q   The first night game in a World Series was played in Pittsburgh in 1971. Who drove in the winning run?

A   *It was between the Pirates and the Baltimore Orioles. Milt May, then with Pittsburgh and later to play with the Tigers, drove in the winning run.*

Q   Has a Tiger ever hit a home run with the bases loaded in a World Series?

A   *Yes, Jim Northrup did it in the sixth game of the 1968 Series.*

Q   What year did the St. Louis Browns move to Baltimore?

A   *1954.*

Q   Name the charter members of the American League.

A   *The American League came into existence in 1901 and the charter clubs were Chicago, Boston, Detroit, Philadelphia, Baltimore, Washington, Cleveland and Milwaukee.*

Q   What was the year of the second expansion in the National League?

A   *The Montreal Expos and the San Diego Padres were added to the National League in 1969.*

Q   What was the year of the third expansion in the American League?

A   *The American League had a third expansion in 1977 when Toronto and Seattle were given franchises.*

Q   What year did the New York Giants and the Brooklyn Dodgers move to California?

A   *In 1958 the Giants moved to San Francisco and the Dodgers to Los Angeles.*

Q   What were the migrations of the Athletics franchise?

A   *The Athletics were transferred to Kansas City from Philadelphia in 1955. They moved again to Oakland after the 1967 season. Kansas City had no team in 1968 but got an expansion team in 1969.*

Q   When did the Boston Braves leave Boston for Milwaukee?

A   *1953.*

Q   What year did the Atlanta Braves come into the majors?

A   *The franchise was moved from Milwaukee after 1965.*

Trivia

Q How many seasons did Hank Greenberg miss because of World War II?

A *Greenberg missed most of 1941, all of 1942, 1943 and 1944, and half of 1945.*

Q Who is the only man to hit home runs in his first two times at bat in a World Series?

A *Gene Tenace of the Oakland A's in 1972.*

Q Where did Willie Horton go to high school?

A *Northwestern High School in Detroit.*

Q Who was known as "The Walking Man"?

A *Eddie Yost, who played third base for the Tigers in 1959 and 1960. He led the league in bases on balls both years.*

Q Where and when did Willie Horton conclude his career?

A *In Seattle in 1980.*

Q Who was the Tiger's regular second baseman immediately after Charlie Gehringer?

A *Jimmy Bloodworth in 1942.*

Q Who replaced Hank Greenberg at first base after Hank broke his wrist in the 1935 World Series?

A *Marv Owen shifted from third to first and Flea Clifton played third.*

Q What Tiger had the longest hitting streak?

A *Ty Cobb hit in 40 consecutive games in 1911. Cobb also hit in 35 games in 1917. John "Rocky" Stone hit in 34 consecutive games in 1930, as did Goose Goslin in 1934 and Ron LeFlore in 1976.*

Q How many times did Norm Cash hit over .300 in his 17-year career?

A *Only once, in 1969, the year he led the league at .361.*

Q Where did former Tiger Joe Ginsberg and Milt Pappas, former Baltimore, Cincinnati, Atlanta and Cubs pitcher go to high school?

A *Detroit's Cooley High.*

Q Who was the first Tiger to hit the ball out of Tiger Stadium?
A *Norm Cash.*

Q How many current or former Tigers are in baseball's Hall of Fame?
A *Twenty-two, including Ernie Harwell, the Tiger's great broadcaster.*

Q Who were the Tiger G-men?
A *The first edition was Goose Goslin, Charlie Gehringer, and Hank Greenberg in the mid-Thirties.*

Q Who was Manager of the Year in the American League in 1987?
A *Sparky Anderson of the Detroit Tigers.*

Q How long have Lou Whitaker and Alan Trammell been the double play combination for the Tigers?
A *They came up together at the end of the 1977 season and have the honor of playing together longer than any Keystone combination in history.*

Q Who was the last Tiger to lead the American League in stolen bases?
A *Ron LeFlore led the league in 1978 with 68 stolen bases.*

Q Who were the pennant-winning managers of the Tigers?
A *The Tigers won the American League pennant in 1907, 1908 and 1909 under Hughie Jennings. They won again in 1934 and 1935 with Mickey Cochrane at the helm. In 1940 Del Baker was the manager, Steve O'Neill in 1945, and Mayo Smith in 1968. Sparky Anderson was the manager in 1984 when they again won the pennant.*

Q Who was the last Tiger to lead the American League in runs batted in?
A *In 1955 Ray Boone and Jackie Jensen of the Boston Red Sox tied for the leadership with 116. Ray is the father of Bob Boone, long-time catcher with the California Angels.*

Q Has Chet Lemon ever played in an All-Star game?
A *Yes. In 1984 he was starting center fielder.*

Trivia

Q What was Sparky Anderson's lifetime batting average?

A Sparky played with the Philadelphia Phillies and hit .218 in 1959. That was his only season in the big leagues.

Q Name the San Diego outfield in the World Series of 1984.

A Tony Gwynn in right, Carmelo Martinez in center, Bobby Brown in left.

Q The Tigers won the pennant in 1945 on the last day of the season. Who finished second?

A The Washington Senators were a game behind the Tigers when the season ended.

Q Who was the first free-agent the Tigers signed?

A Tito Fuentes.

Q Which cities replaced Baltimore and Milwaukee in the American League and in what year?

A St. Louis replaced Milwaukee in 1902 and New York replaced Baltimore in 1903. The same eight clubs had been in place from 1903 to 1954.

Q Who was the winning pitcher in the Tigers' first night game played in Detroit?

A Hal Newhouser, June 15, 1948 defeating Philadelphia 4 to 1. Dick Wakefield hit the only home run of the game.

Q Who was the losing pitcher in the Tigers' first night game?

A Joe Coleman, who took the loss, later pitched for the Tigers, as did his son who was also named Joe.

Q Who was the Earl of Snohomish?

A Earl Averill, who spent most of his career with Cleveland, but played with the Tigers in 1940.

Q How many times has a Tiger player hit 40 or more home runs?

A Seven times. Hank Greenberg hit 40 in 1937, 58 in 1936, 41 in 1940, 44 in 1946. Norm Cash had 41 in 1961, Darrell Evans had 40 in 1985 and Cecil Fielder hit 51 in 1990.

Q   What is the rbi record by a Tiger player?

A   Hank Greenberg drove in 183 runs in 1937, one behind the league record of 184 by Lou Gehrig.

Q   What was the first year Tiger games were broadcast and who was the announcer?

A   Ty Tyson in 1927.

Q   What was the year Detroit was called the City of Champions?

A   1935. The Tigers won the World Series, the Lions won the championship, the Red Wings were the champions and they had a minor league hockey team called the Olympics, who won their championship. Joe Louis was soon to be the next heavyweight champion of the world.

Q   What Tiger pitcher won the most games in 1988?

A   Jack Morris won 15. Frank Tanana and Doyle Alexander each won 14 while Jeff Robinson won 13.

Q   What pitcher had the most victories for the Tigers in 1987?

A   Jack Morris had 18. Walt Terrell had 17 victories and Frank Tanana had 15.

Q   Who led the Tigers in batting and rbi in 1988?

A   Alan Trammell hit .311 and knocked in 105 runs.

Q   Who had the most home runs for the Tigers in 1987?

A   Darrell Evans had 34.

Q   Who hit the most home runs for the Tigers in 1988?

A   Darrell Evans had 22.

Q   Who is the only pitcher to start a World Series game who had never won a game during the regular season?

A   Virgil Trucks started, and finished, and won the second game for the Tigers in the 1945 World Series. Virgil had not won a game during the regular season because he had been in military service.

Q   How many hits did Ty Cobb get in his lifetime?

A   4,191.

Trivia

Q Who was the regular right fielder for the Tigers after Al Kaline retired?
A Leon Roberts took Al's place in 1975.

Q What number did Al Kaline wear when he first came up to the majors in 1953?
A 25. Pat Mullin had number 6 and Al took that over when Pat retired.

Q How many hits did Al Kaline get in his lifetime?
A 3,007.

Q How many times did Ty Cobb lead the American League in batting?
A Twelve, nine of them in a row.

Q What was unusual about Harry Heilmann's leading the American League in batting four times?
A It was always in an odd year. He led the league in 1921, 1923, 1925 and 1927.

Q When did Harry Heilmann start broadcasting for the Detroit Tigers?
A 1934 and he continued until his death in 1951.

Q What was the original name of the ball park at Michigan and Trumbull?
A Bennett Field until 1912.

Q What was the Detroit major league ball park named after 1912?
A From 1912 to 1938 it was known as Navin Field and from 1938 to 1961 it was Briggs Stadium.

Q How long has Paul Carey been broadcasting Tiger baseball?
A Since 1973.

Q Who managed the Lakeland Tigers in 1990?
A Johnny Lipon, the former Tiger shortstop.

Q Who was the last Tiger pitcher to lead the American League with winning percentage?
A In 1968, Denny McLain won 31 and lost 6 and had a .838 percentage.

Q Who was the American League Rookie Pitcher of the Year in 1987?

A *Mike Henneman of the Detroit Tigers.*

Q Did a Tiger relief pitcher ever win the Cy Young Award?

A *Yes, Willie Hernandez in 1984.*

Q What pitcher for the Tigers won 21 games and lost but 5 in the championship year of 1940?

A *Bobo "Buck" Newsom.*

Q What was the first year of the championship playoffs?

A *1969. The Tigers were the last pennant-winner before divisional playoffs began.*

Q Who pitched the pennant-winning game for the Tigers in 1940?

A *Floyd Giebell.*

Q When did Tom Monaghan buy the Detroit Tigers?

A *In the fall of 1983 from John E. Fetzer.*

Q What was the last shortstop-second baseman combination for the Tigers before Lou Whitaker and Alan Trammell?

A *Tito Fuentes was the second baseman and Tom Veryzer was the shortstop in 1977.*

Q What was the last year that players stopped leaving their gloves on the field?

A *1954.*

Q How many saves did Guillermo "Willie" Hernandez have in 1984?

A *32.*

Q When Bob Feller set a new single-game record for strikeouts in 1936, who was his pitching rival?

A *Harry Eisenstat pitched for the Tigers and defeated Feller even though Feller struck out 18 men.*

Trivia

Q Who are the only Tigers to be named the MVP more than once by the BBWAA?

A *Hank Greenberg in 1935 and 1940 and Hal Newhouser in 1944 and 1945.*

Q In 1984 the Tigers were in first place for the entire season. What other teams have gone all year in first place?

A *The 1923 New York Giants; the 1927 New York Yankees; and the 1955 Brooklyn Dodgers.*

Q Where did the Tigers play their home games before the Blue Laws were changed?

A *In Springwell Township, on Dix Avenue at the intersection of Waterman which is now Detroit.*

Q Three of the Tigers broadcasters have been inducted into the Hall of Fame. Who are they?

A *George Kell, Ernie Harwell and Al Kaline.*

Q How many times have the Tigers lost the World Series?

A *They were defeated in 1907, 1908, 1909, 1934 and 1940.*

Q How many home runs did the Kansas City Royals get off Tiger pitching in the 1984 playoffs?

A *None.*

Q When was the first World Series played?

A *1903 between Boston Red Sox and Pittsburgh Pirates with the Red Sox winning in eight games 5 to 3.*

Q Who is the only Tiger beside Ty Cobb to ever hit over .400 in a season?

A *Harry Heilmann hit .403 in 1923.*

Q How many World Championships have the Tigers won?

A *Four, in 1935, 1945, 1968 and 1984.*

Q What former Tiger in the 1954 World Series made a hero out of Willie Mays when Mays made a tremendous catch of his fly ball?

A *Vic Wertz.*

Q What pitcher with the Tigers in 1930 and 1931 later became the broadcaster for the Cincinnati Reds and is in the Hall of Fame?

A *Waite Hoyt.*

Q What year did the playoffs start?

A *1969.*

Q Name the Detroit outfield for the World Series of 1984.

A *Kirk Gibson in right, Larry Herndon in left and Chet Lemon in center.*

Q In the 1987 playoff's Minnesota defeated the Tigers four games to one. Who was the winning pitcher for the Tigers in their lone victory?

A *The third game was won by the Tigers at Tiger Stadium and the winning pitcher was Mike Henneman in relief of Walt Terrell.*

Live the Major League Dream

Feb. 3-10, 1991
Lakeland, Florida

TIGER FANTASY CAMP VIII

Kaline · Horton · Colavito · Lolich · Harwell · Hiller · Grubb · Tresh · Tracewski · Kemp · Stanley · Wockenfuss · McAuliffe · Thompson · Price · Northrup · Wilcox · Rozema

CALL TODAY
313-353-5640

Brought to you by
Sports Fantasies Inc.
19111 W. 10 Mile Rd., Ste. A21
Southfield, Michigan 48075

TRIVIA ANSWERS (from pg. 235)

A 1. First base - Jimmie Foxx, 1932 and 1933.
Second base - Joe Morgan, 1975 and 1976.
Third base - Mike Schmidt, 1980 and 1981.
Shortstop - Ernie Banks, 1958 and 1959.
Outfield - Dale Murphy, 1982 and 1983.
Outfield - Mickey Mantle, 1956 and 1957.
Outfield - Roger Maris, 1960 and 1961.
Catcher - Yogi Berra, 1954 and 1955.
Pitcher - Hal Newhouser, 1944 and 1945.

A 2. During the 1945 regular season, Virgil Trucks had no wins and no losses. But, in game two of the 1945 World Series, Trucks pitched the full 9 innings and was credited with a 4-1 win over the Chicago Cubs.

A 3. Sandy Koufax struck out 15 in 1963, Carl Erskine struck out 14 in 1953, and Howard Ehmke struck out 13 in 1929. When Gibson struck out Norm Cash for his 17th victim, he broke his own record of 16 which he had just set by striking out Willie Horton.

ALUMNI NEWS

One of the most frequently asked questions by Tiger fans is "What ever happened to . . .?" Here are reports on many Tiger fan favorites, some of the lesser-known as well as the famous.

Alumni

Hank Aguirre (1958-1967) is a resident of the Detroit area where he has his own business, the Mexican Industries. He has been a very successful businessman and gives much of his time and money to charity. He is also an outstanding after-dinner speaker.

Eldon Auker (1933-1988) retired in 1975. He has a home on the Indian River in Vero Beach, Florida. He spends most of his time playing golf at the country club of which he is the president. He was voted into the Kansas Hall of Fame in 1969.

Dick Bartell (1940) writes that there is a new book out about him called "Rowdy Richard." Dick is in good health, living in California. Dick can be contacted at 1118 Island Drive, Almeda, CA 94501 if you are interested in information about his book, which may also be available at your local library.

Matt Batts (1952-1954) is in the printing business in Baton Rouge. He has his own plant. Matt's nephew Danny Heep, has been with the Astros, Mets, Dodgers and Red Sox.

John Baumgartner (1953) is vice president of Tractor Trailer Equipment Company in Birmingham, Alabama.

Wayne Belardi (1945-1956) is retired. The Belardi's have three daughters and a son and live in San Jose, California. Wayne would appreciate hearing from some of his fans. His address is 1467 Phantom Avenue, San Jose 95125. Neil Berry (1948-1952) is retired and lives in Kalamazoo, Michigan.

Reno Bertoia (1953-1958 and 1962) teaches modern history at Holy Name School in Windsor, Ontario.

Ike Blessitt (1972) still makes his home in the Detroit area. Ike has one child (4-1/2 years old) and is playing golf and hoping to win the lottery.

Ray Boone (1954-1958) is a scout for the Red Sox and has been for 31 years. He likes in El Cajon, California. He has three sons, including Bob, the record-setting catcher. Bob has a son, Brett, who has signed with Seattle and we may see another Griffey father-son team.

Red Borom (1944-1945) lives in Dallas, Texas, and has an ex-pro baseball players association, a nonprofit group of 240 members.

Steve Boros (1957-1962) is scouting for the Los Angeles Dodgers.

Jim Brady (1956) has three sons who are all pitchers. Mike pitched for Florida State University in the College World Series. Matt pitched for Jacksonville University. Jimmy pitched for his high school and the team won the state championship. Jim's wife, Sheila, is the Director of Continuing Education at Jacksonville University where on September 1, 1989, Jim Brady became the President.

Eddie Brinkman (1971-1974) is scouting for the White Sox.

Gates Brown (1963-1975) has been a sales representative for 18 years for the Summa-Harrison Company in Royal Oak, Michigan. He has two children; Pam is 26 and William Jr. is 25. Gates also has two grandchildren. He lives in Detroit.

Bill Bruton (1961-1964) is now living in Wilmington, Delaware. Billy has retired from Chrysler. Billy hit the first home run in Milwaukee when the Braves moved there from Boston in 1953.

Bob Cain (1951) lives in Euclid, Ohio, a suburb of Cleveland. Bob was the pitcher when Bill Veeck sent up the midget, Eddie Gaedel, in 1951 in St. Louis. He is retired and he and Judy have one daughter and one grandson.

Bill Campbell (1986). Bill, who grew up in Highland Park, Michigan, now lives in Palatine, Illinois. He's in the marketing business. He pitched in the Senior League last winter for Winter Haven and was named the senior pitcher of the week for the week ending January 21. He appeared in four games, pitched nine innings, and did not allow a run while winning two. He was the first Winter Haven Super Sox player to be named either pitcher of the week or player of the week.

Paul Campbell (1948-1950) became a business manager after he retired as a player. He became president and general manager of the Louisville Colonels in the American Association and then scouted for the Cincinnati Reds. Old-timers may remember that Paul was a player-coach for Detroit's Class AAA Toledo club in 1950 and 1951.

Slick Coffman (1937-1939) is living in Birmingham, Alabama.

Rocky Colavito (1960-1964) is retired and living in Pennsylvania. He makes a lot of card shows and personal appearances. He was an instructor in the Fantasy Camp in Lakeland, Florida two years ago.

Joe Coleman, Sr. (1955) and Joe Coleman, Jr. (1971-1976) are living in Ft. Myers, Florida. Joe Jr. is a coach for the California Angels.

Kevin Collins (1970-1971) works with Gates Brown and Jim Price at the Summa-Harrison Company. Kevin is the operations manager there. He has two children; Kelly is 20 and Michael is 16. Kelly is going to Hillsdale College, majoring in Law, and Mike is a sophomore at Clawson High. Kevin has been with Summa-Harrison for 15 years.

Roy Cullenbine (1938-1939, 1945-1947) and his wife, Maxine, live in Mt. Clemens, Michigan. Roy is retired and plays a lot of golf.

Chuck Daniel (1957) is in the trucking business in Memphis, Tennessee.

Don Demeter (1964-1966) lives in Oklahoma City and operates a swimming pool business. He does the baseball chapel service for the local AAA baseball team.

Steve Demeter (1959) is a scouting supervisor for the Pittsburgh Pirates in Ohio, Kentucky and Michigan. Steve has managed, been a hitting instructor, minor league coordinator, and major league coach during the last 18 years with the Pirates. In 1987 he became a scouting supervisor.

Bill Denehy (1971) is now working for the Florida Radio Network in Orlando, Florida. He was a regular member of the FRN Senior Professional Baseball Broadcast team and is now co-hosting a statewide Monday through Friday sport talk show. He is also director of Sales Sports division at the Florida Radio Network in Orlando.

Gene Desautels (1930-1933) and wife Millie have made their home in Flint, Michigan, for many years. They have one boy who is a doctor in California and two daughters who are also living in California. Gene likes to work around the yard and garden and play quite a bit of golf.

Bernie DeViveiros (1927) is now 89 years old. He spent 20 years in the major leagues as a base-running coach. He likes to reminisce about the days when he played with Charlie Gehringer, Harry Heilmann and Heinie Manush. He recalls Babe Ruth hitting some of those 60 home runs, and he remembers batting against Walter Johnson. Bernie has been married for 60 years. He spent 26 years as an instructor with the Tigers and says he's still sliding. Bernie lives in Oakland, California.

Steve Dillard (1978) is an infield instructor for the Houston Astros. He has three sons, 11, 9 and 7 years old. Last winter Steve played in the Senior Professional Baseball League for Bradenton Explorers.

Jim Donohue (1961) is the father of four children and works for Hillerich & Bradsby.

Walt Dropo (1952-1954) lives in the Boston, Massachusetts area. He and his family own a fireworks business, the Washington Fireworks with headquarters in Washington, D.C. They are wholesalers and retailers throughout the United States for fireworks. Walt also is involved in the insurance business, plays a lot of charity golf outings, and he is an instructor in the Red Sox Fantasy Camp.

Paul Easterling (1928 and 1930) is in a hospital in Reidsville, Georgia in poor health. The hospital is Tattnall Nursing Care, Reidsville, Georgia 30453. (Paul would like to receive mail from fans.)

Harry Eisenstat (1938-1939) has been vice president of Curtis Industries, headquartered in Cleveland, Ohio, for the past 22 years. He and his wife of 51 years, Evelyn, have four grandchildren. He makes his home in Shaker Heights, Ohio, a suburb of Cleveland.

Gil English (1936-1937) lives in Greensboro, North Carolina. He was in professional baseball for 46 years, 29 as a major league scout. He is retired and in reasonably good health.

Darrell Evans (1984-1988) started off the 1990 season as a batting coach for the Toledo Mud Hens. He then went to the New York Yankees and finished the season there as batting coach.

Hoot Evers (1941-1956) is a scout for the Detroit Tigers living in Texas.

Bill Fahey (1981-1983) is a coach for the San Francisco Giants.

Al Federoff (1951-1952) recently retired and is living in Allen Park, Michigan, a suburb of Detroit.

Mark Fidrych (1976-1980) still makes his home outside of Boston. He is married and has one child. He makes many charitable events and is still the same old Mark—a joy to everybody he meets.

Hank Foiles (1960) is in the insurance business in Virginia Beach, Virginia.

Paul Foytack (1953-1963) lives in a suburb of Detroit and is a manufacturer's representative.

Tito Francona (1958) retired from baseball in 1970. He has been a parks and recreation director since then. He lives in New Brighton, Pennsylvania and frequently plays golf in alumni golf tournaments.

Bill Freehan (1961-1976) is the coach of the University of Michigan baseball team. He had a very successful career as a manufacturer's representative and in 1990 was appointed coach of Michigan's mens baseball team. He has been quite handicapped by restrictions placed on U-M because of rule infractions by the previous coach. It is thought by some that Bill will some day manage the Detroit Tigers.

Doug Gallagher (1962) lives in Fremont, Ohio. He works for Standard Products in Port Clinton, Ohio, and has three children.

Ned Garver (1953-1956). Ned spent 18 years with a meat-packing company and retired at the end of 1980. He has always lived in Ney, Ohio. He was mayor there for seven years and for more than 20 years was a council member. Ned and his wife have three children and three grandchildren. He spends his winter months in Avon Park, Florida and plays a lot of golf.

Charlie Gehringer (1924-1942), greatest second baseman of all time, now lives in Birmingham, Michigan. He plays golf regularly, and has three holes-in-one to his credit. The Charlie Gehringer Meadow Brook Golf Classic has raised hundreds of thousands of dollars for Oakland University student-athletes and helps preserve Meadow Brook Hall.

Dick Gernert (1960-1961) lives in Reading, Pennsylvania.

Joe Ginsberg (1948-1953) and wife Donna now live in Punta Gorda, Florida. They have one son, Michael. Joe is active with Early Wynn, who is President of the Old-Timers Pension Committee. Joe spends quite a bit of time with Early and also with Hal White who lives in Venice, Florida. Joe loves to play golf.

Ed Glynn (1975-1978) now lives in Virginia Beach, Virginia. He's in sales. He has one daughter who is five years old. He pitched in the Senior League last winter for St. Lucie.

Alumni

Ted Gray (1946-1954) lives in the Detroit suburb of Clarkston. He is now retired.

Al Greene (1979) lives in Detroit where he is a sales rep for General Food. He wants to get into real estate. He and Francisca have two children, Altar Jr. and Amor.

Steve Grilli (1975-1977) is living in Baldwinsville, New York.

Steve Gromek (1953-1957) and wife, Jeannette, live in the Detroit suburb, Beverly Hills. They have two sons, Greg and Carl, both of whom are attorneys. Carl is the Director of the Michigan Court of Appeals and Greg is a partner in one of Detroit's most prestigious law firms. Steve plays golf almost daily in the summer. Steve and Jeanette have five grandchildren.

Johnny Grubb (1983-1987) was the batting coach for the Richmond Braves in 1989. In 1990 he was the roving batting coach for the Atlanta Braves. John still lives in Richmond, Virginia.

Dave Gumpert (1982-1983) lives in South Haven, Michigan, where he has a restaurant. He is married, with three children. Dave coaches baseball and football at South Haven High. He also teaches Physical Education at South Elementary School in South Haven.

Bill Heath (1967) is a certified financial planner with an MBA from the University of Houston. He has his own company, the Center for Financial Planning. Bill resides in Houston. He is past president of Life Time Outs, a Christian professional athlete organization. He is also past president of Pecan Grove Plantation Property Owner Association.

Ray Herbert (1950-1954) is President of the Detroit Tiger Alumni. He and Pat have nine children. He lives in Livonia, a suburb of Detroit and is the last former Tiger to hit an inside-the-park home run, which he did this past summer in an Old-Timers game in Kansas City.

John Hiller (1965-1980) has been elected to the Michigan Sports Hall of Fame. John now resides in Northern Michigan. He is the all-time leader for Tiger pitchers in number of saves. He is still having trouble with his leg and would appreciate any prayers. John appeared in more games, 545, than any other Tiger pitcher.

Billy Hitchcock (1942, 1946 and 1953) is retired and lives in Opelika, Alabama.

Billy Hoeft (1952-1959) is the sales manager for the International Graphics Equipment Company. He and Marge have four children, three boys and a girl. They also have two grandchildren. They live in Livonia, Michigan.

Chief Hogsett (1929-1936) once hit two home runs in one game. He was a longtime roommate of Charlie Gehringer. The Chief resides in Hays, Kansas.

Fred Holdsworth (1972-1974) has been married 17 years and lives in Chelsea, Michigan. They have a son, Tom, 10 years old, and a daughter, Elizabeth who is 12. When Fred quit baseball he completed his college degree at the University of Michigan. He is currently a CPA employed with Arthur Andersen & Company.

Vern Holtgrave (1964) lives in Breezy, Illinois, where Les Mueller used to live.

Johnny Hopp (1952) retired at the age of 53 and spent four years in Naples, Florida; he now lives in Mesa, Arizona. He spends his time golfing, fishing and traveling, even though arthritis has slowed him down a little bit.

Willie Horton (1963-1977) is in the computer business in Detroit. Willie hit his first major league home run off Robin Roberts, as did Jim Northrup. Willie also is the Deputy Director of the Detroit Police Department Athletic League.

Art Houtteman (1945-1953) lives in a suburb of Detroit, Lake Orion. He is in the steel business.

Gary Ignasiak (1973) has six Dairy Queen stores in North Pontiac, Michigan. He also has three children, two boys and one girl, and lives in Waterford, Michigan.

Dalton Jones (1970-1972) loves to play golf, fish and hunt. He lives in Baton Rouge, Louisiana. He has two sons, ages 22 and 24. He was one of the instructors in the Boston Red Sox Fantasy Camp.

Lynn Jones (1979-1983) is a representative for ESR in his home in Pennsylvania.

Al Kaline (1953-1974) still lives in the Detroit area. He does the telecast of the Tiger ball games along with George Kell.

George Kell (1946-1952) has been broadcasting and telecasting Detroit Tiger baseball and games since 1960 with the exception of 1963. He still makes his home in Swifton, Arkansas but comes up to Detroit regularly for his broadcasting.

Steve Kemp (1977-1981) makes his home in Laguna Niguel, California. He has two children, Chris, 3, and Stephanie, 5. He goes to a lot of autograph shows. He played for the St. Petersburg Pelicans in the Senior Professional Baseball League and hit .329 with 12 home runs. He also hit one of the longest home runs ever seen in Florida in the championship playoff game, which the Pelicans won.

Frank Kostro (1962-1963) lives in Denver, Colorado. He is doing credit life insurance and extended warranty business with auto dealers and banks throughout the United States.

Wayne Krenchicki (1983) lives in Palm Harbor, Florida, near St. Petersberg. Wayne is single and does a lot of golfing, fishing and hunting.

Lou Kretlow (1946 and 1948-1949) is semi-retired from the oil business and also has a restaurant. He has three daughters and nine grandchildren. He is a golf professional and plays in a lot of tournaments.

Dick Kryhoski (1950-1951) sells for Northwest Blueprint in Detroit. He has two daughters, 27 and 23 years old. He loves to play golf, fish and garden. Dick spent many years working for Keufel and Esser, where he was manager of the Detroit office.

Eddie Lake (1946-1950) is in California. He doesn't like to travel anymore, but he does play a lot of golf and walks a lot on the course. He has seven grandchildren and three great-grandchildren. Eddie misses the good old days and thinks today's salaries are senseless.

Marvin Lane (1971-1976) still makes his home in the Detroit area.

Frank Lary (1954-1964) is retired from construction work in North Fort, Alabama. He loves to golf and fish.

Fred Lasher (1967-1970) calls Merrillan, Wisconsin, his home. He owns an ice cream cone shop in nearby Hatville, Wisconsin.

Don Lee (1957-1958) lives in Tuscon, Arizona, and is a field representative for the National Association of Professional Baseball Leagues in St. Petersburg, Florida.

Ron LeFlore (1974-1979) makes his home in Sarasota, Florida. He is part-owner of the Jim Rice Baseball School. He expects to open his own baseball school in Naples. Ron has one son, 22, and a daughter, 10. Ron hit .328 in the Senior Professional Baseball League playing for the Bradenton Explorers. He also stole four bases.

George Lerchen (1952) is the general superintendent of the Creco Realty and Development Company. He and his wife Ann have one daughter. They live in Westland, Michigan, a suburb of Detroit.

Don Leshnock (1972) lives in Columbus, Ohio. His son is going to the University of North Carolina on a baseball scholarship.

Johnny Lipon (1942-1952) managed the Lakeland Tigers this year in the Florida State League. John's home is in Houston and he loves to play horseshoes. John is planning on retiring after the 1990 season after a lifetime in baseball.

Dick Littlefield (1952) works for General Motors in Livonia, Michigan at the Inland Division. He is a toolmaker and is retiring in April, 1991. Dick has 3 children and 3 grandchildren. He loves to come to Alumni reunions because he sees so many old friends. Dick spent nine years in the big leagues but was with Detroit only in 1952.

Mickey Lolich (1963-1975) has a donut shop in Lake Orion, Michigan, a suburb of Detroit. He also did cable announcing for the London Tiger games in London, Ontario this past summer. Mickey has three daughters and two grandsons.

Dwight Lowry (1984-1987) lives in Pembroke, North Carolina. He played in Italy in 1988 and 1989. He has two daughters, a 3 year-old and a 4-1/2 year-old.

Don Lund (1949-1954) is still in Ann Arbor with the University of Michigan, where he is the Assistant Athletic Director.

Bill Madlock (1987) lives in West Los Angeles where he works for a Japanese firm. He has four children, a girl 22 years old, and three boys, 18, 15 and 9. In the winter he plays ball for St. Lucie in the Senior League.

Mickey Mahler (1985) lives in Sandy, Utah. He sells Cadillacs in Salt Lake City during the summer. He has one daughter, 6 years old, and a boy, 4 years old. He pitched for Bradenton in 1989-90 in the Senior League.

Jerry Manuel (1975-1976) spent the winter playing in the Senior League for St. Lucie. In the summer, he is the manager of the Jacksonville Expos in the Florida State League. He has four children, two boys, 14 and 12, and two girls, 16 and 6.

Cliff Mapes (1952) quit baseball in 1953 and went to work for a chemical company. He retired after 24 years, then worked at a children's home and on the farm for about five years. He took an early retirement at age 62. He has a hobby of homing pigeons and is involved in an organized racing program. Cliff and his wife of nearly 50 years are in good health, have three children, five grandchildren, and four great-grandchildren, all living nearby. Cliff lives in Pryor, Oklahoma, and enjoys the good hunting and fishing nearby.

Leo Marentette (1965) lives in Toledo, Ohio.

Lew Matlin has retired after a lifetime of baseball from the front office. He has been with the Detroit Baseball Club for 20 years.

Charlie Maxwell (1956-1962) and wife Ann have four children, two boys and two girls, and eight grandchildren. Charlie still makes his home in Paw Paw, Michigan, in the same area where he was raised. He's regional sales manager for Shelby Die Casting in Shelby, Michigan. He travels extensively and loves to play golf.

Eddie Mayo (1944-1948) got a real thrill last summer when the city of Clifton, New Jersey, renamed the Babe Ruth Field located on Clifton Avenue, where Eddie formerly lived, as the Eddie Mayo field.

Dick McAuliffe (1960-1973) is retired. He spends half his time in Naples, Florida, and the other half in West Simsbury, Connecticut. The former left-handed hitter now plays right-handed golf.

Barney McCosky (1939-1946) and his wife Jane now live in Vero Beach, Florida. They have one son, who lives in Troy, Michigan, and a 13-year-old grandson. Barney loves to fish and play golf. He plays in a lot of celebrity golf tournaments and spends summers in Troy.

John McHale, who played with Detroit from 1943 to 1948 and later was General Manager, has been named the 1990 winner of the *Sporting News* Pioneer Award. John is retired and living in Florida. Incidentally, John was an outstanding football player at Detroit's Catholic Central High School and people still rave about his performance in the City Championship Game.

Denny McLain (1963-1970) has a highly rated daily talk show on Detroit station WXYT AM for three hours. He also plays the organ professionally.

Dan Meyer (1974-1976) lives in Danville, California. He has three children. He is now a northern California scout for the Baltimore Orioles. He owns a restaurant in Danville, called the Dog House. He also has a real estate license. Last winter he played for the Bradenton Explorers in the Senior Professional League.

Bob Miller (1953-1956) has been vice president of Barton Brands Limited for 20 years. He's also Chairman of the Board of the Major League Baseball Players Alumni Association. He makes his home near Chicago, Illinois.

Bill Monbouquette (1966-1967) is the minor league pitching coach for the Toronto Blue Jays. He makes his home in Medford, Massachusetts. He has three sons and plays a lot of golf. He is involved in the Boston Red Sox Fantasy Camp.

Jim Morrison (1987-1988) led the Senior Professional Baseball League in home runs with 17. He hit .290 for the season.

Bubba Morton (1961-1963) lives in Falls Church, Virginia.

Gerry Moses (1974) is the owner of the Fanfare Control Food Service Company in the greater-Boston area. He has two children, a daughter, 19, and a son, 16. He plays golf whenever he can and is involved in the Boston Red Sox Fantasy Camp.

Les Moss, who managed the Tigers in the early part of 1979, recently retired after seven years coaching for the Houston Astros. Les is making his home in Orlando, Florida with his brother Perry who coaches the Detroit Drive in the Arena Football League.

Les Mueller (1941 and 1945) is a 22-year season ticket holder for the St. Louis Cardinals. He lives in Millstadt, Illinois, 25 minutes from Busch Stadium. He is retired from the furniture business.

Pat Mullin (1940-1953) is still living in Brownsville, Pennsylvania. He retired in 1985, after 48 years in baseball. Pat has two sons—Pat and Mike. Pat says he's trying to conquer golf and has a 10 handicap.

Russ Nagelson (1970) resides in Little Rock, Arkansas and is currently employed by Shearson, Lehman and Hutton Company as a financial consultant.

Bill Nahorodny (1983) is living in the St. Petersburg, Florida, area.

Hal Newhouser (1939-1953) is retired from the banking business. He's done some scouting for Houston since that time. Hal, with Hall of Fame credentials, still lives in the Detroit area.

Joe Niekro (1970-1972) lives in Mulberry, Florida (just outside of Lakeland). He has a 12-year-old son and a 17-year-old daughter. He loves fishing and playing golf.

Ron Nischwitz (1961-1962 and 1965) is a coaching baseball at Wright State in Dayton, Ohio. His school played in the Rainbow Classic Tournament in March 1990 in Honolulu and went 45-12.

Jim Northrup (1969-1974) televises many of the Detroit Tiger home games along with Larry Osterman. Jim is active in the Fantasy Camp in Lakeland, Florida each year. He is also active in many charities in Detroit and lives in Keego Harbor.

Jimmy Outlaw (1943-1949) lives in Jackson, Alabama. Jim was inducted into the Alabama Sports Hall of Fame in February 1990. He has one son, six grandchildren, and one great grandson. They all live around Mobile, Alabama.

Marv Owen's (1931-1937) son, Skip, writes that Marv is still following baseball. He lives in a senior citizen retirement facility in Santa Clara, California. Marv has his mail sent to Skip & Joan Owen at 1230 Main Street, Santa Clara, California 95050.

Larry Pashnick (1982-1983) is a manufacturer's representative for Ambler Enterprise. He and Denise have one son, Jeffrey John, who is a year and a half old. Larry is active in cystic fibrosis. He is the treasurer for the Tiger Alumni and makes his home in Livonia, Michigan. Larry and Denise are expecting their second child early this fall.

Don Pepper (1966) has a daughter, Dottie Mochrie, who is a fine L.P.G.A. golfer. In 1990, Dottie Mochrie won the Crestar Classic in Chesapeake, Maryland with the second most lopsided margin in LPGA history.

Johnny Pesky (1952-1954) lives in the Boston area and works for the Boston Red Sox during the regular season as a special assistant to General Manager Lou Gorman. He also is an instructor in the Fantasy Camp at Winter Haven.

Jim Price (1967-1971) is the sales manager for Summa Harrison and also runs an outstanding fantasy camp in Lakeland every year. Jim did a series of clinics on the Tigers this summer. He also serves on the Major League Baseball Players Alumni Board.

Alumni 271

Dick Radatz (1969) is involved in industrial packaging in Boston. He also has a two-hour radio talk show on Sunday nights. He is part-owner of the Fantasy Camp in Winter Haven. Dick was born in Berkley, Michigan.

Earl Rapp (1949) has a home in Swedesboro, New Jersey, and scouts the East Coast for the Cincinnati Reds.

Hank Riebe (1942 and 1947-1949) is retired and lives in Euclid, Ohio, a suburb of Cleveland. He plays golf five times a week and visits Tiger Stadium once a year with his children and grandchildren.

Leon Roberts (1974-1975) is in private business in Hurst, Texas. He has one son, 10 years old, and a girl, 14. Leon loves to play golf, hunt and fish. He managed the Toledo Mud Hens two years ago and last year he managed the Winter Haven Super Sox in the Senior League.

Bill Rogell (1930-1939) is playing golf in New Port Richey, Florida. Billy was a councilman for the City of Detroit for many years.

Sol Rogovin (1949-1951) is in New York City.

Dave Rozema (1977-1984) is in the construction business on the east side of Detroit and in St. Clair Shores. He just bought a new home in Grosse Pointe Woods. He has one daughter, Caley, who is three years old. Dave is an instructor in the Fantasy Camp in Lakeland. Dave had a hole-in-one playing in a Tiger Alumni Golf Outing in August.

Jack Russell (1937) is in the oil business in Clearwater, Florida.

Kevin "Hot Sauce" Saucier (1981-1982) is living in Pensacola. He has been with a major-league scouting bureau for the last five years.

Fred Scherman (1969-1973) still makes his home in Brookville, Ohio. He is the manager of IAMS Pet Food Company. He flies a private plane for business and pleasure. Fred does a lot of work with promising young ball players. Fred and his wife Frankie have a daughter, Andrea, and a son, Fred.

Chuck Scrivener (1975-1977) is the manager of the Old Ball Park in Livonia—a very popular baseball memorabilia store. (Phone 313/261-4810.)

Heinie Schuble (1929-1935) is in ill health and would love to have any news sent to him. He lives at 1802 Florida Street, Baytown, Texas 77520. (Heinie was a little fellow who played shortstop for the Tigers back in the early '30s. He really could hit off Herb Pennock, one of the great pitchers of all time.)

Frank Secory (1940) played only one game for the Tigers but umpired for 18 years in the National League. Frank and Vonda live in Port Huron, 55 miles from Detroit. Frank is in the Western Michigan University Hall of Fame, the Muskegon High School Hall of Fame, and the Grand Haven Hall of Fame.

Ron Shoop (1959) lives in Rural Valley, Pennsylvania, where he grew up, and works for the Pittsburgh Brewing Company.

Lou Skizas (1958) retired last year as assistant baseball coach at the University of Illinois. He's in good health and keeps in good shape by doing aerobics. He has one son, who resides in Kansas City.

Jim Small (1955-1957) and his wife Betsy have three children, two boys and one girl; they are really not children, at ages 30, 28 and 18. Jim lives in beautiful Canadian Lakes, Michigan, three doors down the street from Ray Herbert. Jim owns a real estate company, Lakes Realty, specializing in recreational property. (Jim can be reached at 616/972-8300.)

Elias Sosa (1982) lives in Phoenix, Arizona. He coached the Montreal Expos in 1988. He has a 5-year-old daughter. He won three and lost four for the St. Petersburg Pelicans in the Senior Professional Baseball League last winter.

Rusty Staub (1976-1979) has a restaurant in New York City.

Mickey Stanley (1964-1978) lives in Brighton, Michigan. Mickey is a manufacturers representative for an automotive company. He plays golf as often as he can. He has one grandson and is expecting another. He and Ellen have been married for 29 years. In a golf outing last summer at Wabeek Country Club Mickey hit one drive 350 yards. He would have been tough if he had taken up golf instead of baseball.

Marlin Stuart (1949-1952) is confined to bed after three strokes. Mrs. Stuart writes that she is able to keep him at home. Marlin was a heavy-equipment operator at the time of his illness. They live on a farm in Arkansas, have a son, Richard, two granddaughters, and a great-grandson. They have been married for 50 years. Marlin would appreciate letters sent to him at Route 1, B133, Paragould, Arkansas 72450.

Gary Taylor (1969) has a jewelry store in Dearborn, Michigan. Gary is the father of two children—one girl and one boy. He loves to play golf.

Bud Thomas (1939-1941) bought a farm in 1934 in North Garden, Virginia, and still lives there. He and Dorothy have been married for 56 years. He has five grandchildren and three great-grandchildren. One of his grandsons was the starting center fielder for four years at the University of Virginia.

Tom Timmerman (1969-1973) and his wife Ruby have two children, one boy and one girl, and one grandchild. Tom is territorial manager for the Yale Material Handling Company. He lives in Milford, Michigan, a suburb of Detroit.

Dave Tobik (1978-1982) is director of industrial sales for Five Star Temporaries in St. Louis. He and wife Ann have two daughters.

Tom Tresh (1969) has seven children and three grandchildren. He represents Western Diversified Company for new accounts in Mt. Pleasant,

Michigan. He is also the assistant baseball coach at Central Michigan University. He has invented a Slide-Rite, a device to teach people how to slide. It consists of a durable nylon sliding pad with a 1-1/4-inch-thick open self-foam cushion, inside mat, and a nylon top sliding sheet. (Tom Tresh can be contacted at Central Michigan University for further information.)

Virgil Trucks (1941-1952 and 1956) has spent some of his time in Birmingham, Alabama, scouting for the Tigers in that area. He retired from the Civic Center Parks and Recreations in Leeds, Alabama. He works on many charitable golf tournaments. Virgil recently moved to Punta Gorda, Florida. He is an instructor in the Lakeland Fantasy camp each winter.

John Tsitouris (1957) is living in Monroe, North Carolina.

Bill Tuttle (1952 and 1954-1957) lives in Blue Springs, Missouri. He had a heart attack in 1985, but is in fine condition now. Bill plays a lot of golf and likes to go fishing whenever he can find time. He works part-time as a supervisor for General Motors Services. Bill has 15 grandchildren.

Pat Underwood (1979-1983) lives in Kokomo, Indiana, with his wife and two sons, Ryan, 6, and Evan, 4. Pat recently was graduated from Indiana University and is now with Delco Electronics.

Al Unser (1942-1944) is in Decatur, Illinois. Al is the father of Del and the father of eight, all of whom were graduated from college.

Ozzie Virgil (1958-1961) lives in Glendale, Arizona. He was with the Seattle Mariners two years ago. He plays a lot of golf and loves to fool around with model airplanes. Last winter he coached in the Senior Professional Baseball League. His son, Ozzie, is also a major leaguer. Ozzie, Sr. figured in a key play in the 1984 World Series while a third-base coach for the San Diego Padres.

Mark Wagner (1976-1980) lives in Westland, Michigan, with his wife, Beverly. He is superintendent of a construction company. They have two children, Megan, 8, and Mark, 7, and recently moved from Ashtabula, Ohio.

Tom Walker (1975) has four children. He's a senior account executive with Hill Romm Company in Batesville, Indiana. Tom's home is in Pittsburgh.

Jon Warden (1968) lives in Loveland, Ohio.

Don Wert (1963-1970) has moved to New Providence, Pennsylvania.

Hal White (1941-1952) lives in Venice, Florida, and sees a lot of Joe Ginsberg, Early Wynn and Joe Coleman, playing golf with them once a week. Hal is retired and the father of nine children, 20 grandchildren, and three great-grandchildren.

Dave Wickersham (1964-1967) is a financial consultant for Equitable Life in Overland Park, Kansas.

Milt Wilcox (1977-1985) has a television show in Detroit, has a baseball camp, and is very active in many charities. He lives in a suburb of Detroit.

Earl Wilson (1967-1970), the "Duke," has his own company—Autotech Inc. in Farmington Hills. He lives in Southfield, Michigan.

Red Wilson (1954-1960) recently retired from his job with the Valley Bank of Madison, Wisconsin. He still lives in Madison and will spend the wintertime in the south. He loves to play golf, hunt and fish.

Casey Wise (1960) is an orthodontist in Naples, Florida.

Eddie Yost (1959-1960) still resides in Wellesley, Massachusetts.

Bill Zepp (1971) is a market representative for Chrysler. He and Cheryl have two children, a daughter, 16, and a son, 12. Bill loves to play golf. They live in Plymouth, Michigan, a suburb of Detroit.

Gus Zernial (1958-1959) lives in Fresno, California.

TIGER ALUMNI NEWS

Former Tigers **Milt Wilcox** (1977-1985) and **Jim Morrison** (1987-1988) distinguished themselves in the senior professional baseball league last winter. Milt won 12 games and lost but 3. Jim led the league in home runs with 17. **Mickey Mahler** (1985) won 8 and lost 7 for Bradenton and had a 3.49 earned run average. Milt Wilcox's earned run average was 3.19. **Bill Campbell** (1986) won 6 and lost 2 and led the league with a 2.12 earned run average.

In the last five years these gentlemen have passed away:

Johnny Bero, Archie McKain, Syl Johnson, Bob Nieman, Bob Scheffing, "Little Joe" Sullivan, George Uhle, Dick Wakefield, official scorer **Eddie Browalski,** and grounds keeper **Lefty Conway.** Also, **Hank Greenberg, Frank O'Rourke, Paul Richards, "Good Kid" George Susce, Joe Sparma, Jack Warner** (Jack once beat Ty Cobb in a foot race), **Big Ed Wells, Jo-Jo White** and **Skeeter Webb. Johnny Hand** (the old club house man), **Harvey Kuenn, Don Heffner, Joe Orengo, Frank Skaff, Ben Steiner, "Boom Boom" Beck, Joe Burns, Don McMahon, Tom Morgan, "Bots" Nekola, George Smith, John Skurski, Tony Renza, Hugh Wise, Jim Brideweser, Charlie Keller, Rip Sewell, "Doc" Cramer,** and **Billy Martin.**

Alumni

Former Tigers who are now coaching in the majors include:

- **Jackie Moore** (1965), with the Reds.
- **Larry Rothschild** (1981-1982), with the Reds.
- **Ron Perranoski** (1971-1972), with the Dodgers.
- **Gene Lamont** (1970-1975), with Pittsburgh.
- **Milt May** (1976-1979), with Pittsburgh.
- **Mike Roarke** (1961-1964), with the Cardinals.
- **Pat Dobson** (1967-1969), with the Padres.
- **Bill Fahey** (1981-1983), with the Giants.
- **Richie Hebner** (1980-1982), with the Red Sox.
- **Joe Coleman** (1971-1976), with the Angels (his dad was with Detroit in 1955).
- **Duffy Dyer** (1980-1981), with the Brewers.
- **Rusty Kuntz** (1984-1985), with Seattle.

TRADES

The Tigers have made many trades over the last 65 years. Some have been controversial while others hardly raised an eyebrow. Some proved to be good for the Tigers; others did not. One thing is certain: when a favorite is traded, every fan has an expert opinion.

The most important trades involving Tigers are analyzed here. Would you have traded Barney McCosky? Hank Aguirre? Steve Demeter?

A REAL CLUNKER

The Tigers have made many trades over the years, and going back to 1927, they made one of the worst possible. At the end of the 1927 season they traded Heinie Manush and Lu Blue to the St. Louis Browns for Harry Rice, Elam Vangilder and Chick Galloway. Manush had won the batting championship in 1926 with a .378 average. He slumped in 1927 to .298, then after the trade to St. Louis he came back and hit .378, missing the batting championship by one point to Goose Goslin. Heinie played 17 years in the majors and wound up with a lifetime batting average of .330. Blue, who had been the Tigers first baseman for seven years, played three years for the Browns, two with the White Sox, and finished his career with Brooklyn in 1933. He had a lifetime batting average of .287.

Harry Rice, who the Tigers received in exchange, hit .302 in 1928, and .304 in 1929. He was traded to the Yankees in 1930. Chick Galloway played 53 ballgames for the Tigers in 1928, hit .264 and was out of baseball after that. Vangilder won 11 and lost 10 in 1928, and in 1929 did not win a game.

Truly, a terrible trade for the Tigers.

WE GOT GEORGE

Jackie Tavener was a little shortstop, only 5'5", who batted left handed, and took Topper Rigney's place at shortstop for the Tigers in 1925. After the 1928 season he was traded, along with Ken Holloway, to the Cleveland Indians for George Uhle.

Jackie played one year with the Indians and wound up his career in 1929 with a .255 lifetime batting average. Holloway had been a pitcher with the Detroit organization for seven years. He won six and lost five when he went to Cleveland in 1929. He concluded his career in 1930, while George Uhle, an Indian since 1919, came to Detroit, won his first nine games and wound up winning 15 and losing 11. He won 12 in 1930 and 11 in 1931. He went to the Giants, then to the Yankees, and then back again to Cleveland. He finished his 17-year career in 1936 with 200 lifetime wins.

Clearly, a great trade for Detroit.

THE DALE ALEXANDER/ROY JOHNSON/ EARL WEBB TRADE

Dale Alexander was a 6' 3", 220-pound first baseman who was one of the poorest fielding first basemen of all time. He came up to the Tigers in 1929 and hit .343, .326 in 1930, and .325 in 1931.

In 1932 the Tigers got a first baseman by the name of Harry Davis who was a great-fielding first baseman. At the same time, Alexander's inadequacies in the field caused much concern to Bucky Harris, the manager of the Tigers. In June 1932, the Tigers traded Alexander, along with outfielder Roy Johnson, to the Boston Red Sox in exchange for Earl Webb. Alexander went on to lead the American League in batting with a .367 batting average. In

1933 he played in only 94 games and the Red Sox gave up on him, even though he could hit, because his fielding was so poor.

Roy Johnson, an outfielder, was also a poor fielder. He had a strong arm but no one knew exactly where the ball was going. Roy continued to play for the Red Sox through 1935, then went to the Yankees, then the Boston Braves.

Earl Webb had been an outfielder in the National League in the '20s and came to Boston in 1932. He is remembered mainly for the fact that he hit 67 doubles in 1931 when he was with the Boston Red Sox, which is still a major league record for most doubles in one season. With the Tigers, he played in merely six games in 1933 and wound up his career with a .306 lifetime batting average.

The trade didn't amount to much for either ball club but the edge went to Boston.

"MUCH ADO ABOUT NOTHING"

On May 30, 1930, the Tigers made a deal with the New York Yankees. They traded a pitcher, Ownie Carroll, and Yats Wuestling and Harry Rice for Mark Koenig and Waite Hoyt. Hoyt, who had been a great pitcher for the Yankees, spent the balance of 1930 and part of 1931 with the Tigers, winning 12 games and losing 16. Koenig was the regular shortstop for the Tigers for the balance of 1930 and in 1931.

Carroll, who had been a sensation at Holy Cross College, pitched in only 10 games for the Yankees, winning none and losing one. Wuestling played 25 games with the Yankees and that completed his major league career. Rice finished the 1930 season with the Yankees, then went to Washington and Cincinnati, concluding his career in 1933.

There was much ado about this trade when it was made, but it was "Much Ado About Nothing."

WE LOST THE "EARL"

Fred Marberry, better known as "Firpo," had been a pitcher for the Washington Senators for 10 years (1923-1932) when the Tigers traded Earl Whitehill for Marberry's services along with Carl Fischer. Marberry won 16 games the next season for the Tigers and 15 the season after that. He had been primarily a relief pitcher with Washington. In fact, he was generally considered one of the first great relief pitchers.

Whitehill, who had been an excellent pitcher for the Tigers, pitched for Washington for four years, won 22 games in 1933, went to Cleveland in 1937 and then to the Cubs in 1939. Whitehill won 218 during his big league career. Fischer pitched for Detroit in 1933, 1934, and the start of 1935. He won 17 games and lost 20 for the Tigers in those seasons.

This trade was pretty good for both teams.

COOKING UP A GOOSE DEAL

There was some criticism when the Tigers traded Johnny "Rocky" Stone in December 1933 to the Washington Senators for Goose Goslin. The Goose was getting up in age—he would be 33 years old when the season started in 1934. He had been a hero of the Senators in the World Series of 1924. But it turned out to be one of the great deals for the Tigers.

Goslin played for Detroit until 1937. He was the hero of the World Series in 1935. Stone played for the Senators for five years. He wound up with a lifetime batting average of .310. But his major league career was shortened by the fact that he came down with tuberculosis.

This was a mighty good deal for the Tigers.

A GOOD DEAL, IN GENERAL

One of the greatest deals the Tigers have ever made was August 4, 1934, when they picked up General Crowder on waivers from the Washington Senators. Crowder went on to win 5 and lose 1 for the Tigers in 1934, and in 1935 he won 16 and lost 10.

A FILL-IN FOR HAMMERIN' HENRY

In the spring of 1936 Hank Greenberg broke his wrist and was sidelined for the rest of the season. The Tigers badly needed a first baseman, so they traded pitcher Chief Hogsett to St. Louis for Jack Burns. Burns had been the regular first baseman for the Browns since 1931 and he played 138 games for the Tigers in 1936, finishing with a batting average of .281 for the season. That was his last year in major league baseball. He had no chance to be the regular first baseman with Hank Greenberg returning.

Hogsett, who had been with the Tigers since 1929, went on to the Browns and won 13 and lost 15 games during that season for the Browns. He also pitched in St. Louis in 1937, and 1938 with Washington. He came back during the war for a brief time with the Tigers in 1944.

It was a good trade for both clubs. Hogsett was a good relief pitcher, but Detroit badly needed somebody to take Greenberg's place and Burns did the job adequately.

IT BROKE THE FANS' HEARTS

On December 2, 1937, the Tigers traded Marv Owen, Mike Tresh, and the people's choice of Detroit, Gee Walker, to Chicago for Vern Kennedy, Tony Piet and Dixie Walker. Gee Walker had been an extremely popular player with the Tigers and many of the fans resented the trade. However, Gee or Jerry, as he was also known, played only two years with the White Sox, then went on to Washington, Cleveland and Cincinnati, completing a 15-year career in the majors in 1945. Owen played full-time in 1938 with the White Sox and in 58 games in 1939; in 1940 he went to the Boston Red Sox for only 20 games. Mike Tresh went on for a 12-year career in the American League, playing with the White sox for 11 years. Mike is the father of Tom Tresh, who later played for the Tigers and became a baseball coach at Central Michigan University.

Vern Kennedy won his first nine games with the Tigers and never did anything after that. Tony Piet concluded his eight-year career in the majors that season with the Tigers playing in only 41 games. Dixie Walker only played a season and a half for the Tigers before he went on to Brooklyn and became the people's choice in Brooklyn. He wound up his career in 1949 with Pittsburgh.

Clearly, a much better deal for Chicago.

GOOD-BYE, ELDON—HELLO, PINKY

Eldon Auker was one of the better pitchers for the Tigers from 1933 through 1938. Then he was traded to the Boston Red Sox, along with Jake Wade and Chet Morgan in exchange for Pinky Higgins and Archie McKain. Auker had four more good years with Boston and St. Louis in the American League before retiring. Higgins was the Tigers regular third baseman through the 1944 season. In 1945 he was in the service and in 1946 he went back to Boston. He had a .292 lifetime batting average and was a very good fielding third baseman. Chet Morgan never played for the Red Sox. Jake Wade stuck around until 1946 with Boston, St. Louis, White Sox, Yankees and Senators, and won a total of 27 games during his eight-year career. Archie McKain won a total of 12 games for the Tigers during 1939, 1940 and 1941. He later went to the Browns and retired from baseball after the 1943 season.

I would call this one best for Detroit.

THE MAN WHO CAME TOO LATE

Earl Averill came to the Tigers from Cleveland in exchange for Harry Eisenstat during the 1939 season. Earl was nearing the end of a great career. He played with the Tigers through 1940 and then went to the Boston Braves in 1941 where he completed a 13-year career in the majors. He hit .262 for the Tigers in 1939 and .280 in 1940.

Eisenstat stayed with the Indians through the 1942 season. He won a total of 10 games and lost 13 during his four years with the Indians. Eisenstat is best remembered as the man who beat Bob Feller when Feller struck out 18 Tigers in 1938.

Edge—the Tigers.

A BIGGIE WITH THE BROWNS

In May 1939, the Tigers and the St. Louis Browns completed one of the biggest deals in manpower in major league history. The Tigers sent six players to St. Louis in return for four. The Tigers traded Vern Kennedy, Bob

Harris, George Gill, Roxie Lawson, Chet Laabs and Mark Christman. In return, they received Beau Bell, Red Kress, Jim Walkup and Bo Newsom.

Bo Newsom won 17 games the first year he was with the Tigers and 21 the second. He was also the hero of the 1940 World Series, winning two games and narrowly missing winning a third. Beau Bell only played a half a season with the Tigers. Red Kress was near the end of his career and only played two years as a utility man. Jim Walkup won no games and lost two in one year with the ball club.

On the Browns side, Vern Kennedy pitched for six more years. His best year was a 12-17 slate in 1940. Bob Harris pitched three years, twice winning over 10 games. George Gill, Roxie Lawson and Mark Christman did nothing of importance. Chet Laabs played for eight years and batted .262 lifetime. He also hit two dramatic home runs in 1944 which deprived the Tigers of the pennant that season.

Because of the work of Bo Newsom, the Tigers had the best of it.

ROGELL FOR A PENNANT SPARK

Billy Rogell was one of the finer shortstops the Detroit Tigers ever had. He played with them from 1930 through 1939. At the end of 1939 he was traded to the Chicago Cubs for Dick Bartell. Bartell had played for many years in the National League and was a very peppery shortstop and a good one. In fact, many feel that Bartell belongs in baseball's Hall of Fame. The trade was very beneficial for the Tigers; Rogell had reached the end of the line and Bartell provided a spark that helped ignite the Tigers to win the pennant in 1940.

DICK FOR DICK

Dick Wakefield was the first bonus baby of the Detroit Tigers, receiving approximately $51,000 to sign with the Bengals. He was a graduate of the University of Michigan and the son of a former major league ballplayer, Howard Wakefield. Dick signed with the Tigers in 1941 and he was with them through 1949, outside of the war years. Dick was an outfielder and a long-ball hitter. After the 1949 season he was traded to the New York Yankees for Dick Kryhoski.

Kryhoski was a first baseman who played in Detroit for two years before going in another trade to St. Louis. Dick Kryhoski alternated with Don Kolloway at first base during the 1950 and 1951 seasons. Wakefield could have been a great ballplayer but did not seem to have his heart in it. He didn't care for baseball like most people do. He had the ability but not the heart.

A good trade for the Tigers.

THANKS, WASHINGTON

In December 1941, the Tigers secured the services of Doc Cramer and Jimmy Bloodworth. In exchange they gave to the Washington Senators Frank Croucher and outfielder Bruce Campbell. Bloodworth then had the distinction of replacing the great Charlie Gehringer at second base, who had called it a career and gone into the military service. Jimmy was the regular second baseman for the Tigers through 1942, 1943, and then after the war in 1946.

Doc Cramer played for the Tigers for seven years, finishing his career in 1948. The first 4 years he played regularly. He had a .296 lifetime batting average. Bruce Campbell played only one year with Washington, hit .278, and then retired from major league baseball. Frank Croucher played just 26 games for the Senators in 1942 and that was his last year in the big leagues.

Score that trade a very big plus for the Tigers.

WE LOOKED GOOD ON THIS

On April 27, 1945, the Tigers secured Roy Cullenbine from the Cleveland Indians in exchange for Don Ross and Dutch Meyer. Roy was nearing the end of his 10-year career in the major leagues but he was a great factor in the Tigers winning the pennant and the World Championship in 1945 and then hit .335 in 1946. Roy set the Detroit record for most base on balls in one season when he walked 137 times in 1947. Don Ross only played 10 games with the Indians in 1945 and 55 games in 1946. Meyer played 130 games and batted .292 for the Indians in 1945 and concluded his six-year career in the majors in 1946 with the Indians hitting .232 that season.

This was another trade that was very good for the Tigers.

GOOD-BYE TO RUDY

The war was over. The Boston Red Sox needed a first baseman and the Detroit Tigers needed a shortstop. The Red Sox had two shortstops: Johnny Pesky, returning from the service, and Eddie Lake. The Tigers had Hank Greenberg coming back from the service. Greenberg had played in the outfield but he was getting older and thought it would be best for him to go to first base. So the Tigers traded Rudy York to Boston for Eddie Lake.

Eddie was the regular shortstop for the Tigers in 1946 and 1947, and played through 1950. He retired after the 1950 season. York played for the Red Sox in 1946 and batted .276. In the middle of the 1947 season he went to the Chicago White Sox and then in 1948 he went to the Philadelphia Athletics where he concluded his 13-year career.

Call this trade a wash.

AN OLD FAN FAVORITE FOR A FUTURE HALL OF FAMER

The Tigers got George Kell in a trade for Barney McCosky in May 1946. George went on to become one of the finest third basemen in baseball history, a league-leading batter, and eventually a Hall of Fame inductee. McCosky was an excellent outfielder and good hitter, and had a lifetime batting average of .311 for his 11 years in the majors. His career was shortened by a back injury in the first night game ever played at Tiger Stadium and he never was quite the ballplayer that he had been before that.

This was a super trade for the Tigers, especially considering Barney's injury. Despite the injury, Barney had a lifetime average of .312.

TEBBETTS FOR WAGNER

On May 20, 1947, the Tigers traded long-time catcher Birdie Tebbetts to the Boston Red Sox in exchange for another catcher, Hal Wagner. Birdie played with the Red Sox for four years before finishing his career with the Indians in 1951 and 1952. Wagner caught for Detroit the rest of 1947 and part of 1948, before going to the Phillies where he finished his career in 1949.

Boston got the best of this trade.

YOU CAN'T WIN 'EM ALL

On November 10, 1948, the Detroit Tigers and Chicago White Sox made a trade which will go down in history as the worst trade the Tigers ever made. They traded Billy Pierce, a left-handed pitcher, to Chicago for Aaron Robinson, a catcher. They also sent $10,000 along with the deal. The White Sox had wanted Teddy Gray, a left-handed pitcher, or Art Houtteman, a right-handed pitcher. But the Tigers had refused to give either one of them up and the Sox finally decided to go along with Pierce. Pierce had a physical ailment and they were a little afraid it might shorten his career.

Billy went on to pitch 13 years for the White Sox and three years after that with the San Francisco Giants. He won 211 games during his 18-year career. Twice he won 20 games. He was the winning pitcher in an All-Star game.

Although Aaron Robinson caught for Detroit for 2-1/2 seasons, the power the Tigers expected wasn't there. He had only 61 home runs in his eight-year career in the majors, and had a .260 lifetime batting average. Robinson also was involved in a play in a crucial game in 1950 with the Cleveland Indians which has gone down in history as "Robinson's rock."

The deal was terrible for the Tigers. But, strangely enough, many people, myself included, thought when the trade was first announced that it would be a good deal for the Tigers because Pierce was small, had trouble with his control, and had a physical impairment, while Robinson was a big, strong left-handed hitter. It didn't work out that way.

A PRIDDY GOOD ONE

In December of 1949, the Tigers sent $100,000 and pitcher Lou Kretlow to the St. Louis Browns in exchange for Gerry Priddy, a second baseman. The Tigers were in dire need of a second baseman. Priddy played the position for four years for the Tigers.

Kretlow only appeared in nine games for the Browns, had no victories and two defeats. He went on later to the White Sox and then back to the Browns, was with the Browns when they moved to Baltimore, and then finished his career in 1956 with Kansas City.

This was a victory for the Tigers.

SUGAR AND SAUL

On May 15, 1951, the Tigers traded Saul Rogovin to the Chicago White Sox in exchange for Bob "Sugar" Cain. Bob won 11 games and lost 10 for the Tigers the 1951 season and he went on to the Browns and then back to the White Sox before completing his career in 1954. Bob was well remembered as the pitcher who pitched against Eddie Gaedel, the midget that Bill Veeck sent up to bat in 1951.

Rogovin won 11 and lost seven for the White Sox in 1951 and stayed with them until 1955 when he went to Baltimore and then went over to the Phillies. He had an eight-year career.

The White Sox came out on top.

A NOD TO THE BROWNS

A seven-player trade was made with the St. Louis Browns before the 1952 season. The Tigers received first baseman Ben Taylor, catcher Matt Batts, pitcher Dick Littlefield, and outfielder Cliff Mapes. In exchange they sent first baseman Dick Kryhoski and pitchers Bob Cain and Gene Bearden to the Browns.

Cain and Kryhoski had pretty good years so St. Louis gets the nod on this one.

A WIN-WIN PROPOSITION

George Kell figured in one of the biggest trades the Tigers ever made when the Tigers traded him to Boston in the middle of 1952, along with Hoot Evers, Johnny Lipon and Dizzy Trout. In exchange the Tigers received Walt Dropo, Freddie Hatfield, Don Lenhardt, Johnny Pesky, and Bill Wight. This was one of the largest trades the Tigers ever made.

All the ballplayers involved were good ones and the trade benefitted both teams.

TIE WITH THE BROWNS

In August 1952 the Tigers sent Dick Littlefield, Marlin Stuart, Don Lenhardt and Vic Wertz to the St. Louis Browns in exchange for Jim Delsing, Ned Garver, Dave Madison and Bill Black. Wertz and Garver were the principals in this deal. Ned pitched four years for the Tigers, winning 14 games in 1954 when the Tigers had a very poor ball club. He wound up his career in 1961 with the Los Angeles Angels.

Vic Wertz went on to play with the Browns and moved with them to Baltimore in 1954 and then went to Cleveland in the same year. He later played with the Boston Red Sox, came back again with the Tigers, and wound up his career in 1963 with the Minnesota Twins. He had a lifetime batting average of .277 with 266 home runs.

Call this one a draw.

THIS DEAL WAS A BROWN-OUT

On December 4, 1952, the Tigers traded Virgil Trucks, Hal White and Johnny Groth to St. Louis and received in exchange Owen Friend, Bob Nieman and J. W. Porter. Trucks went to the White Sox during the season and won 20 games and lost 10. He came back to Detroit in 1955 in another trade for Bubba Phillips. Hal White won 6 and lost 5 in 1953 and completed his career in 1954 without winning or losing a game. Johnny Groth played seven more years. He hit .253 with St. Louis in 1953 and then went to Chicago, Washington, and Kansas City before coming back to the Tigers.

Owen Friend played a half season with the Tigers. Bob Nieman played two years with Detroit and hit .281 and .263. J. W. Porter played part-time with the Tigers for three seasons.

Neither team did too well on this trade.

A BIG ONE WITH CLEVELAND

Steve Gromek, Ray Boone, Al Aber and Dick Weik came to the Tigers in a big deal with Cleveland on June 15, 1953. The Tigers gave up Art Houtteman, Joe Ginsberg, Owen Friend, and Bill Wight. Gromek had several good years with the Tigers, winning 18 games in 1954. Boone became the regular third baseman and tied for the American League leadership in runs batted in with 116 in 1955 with Jackie Jensen of the Boston Red Sox. Aber spent almost five successful years with the Tigers as a relief pitcher. Weik pitched during 1953 and 1954 for the Tigers.

Art Houtteman went on to pitch for Cleveland from 1953 to 1956. In 1957 he went to Baltimore where he concluded his career. He won 15 games for the Indians in 1954 when they won the American League pennant. Owen Friend completed the season with the Indians and played two more years in the major leagues. Bill Wight, who had a great pickoff move, spent the balance of the season with the Indians, winning two and losing one. He played in the majors for four more seasons. And Joe Ginsberg went on to play 10 more years in the big leagues with the Indians, Athletics, Orioles, White Sox, Red Sox, and finally wound up as a catcher for the New York Mets.

Advantage Detroit.

BACKSTOP FOR BACKSTOP

On May 29, 1954, the Tigers traded Matt Batts to Chicago White Sox for Red Wilson. Matt finished the season with the White Sox and then went to the Reds for 1955 and 1956 playing in only 29 games in those two seasons and he played in 55 games with the White Sox in 1954 after he was traded by the Tigers.

Red Wilson stayed with the Tigers until the middle of the 1960 season when he went to Cleveland. Red had a lifetime batting average of .258 and in 1958 with the Tigers he hit .299.

This was a victory for the Tigers in the trade department.

EVEN-STEVEN

On December 6, 1954, the Tigers secured the services of Ferris Fain, Leo Cristante and Jack Phillips. They made a trade with the Chicago White Sox and gave up Ted Gray, Bob Nieman and Walt Dropo. Fain, who had been the batting champion in 1951 and 1952, played only 58 games for the Tigers then went on to Cleveland. Jack Phillips played parts of three seasons with the Tigers at first base. Leo Cristante, a Detroit boy, appeared in 20 games in 1955 with the Tigers, was not credited with a win and was charged with one defeat.

Dropo played more than three seasons with the White Sox. Teddy Gray, hampered by a sore arm, pitched for the White Sox, the Indians, the Yankees and Baltimore, all in 1955, winning one and losing two. Bob Nieman played 99 games with the White Sox in 1955 and went on to Baltimore in 1956. He later went to the St. Louis Cardinals, the Cleveland Indians and the San Francisco Giants.

Neither team gained nor lost much with this trade.

BEST FOR CHICAGO

On June 14, 1957, the Chicago White Sox sent Dave Philley to Detroit in exchange for Earl Torgeson. Philley played the balance of the season with Detroit, being used mainly as a pinch-hitter and hitting .418. He was sold to the Phillies at the end of the year while Torgeson played for the Sox until 1961.

Give the edge to Chicago.

Trades ———————————————————————— 289

QUANTITY GALORE

On November 20, 1957, the Tigers made the biggest deal in their history, receiving six players from Kansas City in exchange for seven. The Tigers received Billy Martin, Gus Zernial, Tom Morgon, Lou Skizas, Tim Thompson and Mickey McDermott. In exchange, they sent to Kansas City Bill Tuttle, Jim Small, Duke Maas, John Tsitouris, Frank House, Kent Hadley and Jim McManus.

None of the six Tigers received in this deal distinguished themself playing for Detroit. Billy Martin played for Detroit for only one year and hit .255. Gus Zernial played part-time for two years. Lou Skizas played briefly, hit only .242 and Tim Thompson played in four games. Mickey McDermott did not win nor lose a game and Tom Morgan won six and lost 11 in three seasons.

Bill Tuttle played in 25 games for Kansas City for more than three seasons before being traded again to Minnesota. Jimmy Small appeared in only two games for Kansas City and then retired from baseball. Frank House played two seasons for Kansas City before going to the Cincinnati Reds and then coming back to Detroit in 1961. Kent Hadley played 113 games in 1959 and then went to the Yankees where he finished his career in 1960. Jim McManus played in only five games for Kansas City in 1960 and didn't play in any in 1958 or 1959. Duke Maas appeared in 10 games for Kansas City, winning four and losing five before being traded again to the New York Yankees. John Tsitouris was with Kansas City for three years, won four and lost five before going to Cincinnati where he played for seven years.

There was a lot of volume in this trade but not too much quality.

DETROIT GETS HANK & JIM

Hank Aguirre and Jim Hegan came to the Tigers from Cleveland in February 1958 in a trade for Hal Woodeshick and J. W. Porter. Hank had several good years with the Tigers leading the league in 1962 with a 2.21 e.r.a. He won 16 ball games that year. He stayed with the Tigers through 1967. Jim Hegan played half the 1958 season with the Tigers and then went to the Phillies.

J. W. Porter spent two seasons in the major leagues after leaving Detroit, batting only .200 in 1958 and .223 in 1959. Woodeshick pitched for Cleveland in 1958; later went to Washington; came back to Detroit; then went to Houston and to the St. Louis Cardinals.

Detroit got the best of this deal.

MOSSI MADE IT GOOD

On November 20, 1958, the Tigers secured Don Mossi, Ray Narleski and Ossie Alvarez from the Cleveland Indians in exchange for Billy Martin and Al Cicotte. Mossi was an excellent pitcher for the Tigers for five seasons. He won 17 games in 1959, 15 in 1961. He finished his career in 1965 with Kansas City. Narleski only pitched one year for the Tigers, won four and lost

12. Alvarez only played eight games for the Tigers and that was the end of his major league career.

Cicotte pitched three more years in the major leagues and ended his career in 1962. Billy Martin, who had played one year with the Tigers, then went on to play with Cleveland one year, Cincinnati a year and Milwaukee and Minnesota completing his 11-year career at the end of 1961.

The savvy Mossi gave the Tigers the better of the trade.

A BIG ONE WITH THE SENATORS

In December 1958, the Tigers got Eddie Yost, Rocky Bridges, and Neil Chrisley from the Washington Senators in a straight trade for Reno Bertoia, Ron Samford and Jimmy Delsing. Yost was a regular third baseman for the Tigers for two seasons. He was near the end of his career when he came to the Tigers. He played 18 years in the big leagues and he finished his last two years with the Los Angeles Angels. Bridges played one season as the regular Tiger shortstop before going on to Cleveland. Chrisley played two years for the Tigers before going on to the Milwaukee Braves. He failed to distinguish himself and wound up his five-year career in the major leagues in 1981 with a lifetime batting average of .210.

Reno went on to play two years with Washington, then went with the club when they moved to Minnesota, later played with Kansas City, and then came back to Detroit. He wound up his 10-year major league career with a .244 batting average. Samford played one season with Washington after the trade and finished his major league career in 1959 with a .219 lifetime average. Delsing wound up his 10-year major league career with Kansas City in 1960.

The play of Eddie Yost gave the Tigers the advantage of this trade.

A REAL BAD ONE

In March of 1959, the Cleveland Indians traded Larry Doby to Detroit for Tito Francona. Doby only lasted 18 games with Detroit while Francona played six years with Cleveland and six more in the majors afterward.

Quite a disappointment for Detroit and it was super for the Indians.

EVEN WITH THE RED SOX

May 2, 1959, the Tigers traded Billy Hoeft to the Boston Red Sox in exchange for Dave Sisler and Ted Lepcio. Billy went on to pitch eight more years in the big leagues. He was a good pitcher for Boston and then Baltimore, San Francisco, Milwaukee, Chicago Cubs and back again to San Francisco.

Dave Sisler was an excellent relief pitcher for the Tigers in 1959 and 1960. Lepcio finished up the 1959 season with the Tigers and then went to the Phillies, the White Sox and the Twins.

Score this trade about even.

A REAL DANDY

Unquestionably, the greatest trade in Detroit Tiger history was made on April 12, 1960 when the Tigers secured the services of Norm Cash from the Chicago White Sox in exchange for Steve Demeter. Cash played for the Tigers for 15 years, had a lifetime batting average of .271, and hit 377 home runs (all but four of them hit for Detroit). He led the American League in batting with a .361 average the year after he came to Detroit from Cleveland.

Steve Demeter played four games for Cleveland in 1960 and spent the rest of his baseball playing career in the minor leagues.

This was one of the great trades of all time for any club, and for the Tigers it was the best they ever made.

A HAMBURGER FOR A STEAK, SAID THE ROCK

On April 17, 1960, the baseball world was astounded by a trade by the Detroit Tigers and the Cleveland Indians. The Tigers traded batting champion Harvey Kuenn for Rocky Colavito. Colavito had been the home run champion in 1959. There was considerable speculation as to which team got the better of the deal, but Harvey played only one year with the Cleveland Indians and hit .308; Colavito spent four seasons with the Tigers before moving on to Kansas City.

The edge? The Tigers.

THERE WILL NEVER BE ANOTHER LIKE THIS

The weirdest trade in Tiger history was the one where the Tigers and the Cleveland Indians traded managers. In 1960 Frank Lane was the general manager of the Cleveland Indians and he had Joe Gordon as his manager. The Tigers field manager was Jimmy Dykes and their general manager was Bill Dewitt.

Dewitt and Lane loved to make deals. They got together and decided it would be a great deal to trade managers. So in August of 1960, Gordon came to Detroit and Dykes went to Cleveland. Gordon quit at the end of the season and later managed Kansas City. Dykes, who managed just about everybody at one time or other, continued managing through 1961.

Neither club gained anything but publicity from this deal.

A GREAT DEAL

On December 7, 1960, the Tigers traded Frank Bolling and Neil Chrisley to the Milwaukee Braves in exchange for Billy Bruton, Terry Fox, Dick Brown and Chuck Cottier. Bolling played five years for the Braves. Chrisley played 10 games for Milwaukee and completed his career there in 1961.

Bruton played four years for the Tigers in center field and is one of the finest defensive center fielders of the modern era. Fox was an excellent relief pitcher for the Tigers for five seasons. Dick Brown caught for the Tigers for two seasons before going to Baltimore. Chuck Cottier played only 10 games for the Tigers before going to Washington for five more years. This was another good trade for the Tigers.

SO LONG, PAW-PAW

Charlie Maxwell was one of the all-time favorite Tiger players. He came from Paw Paw, Michigan, and had a penchant for hitting home runs on Sunday. He hit 148 during his major league career and about one-fourth of those came on the Sabbath.

On June 25, 1962, Tiger fans were saddened to hear that Charlie was traded to Chicago for Bob Farley. Charlie only played another year or two, but it was a sad thing for fans who really appreciated this outfielder. And Farley never did anything for the Tigers.

BOROS FOR ANDERSON

In November 1962, the Tigers traded Steve Boros to the Chicago Cubs in exchange for Bob Anderson. Steve played with the Cubs in 1963 and with the Cincinnati Reds in 1964 and 1965. Anderson won three games and lost one in 1963 with the Tigers and that was the end of his major league career.

No blood.

LUMPE MADE IT A GOOD DEAL

November 18, 1963, the Tigers traded Rocky Colavito, Bob Anderson, and $50,000 to the Kansas City ball club in exchange for Jerry Lumpe, Ed Rakow and Dave Wickersham. Colavito played the 1964 season for Kansas City and then moved back again to the Cleveland Indians from whence he had come. Lumpe was the Tigers' regular second baseman for the next three seasons and played part of 1967. He was a good one. Rakow pitched for the Tigers in 1964 and won eight and lost nine. Wickersham won 19 games in 1964 and pitched four more seasons, never winning more than nine.

Give the nod to the Tigers.

WE LOSE BUNNING

In December 1963, the Tigers traded Jim Bunning and Gus Triandos to the Phillies for Don Demeter and Jack Hamilton. Demeter played for only two full years with the Bengals; Hamilton pitched for the Tigers in parts of two years, winning one game and losing two.

Bunning spent a total of 17 years in the majors. He pitched for the Phillies for four years, went to Pittsburgh, Los Angeles, and back again to the Phillies. He won 20 games for Detroit in 1957, on four other occasions he won 19, and three others he won 17. He won a total of 224 games and lost 184, winning 118 in the American League and 106 in the National League.

He pitched a perfect game when he was with the Phillies, and as the father of seven children, it was only proper that he pitched it on Father's Day. That was a great trade, but not for Detroit.

HERE COMES THE DUKE

On June 14, 1966, the Tigers traded Julio Navarro and Don Demeter to Boston for Earl (Duke) Wilson and Joe Christopher. Christopher never played for the Tigers but Earl Wilson went on to pitch for the Tigers for five years. He won 18 games in 1966, 13 of them for the Tigers and five for the Boston Red Sox, and he was a 22-game winner in 1967. In addition to being a good pitcher, Earl was a very good hitter. He hit 35 home runs during his major league career.

Navarro won only seven ball games during a six-year career in the major leagues. Demeter finished the 1966 season with the Red Sox and was traded in 1967 to Cleveland, where he finished his major league career. In 11 years he had a lifetime average of .265.

This trade was surely one of Detroit's better ones.

TRIXIE FOR THE VULTURE

Dick Tracewski, it seems, has been with the Tigers forever but that is not true. He came to the Tigers in December 1965 in a straight trade with the Dodgers for Phil "The Vulture" Regan. Regan had been with the Tigers for six seasons and had won 15 games back in 1963. He went to Los Angeles in the trade for Tracewski, and in his first year he won 14 and lost 1, all in relief. He became one of the better relief pitchers in the majors and pitched in the majors for 13 years.

On the field, the Dodgers came out best, but Tracewski has been with the Tigers since the trade. He retired after the 1969 season as a player and has been a coach ever since. Dick was a good utility infielder and a good man to have around when we got him. He was with the club in the 1968 World Series.

PRICE IS RIGHT

The Tigers purchased the contract of Jim Price from the Pittsburgh Pirates before the 1967 season. Jim then played five years as a back-up catcher to Bill Freehan. He had a .214 lifetime batting average. He was with the Tigers in the 1968 World Series.

A good move for Detroit.

HEAVY LUMBER COMES TO DETROIT

Eddie Mathews was one of the great sluggers of all time, finishing a 17-year career in the majors with 512 home runs. He came to the Tigers in a straight trade for Fred Gladding in 1967. Gladding was a pitcher and possibly the worst hitter of all time (although Hank Aguirre also has a good case). Fred was with the Tigers before the days of the designated hitter when pitchers batted. He went to bat 40 times during his career with the Tigers and never got a hit. When he went to Houston he went to bat 23 times more and got one hit. His batting average for his 13 years in the majors was .016. Fred pitched with the Houston ball club from 1968 through 1973.

Mathews was a great help to the Tigers in winning the pennant in 1968, his final year as a player in professional baseball.

Gladding did a good job for Houston, and though Mathews helped the Tigers, score this one for Houston.

WE COULD HAVE USED JOE

The Tigers got Joe Niekro in December 1969 in a trade with San Diego for Pat Dobson and Dave Campbell. Joe stayed with the Tigers for three years and then was sold to Atlanta. He played with Atlanta, Houston, New York Yankees and Minnesota Twins for almost 20 years after that.

Neither Campbell nor Dobson put together consistent good years for the Tigers, and it was a shame that the club let Niekro go.

A DRAW

In December 1969, the Tigers picked up Dalton Jones for Tommy Matchick. Matchick played three more years with Kansas City, Boston, Milwaukee and Baltimore, while Jones played three years with the Tigers and then finished up with Texas.

Nobody gained too much nor lost too much.

A GREAT ONE FOR DETROIT

After the 1970 season, just before the World Series, the Tigers astonished the baseball world by making a deal with the Washington Senators. They traded the once-great Denny McLain along with Don Wert, Elliott Maddox, and Norm McRae. The Tigers received Aurelio Rodriguez, Jim Hannan, Joe Coleman and Eddie Brinkman.

McLain went on to win 10 games and lose 22 for Washington in 1971. Then he went to Oakland and Atlanta and finished his career in 1972. Wert, who had been the Tiger regular third baseman since 1963, played in only 20 games for Washington in 1971 before retiring from major league baseball.

Joe Coleman was a fine pitcher for the Tigers for five seasons, twice winning 20 games or more. Rodriguez was the third baseman for the Tigers for nine seasons and a mighty good one. Eddie Brinkman played shortstop for the Tigers for four years.

The Tigers surely got the best of this deal by a wide margin.

Trades 295

UNFILLED HOPES

Bill Zepp came to the Tigers from Minnesota in the 1971 season. The stylish hurler had won nine games and lost four for the Twins the year before, and he won one game and lost one for the Tigers in 1971. His career was shortened because of the same arm trouble that Tommy John later overcame with pioneering surgery. Bill came to the Tigers in a straight trade for Bob Adams and a minor leaguer named Art Clifford.

SHORT BUT SWEET

Jim Perry came to the Tigers in March of 1973 from the Minnesota Twins in exchange for Dan Fife, a former University of Michigan pitcher, and a lot of cash. Fife pitched for the Twins for two years, appearing in 14 games, winning three and losing two, while Jim Perry won 14 games and lost 13 for the Tigers in 1973. Perry finished his major league career with Oakland in 1975. He pitched for 17 years in the big leagues and won 215 games.

SO LONG, DICK—YOU WERE A DANDY

Dick McAuliffe played with the Tigers from 1960 through the 1973 season. After that season he was traded to the Boston Red Sox in exchange for outfielder Ben Oglivie. Dick, one of the better second basemen the Tigers ever had, was nearing the end of his career. He played only 100 games for Boston in 1974 and finished the next season with just seven games.

On the other hand, Oglivie played the outfield for the Tigers for four years and then went to Milwaukee where he played for another nine years.

Detroit got the best of this one.

WOODY WAS GREAT

Terry Humphrey came to the Tigers from Montreal at the end of the 1974 season along with Tom Walker in exchange for Woody Fryman. Fryman came to Detroit during the 1972 season and won 10 and lost three during the rest of that season for the Tigers. He was a most valuable addition in their winning the Eastern Division Championship.

MICKEY FOR RUSTY

In December 1975 the Tigers traded Mickey Lolich and Billy Baldwin to the New York Mets in exchange for Rusty Staub and Bill Laxton. Actually, it was really a deal for Lolich for Staub. Both Lolich and Staub had great careers. Mickey won 20 games or more twice with the Tigers, and he won 217 in his 16-year career. Staub was a .279 hitter in his 23-year career in the majors. Staub was a great pure hitter and an excellent clutch hitter. But who in Detroit will ever forget Mickey Lolich in the 1968 World Series?

Both players were near the end of their careers—give it a draw.

A DEAL WITH THE ASTROS

On December 6, 1975, the Tigers traded Leon Roberts, Terry Humphrey, Gene Pentz and Mark Lemongello to Houston in exchange for Dave Roberts, Milt May and Jim Crawford. Dave Roberts had a good year with the Tigers in 1976, winning 16 and losing 17. He was traded away from Detroit to the Cubs in 1977. Jim Crawford spent three years with the Tigers and won 10 and lost 19 in those three years. Milt May was the regular catcher for the Tigers from 1976 to the middle of 1979.

Leon Roberts hit .289 for Houston in 1976 and then he played with Houston again in 1977; in 1978 he went to Seattle, then to Texas, Toronto and Kansas City. Terry Humphrey had played in only 18 games for the Tigers in 1975. He never played a game for Houston, having been traded by the Astros to California for the 1976 season. Gene Pentz pitched three years for Houston and won eight and lost five.

The Tigers got the best of that deal.

FAREWELL TO WILLIE

Willie Horton was one of the all-time sluggers for the Tigers. He played 18 years in the major leagues and hit 325 home runs. He was traded to Texas in 1977 for Steve Foucault. Willie was nearing the end of his career and had lost power.

Foucault won seven games for the Tigers in 1977. In 1978 he went to Kansas City.

This trade is graded a tie.

WE GOOFED

In December of 1977, the Tigers obtained Jim Slaton and Rich Folkers from Milwaukee in return for Ben Oglivie. Folkers never pitched for the Tigers and Jim Slaton won 17 games and lost 11 for the Tigers in the 1978 season, declared himself a free agent and went back to the Milwaukee Braves where he pitched through 1983. He went to California in 1984 and later came back to the Tigers in 1986 for a brief session.

Oglivie played nine years for the Braves, was an outstanding hitter, and wound up his career in 1986.

This was truly a bad trade for the Tigers.

LOPEZ DID THE JOB

One of the better trades the Tigers have ever made was in securing the services of Aurelio Lopez and Jerry Morales from the St. Louis Cardinals in December 1978. The Tigers gave up Bob Sykes, a left-handed pitcher and a minor leaguer named Jack Murphy (who never did play in the big leagues). Sykes won 12 games and lost 13 in three years with the Cardinals, while Lopez was a great relief pitcher for the Tigers for seven years.

Truly, a plus for the Tigers.

HEBNER COMES TO TOWN

Before the 1979 season, the Tigers gave up Jerry Morales and Phil Mankowski to the New York Mets in exchange for Richie Hebner. Morales played one year for the Tigers, hit .211, then went on and played four more years in the majors. Phil Mankowski played 8 games in 1980 and then 13 in 1982. Hebner batted .290 for the Tigers in 1980 and in 1981 he batted .226 before going to Pittsburgh in 1982.
Credit this one to the Tigers.

THE CHAMP WAS A CHAMP

On May 25, 1979, the Tigers made a deal with the Cincinnati Reds, obtaining the services of Champ Summers in exchange for pitcher Sheldon Burnside. Champ only played three years with the Tigers, 1979 through 1981, but was an extremely popular player and delivered many a clutch hit. He had 21 home runs in 1979 and 17 in 1980. He dropped off to three in 1981.

Burnside pitched in only seven games for the Cincinnati Reds and gained one victory and no defeats.

Clearly, this was a great trade for the Tigers.
Ron LeFlore was traded to Montreal in December 1979 in exchange for Don Schatzeder. LeFlore was nearing the end of his nine-year career in the majors and played only one season with Montreal and then went to the White Sox for two years.

Schatzeder won 11 games and lost 13 for the Tigers in 1980, and in 1981 he won six and lost eight. He went on to pitch in the National League, first to San Francisco, then Montreal. Neither team gained nor lost too much from this deal.

ROOFTOP JASON IS SWAPPED

On May 27, 1980, the Tigers traded Jason Thompson to California in exchange for Al Cowens. Jason spent seven more years in the big leagues, one with California, five with Pittsburgh, and one with Montreal. Cowens played for the Tigers for two seasons, then went to Seattle for five.

Neither player stayed with their selected team long enough to make this trade a winner.

SAUCED UP

After the 1980 season the Tigers traded shortstop Mark Wagner to the Texas Rangers in exchange for pitcher Kevin Saucier. Kevin pitched for the Tigers in 1981 and 1982. He won 15 games and lost 11 in his five-year major league career. Mark played three years for Texas and one for Oakland after leaving Detroit.

A LEMON, THIS

On November 27, 1981, the Tigers traded outfielder Steve Kemp to the Chicago White Sox in exchange for outfielder Chet Lemon. Steve played with the White Sox for one year, then went to the Yankees for two years and Pittsburgh for two years. Lemon was still with the Tigers in 1990.

Another win for the Tiger traders.

LARRY HELPED

December 9, 1981, the Tigers secured the services of Larry Herndon from the San Francisco Giants in exchange for Mike Chris and Dan Schatzeder. Larry played for eight seasons for the Tigers, hit a very valuable home run to defeat Toronto in the final game of the season in 1987 as the Tigers won the Eastern Division Championship that day.

Chris pitched parts of two innings with San Francisco and was charged with two defeats and no victories. He appeared in 16 ball games in the two seasons. Schatzeder was in 13 games for San Francisco in 1982, then went to Montreal, the Phillies, and Minnesota.

Truly, the Tigers got the best of this deal.

GO WEST, CHAMP

On March 4, 1982, the Tigers completed a deal with the San Francisco Giants. They traded Champ Summers for Enos Cabell. Champ spent three years playing part-time for San Francisco and then one year with San Diego. Cabell was a regular first baseman for the Tigers in 1982 and 1983, batting .261 in 1982 and .311 in 1983. He left the Tigers after the 1983 season as a free agent and went to Houston.

This was a good deal for the Tigers.

GOOD GRUBB FOR US

Johnny Grubb came to the Tigers from Texas in a straight trade for Dave Tobik just before the 1983 season started. John played with the Tigers for five years and contributed greatly to the Tiger success in 1984 when they won the World Championship. Dave pitched for Texas 1983 and 1984 and finished his career in 1985 with Seattle. He won four games and lost seven during his career with Texas and Seattle.

Clearly, this was a good trade for the Tigers.

A DANDY

In March of 1984, the Tigers secured Dave Bergman and Guillermo Hernandez. The Tigers gave up Glenn Wilson and John B. Wockenfuss. Hernandez saved 32 games for the Tigers in the 1984 season, 31 in 1985, and 24 in 1986 and became one of the great relief pitchers of our time. Bergman remained a steady first baseman through the 1990 season.

Wockenfuss played two years for Philadelphia and Glenn Wilson had several good years in the National League. However, the deal was all Detroit's.

It was one of the great all-time deals for the Tigers.

ANOTHER DANDY

On June 20, 1985, the Tigers secured the services of Frank Tanana from the Texas Rangers in exchange for Duane James. Frank has been a good asset since reporting to the Tigers.

A great trade for Detroit.

STILL WAITING

On October 7, 1905, the Tigers traded Juan Berenguer, Scott Medvin and Bob Melvin to San Francisco for Matt Nokes, Dave LaPoint and Eric King.

As most of these players are still active, the jury is still out.

HEATH MADE IT FOR DETROIT

On August 10, 1986, the Tigers sent first baseman Mike Laga and pitcher Ken Hill to the Cardinals in exchange for catcher Mike Heath. Heath has done a good job and made it a good deal for the Tigers.

A TRADE THAT WON A CHAMPIONSHIP

Doyle Alexander came to the Tigers in a trade for John Smoltz in 1987. He won nine games and lost none during the balance of the season. Without Alexander the Tigers would never have won the East Division Championship that year.

Whatever happens in the future for young Smoltz, who is now with Atlanta and doing an excellent job, it was a tremendous trade for the Tigers.

KNIGHT TIME

In February of 1988 the Tigers traded Mark Thurmond to Baltimore for Ray Knight. Ray was near the end of his career and only played the 1988 season. Thurmond went on to Baltimore for the 1988 and 1989 seasons. There wasn't much to choose on this trade.

THE RETURN OF DANNY BOY

The Tigers acquired Gary Pettis from California before the 1988 season. Gary is one of the best defensive outfielders baseball has ever seen—a brilliant centerfielder. He was not much of a hitter, but his fielding more than made up for his lack of power at the plate. The Tigers traded Dan Petry, who had been troubled with arm problems for the past two years.

The Tigers got the better of the deal but it's quite possible that Petry could come back.

FRED LYNN FIASCO

At the end of August 1988, the Tigers secured from Baltimore the services of Fred Lynn. In exchange they gave Baltimore three minor leaguers. At the time, many people thought this would be the difference between winning and losing the divisional title. Up to that time the Tigers were in the race. But Lynn batted .222 for the 27 games he played in for the Tigers in 1988 and .241 in the 1989 season. Lynn, who had been one of the finer hitters in the majors in his 14 years prior to coming to Detroit, delivered only a couple clutch blows for the Tigers.

This deal didn't help the Tigers at all.

JONES FOR SHERIDAN

In the summer of 1989 the Tigers traded Pat Sheridan to San Francisco in exchange for Tracy Jones. Neither Sheridan nor Jones distinguished themselves much after the trade.

MINOR TRADES

In the past three or four years the Tigers have made quite a few trades that were not of major importance, including:

- The California Angels and Detroit Tigers made a deal in 1987 where California received Dan Petry in exchange for Gary Pettis. After the 1989 season Pettis became a free agent and went to Texas, and Petry came back to Detroit also as a free agent to turn in some surprisingly strong outings.

- In February 1988 the Tigers secured the services of Ray Knight in exchange for Mike Thurmond. The Tigers got Thurmond in a trade with Dave LaPoint with the New York Yankees on July 9, 1986.

- In October 1988 the Tigers traded Walt Terrell to San Diego. Terrell later went to the New York Yankees, Pittsburgh Pirates, and came back to Detroit in the summer of 1990 on waivers.

- On March 3, 1989 the Tigers traded the popular Tommy Brookens to New York for Charlie Hudson, the promising Eric King to the White Sox for Ken Williams, and Luis Salazar to San Diego for Mike Brumley.

- On July 28, 1989 the Tigers traded Keith Moreland to Baltimore for Brian DuBois.

- Detroit secured the services of Larry Sheets on January 10, 1990 from Baltimore in exchange for Mark Brumley, which could pan out for the Tigers.

- In the summer of 1990 the Tigers traded Tracy Jones to Seattle for Darnell Coles. Previously the Tigers had obtained Jim Morrison in exchange for Darnell Coles and Morris Madden on August 9, 1987.

- In 1990, Detroit traded once-promising Matt Nokes to the Yankees for Clay Parker and Lance McCullers.

Only time will prove the merits of these deals in Tiger history.

STORIES

Baseball has a more colorful history than any other American sport. That's because since its first day, baseball has been filled with colorful characters. Many of them wore the old English "D" of the Tigers or displayed their talents on teams visiting the corner of Michigan and Trumbull.

In 1989, when the Tigers were having so much difficulty getting runs across the plate, Hoot Evers, who was scouting in Texas, called Sparky Anderson. Hoot said, "I have just seen the greatest young pitcher I have ever seen. He struck out 27 batters, did not allow a hit, and did not walk a man. In fact, only one man even got a foul ball off him. We should sign this kid right away." Sparky answered quickly. "The heck with the pitcher. Get me the guy who got the foul ball."

⚾ ⚾ ⚾

Alan Trammell was in a Catholic church just before the fifth game of the World Series against the San Diego Padres. Trammell saw Dick Williams, the manager of the Padres, come in and light four candles. When Trammell got to Tiger Stadium, he went in and told Sparky Anderson. Sparky immediately changed back into his street clothes, took a taxicab down to Saint Aloysius Church, and lit eight candles. He told Trammell, "If Williams thinks he can get lucky with the Lord by lighting four candles, I'm going to light twice as many." The final score of the game was 8 to 4.

⚾ ⚾ ⚾

Everybody knows that Margaret Mitchell wrote *Gone With the Wind*, but few know that her paperboy was Ernie Harwell.

⚾ ⚾ ⚾

The Chicago White Sox had a pitcher back in the twenties named Sloppy Thurston. Sloppy won 20 games for the White Sox one season, although the White Sox finished last. When Sloppy got his contract for the next season, there was no raise in it. He immediately contacted the White Sox and said, "Hey, I won 20 games. I think I deserve a raise." The answer was, "Sloppy, we could have finished last without you."

⚾ ⚾ ⚾

Joe Engle owned and ran the Chattanooga ball club in the minor leagues for many years. One year a rookie wrote to him and said, "pay me $3,000 a year or I'm out." Joe telegrammed back, "1, 2, 3, 4, 5, 6, 7, 8, 9, 10. You're out."

⚾ ⚾ ⚾

Some years back I put out a book called *Tiger Facts* and I was delighted to get an order for two copies from a library in Uppsala, Sweden. I immediately mailed them two copies and told all my friends about it. I was really proud of the fact that my book would be in a library in Sweden. I planned on going there someday. Two weeks later the books came back in the mail with a note: "We thought it was about the animal 'tiger'."

⚾ ⚾ ⚾

In 1945 the World Series opened in Detroit. After the first three games, the next four were played in Chicago. I was in the Army, stationed at Fort Sheridan, 25 miles outside the city of Chicago. For the Sunday game I took the train to Wrigley Field. I got off the train, wondering how I was going to get into the ball park. I didn't have much money so I walked around the park until I saw a group of servicemen who were Military Police. They were all going to be admitted to the ball park with the idea that they would be checking to see that the servicemen all behaved. I got in the middle of the group, and, sure enough, they took us all in.

When I got into the ball park I drifted away from the MPs and then wondered what I should do for the next three hours before the game. I didn't want anybody coming up to me and asking for my ticket. So I went into the latrine and stayed there for two hours. Eventually, I ventured out to the stadium and watched the Tigers beat the Sox.

⚾ ⚾ ⚾

I got out my old autograph book the other day. It goes back to the late twenties and early thirties. I saw some names in it that really brought back memories. Those were the days when the ball games all started at 3 p.m. and were over by 5 p.m. I used to wait for the players to come out and shake hands, and then get their autographs. In my book I have such Hall of Famers as Connie Mack, Bucky Harris, Chuck Klein, Al Simmons, Waite Hoyt, Heinie Manush, Walter Johnson, Sam Rice, Jimmie Foxx, Ted Lyons, Paul Waner, Rick Ferrell, Lloyd Waner, Earl Averill and, of course, Charlie Gehringer, among others.

Years later, when I went to work for the Tigers, one of my pleasant duties was to go into the Tiger clubhouse and Tiger dugout before a game and get autographs for youngsters. We'd also take in 13- or 14-year-old boys who had won a contest or had been chosen that day to be the honorary bat boy, and get the players' autographs. The Tigers were always very obliging and I enjoyed doing it very much.

I particularly remember Lynn Jones. Lynn was an outfielder with the Tigers in the Eighties and he would always find out the name of the boy I was bringing around to get autographs. Lynn would then come up and say to me, "Fred, is this Bill Bush? I heard he was coming down today and I sure did want to meet him. Bill, I'm Lynn Jones and it's certainly a pleasure." The boy would grin and it was beautiful. There are a lot of youngsters in this world today with a special place in their heart for Lynn Jones.

There are three important days in the year for me. One, of course, is Christmas; another is St. Patrick's Day; and the third, and probably the most important, is Opening Day. All in all, Opening Day is a wonderful day because hope springs eternal in the human breast. We think that Ray Oyler is going to be another Joe Cronin; that Tito Fuentes will be another Charlie Gehringer; that everything is going to be rosy.

Opening Day is a tradition in Detroit where we all feel that the Tigers will overcome despite any weaknesses they may have. The Tiger true believer is convinced the boys will win over all and bring the pennant back to Michigan and Trumbull where it belongs.

Many times Opening Day is rainy or snowy. That was the case back in 1962 when the Tigers played the Yankees. As we walked to our seats which happened to be right behind the Yankee dugout, the Yankee players were turned around looking at the stands and waving towels and saying, "Go home, go home, it's too cold to play." They were absolutely right. We won the game that day because Frank Lary, the pitcher, hit a key triple. But in running the bases, he hurt his leg. That threw off his stride and he strained his arm. It was the beginning of the end for Yankee killer Lary. That was probably the most costly Opening Day victory ever for Detroit.

While I worked for the Tigers, I grew to dread Opening Day because I got so many phone calls from friends, acquaintances, and people I barely knew who wanted tickets for Opening Day. It became impossible to satisfy them. At the same time these phone calls were coming in, I was selling season tickets and Red Willis, the ticket manager, had a rule that he wanted every potential season ticket buyer to have a look at their seats before they bought them for the season. This was a good rule because we knew the people would then be satisfied.

Then, I got a call from a bar owner in Ecorse. He said he couldn't come out but if I would come to Ecorse and show him on a map where the seats would be he would make the purchase. That day I was having lunch with John Mulroy from the University of Detroit. I called John and said we've got to go down to this bar. So John and I went to Ecorse and I bought a drink for the house. I showed the owner exactly where the seats would be and he said that was fine, he liked them very much. I told him the price and he said, "Wait a minute, I just want those for Opening Day, I don't want them for the season." John Mulroy looked at me and laughed like the dickens and said, "Fred, I'll never tell anyone." I said, "Go ahead and tell everyone, it's the funniest thing that's ever been pulled on me."

Once upon a time the Tigers had an outfielder who became more famous in the National League, but he had a brief cup of coffee with the Tigers. His name was Babe Herman. One day Babe was complaining to his teammates that his son was having trouble in school. The boy didn't seem to get along well and didn't seem to learn much. One of the players suggested that Babe get an encyclopedia. Babe answered, "Let him walk to school like I did, he doesn't need an encyclopedia."

Charlie Gehringer was probably the greatest second baseman who ever lived. He came from a little village outside of Lansing called Fowlerville. One day when Charlie was at the height of his career, a traveling salesman stopped at a restaurant in that village and had a cup of coffee. Not knowing the area, he asked the counterman where he was. The restaurant owner said to him, "You're in Fowlerville." The salesman said, "Oh, this is where Charlie Gehringer is from." The owner said, "No, he's always tried to pass himself off as a city boy but he's actually from a farm three miles out."

Stories

In the late Twenties there were two prospects in Hattiesburg, Mississippi. Their names were Gerald and Harvey Walker and they both had great promise to be future major leaguers, which they did become. One day a Yankee scout came to Mrs. Walker and made an offer to sign both of the ballplayers. It was a much more generous offer than she had had before, but refused it and said her boys would sign with the Tigers. "I don't want anything to do with those Yankees," she said. "I'm a southerner and to me all Yankees are poison."

Around 1930 a young fellow came up to the Tigers by the name of Parker. His nickname was "Salty." The first day Salty joined the Tigers there was a notice on the bulletin board that there was going to be a party and all Tigers were invited. Chevrolet was going to throw a dinner and everyone who could make it was expected to come. Only four of them showed up—including Salty Parker. All the players who attended the party received brand new automobiles.

Many years ago we had an infielder named Frank Sigafoos. Frank didn't play too long in the big leagues but one day when the Tigers were in St. Louis, Sigafoos hit the ball into the left field stand for a home run. As he rounded third and came into home plate with a big smile on his face, the umpire greeted him with, "Sorry, Sigafoos, you'll have to bat over again. The pitcher balked just before he threw the pitch that you hit into the stands." The ruling in those days was that he had to pitch again. Sigafoos never got another home run. He died a few years back and he went to his grave never having hit a home run that made it into the record books.

Freddie Hutchinson was a great pitcher for the Tigers. He also later managed Detroit, the St. Louis Cardinals and the Cincinnati Reds. Hutch was known for his fiery temper.

In those days the Cincinnati Reds were playing their home games every afternoon and the heat was terrific. It was 100 degrees in the shade and there wasn't much shade and all the players were complaining about it. Hutch turned to them one day and said, "The next player to complain about the heat is going to be fined $250." The next day Art Fowler was pitching for the Reds and as he came into the bench during the sixth inning, he sat down on the bench, put his arms out to his side, put his feet out and just as Hutch walked by, said, "My God, it's hot." Fowler looked up at Hutch and said, "And that's exactly the way I like it."

Many years back Harry Heilmann, remembered both as a great-hitting outfielder for the Tigers and as a great Tiger broadcaster, was playing right field. He was sitting in the hotel preparing to go to the ball park one Sunday afternoon when a minister walked up to him and said, "Son, you shouldn't be playing ball on Sunday, it's terrible. It's the Lord's day, you should keep it only for church and prayer." Harry looked at him for a moment and said, "Wait a minute, you do your work on Sunday." The minister said, "Yes, but I'm in the right field." Harry said, "That's where I play, and isn't that sun hell?"

Ferris Fain was a very good first baseman for the Philadelphia Athletics. He later played with the Tigers, but at this particular time he was playing first base for the A's and there were runners on first and third for the Tigers and the ball was hit to Fain. He looked around, as if he didn't know what to do, and finally threw the ball into center field. The runner who had been on first went all the way to third and the runner who had been on third scored. Connie Mack, then manager of the Athletics, admonished Fain in the clubhouse after the game, saying "Ferris, what in the world were you doing?" Ferris said, "What should I have done, stuck it in my pocket?" Mr. Mack said, "Ferris, that would have been better."

The Cleveland Indians had a ballplayer called Rube Lutzke who was right proud of his hitting. One day he got four hits in the game and when he came home his wife greeted him at the door and he said, "Boy, honey, I really can hit. I had four hits in four times at bat today. You should have seen them—two screamers right over third base, one went into the stands and was a home run, and the other was a double down the left-field line."

The next day they played a double-header. Rube didn't get a hit in eight times at bat. When he came home his wife greeted him at the door saying, "Well, how's my heavy-hitting hero today?" Rube said, "Look, you take care of the cooking and I'll take care of the hitting."

It was Ascension Thursday in 1927, a holiday for boys and girls in Roman Catholic schools. I had saved up my money and I had sixty-two cents: twelve cents for streetcar fare and fifty cents for the ball game and I went down to what was then Navin Field. It was the first ball game I had ever gone to by myself.

I was the first paid admission into the ball park. I paid my fifty cents and went out to the old center field bleachers. In a few minutes a ball was hit there during batting practice. Naturally, I got the ball as I was the only person around. A little while later I got talking to one of the ballplayers on the Chicago White Sox and I asked him for a ball and he gave it to me. He became an immediate hero to me. I found out later his name was Ted Lyons, one of the great pitchers of all time and now a member of baseball's Hall of Fame.

Just before the game was scheduled to start, it was the custom in those days for the outfielders to throw the last ball they received in practice into the stands. I looked at the Tiger's center fielder, whose name was Heinie Manush, and said "How about a ball, Heinie, there's no business here." Heinie looked at me and said, "Here's one for you kid, I hope business picks up." And he threw the ball right to me. Even though the Tigers got beat by Ted Blankenship 4-3, I went home that night as happy as a little boy could ever be, carrying my three baseballs. My Dad, who had been going to ball games all his life, just couldn't believe it. It convinced my mother that I was old enough to go down to the ball park by myself.

It was the second time that I had seen the Tigers play, the first time being the day after the season opened in 1927 when the Tigers lost to the St. Louis Browns 15-10. Mr. Zander, next door, had taken me to the ball game and I was very disappointed because we lost and also because I did not see a home run. My second ball game was the day Lindberg landed in Paris. I went down with my cousin Jack and my Uncle George, and the Tigers lost 4-3. They came around with megaphones around the seventh inning and announced that Lindberg had landed in Paris (there was no public address system in those days). I was annoyed that they disturbed the ball game even for a fraction of a minute with that announcement.

One ball game that I was lucky enough to see was one day when I skipped school. On May 31, 1927 the Tigers won 1-0. Johnny Neun had an unassisted triple play in the ninth inning. There were two runners on and the batter hit the ball to Neun who was playing first base. John grabbed the line drive and tagged the runner who had been on first and was now halfway between first and second; Nuen then raced to second base, beating the runner who had been on second and trying to go to third base.

The unassisted triple play didn't mean as much to me as the fact that I had finally seen the Tigers win a ball game. The pitcher for the Cleveland Indians that day was Garland Buckeye, who was a great big left-hander who played for five or six years in the major leagues, mainly with the Indians.

⚾ ⚾ ⚾

My first recollections of baseball were in the early twenties. We lived on Elmhurst Avenue, three doors from work. There were no radio broadcasts in those days and Walter Hallis and I would stand on the corner waiting for men to get off the bus. They would be carrying either a *Detroit News* or a *Times* (we had three newspapers in those days) with a headline about the results of the ball game. We would ask them as they got off the bus how the ball game came out. Our second question was always the same thing, "How many runs did Cobb make?" We didn't care about the score of the ball game, we didn't care who pitched, but how many runs did Cobb make—that was most important to us.

I went to every ball game I could from 1927 until the day I started working. I got admittance through my friend, by mentioning a Mr. O'Keefe who owned a nearby blind pig. Sometimes I would pick up papers along the field or in the stands to get a pass.

⚾ ⚾ ⚾

After the game I would always wait for the players, and some of them were very good to me. Heinie Manush would give me a ball every time he came to town. He was traded on December 13, 1927, to the St. Louis Browns and I cried when I heard the news. The Browns could come to Detroit each season for 11 games and I would see most of them, and after each game Heinie would give me a ball. Red Kress, who played for St. Louis, also gave me balls. Ted Lyons, who had become my hero when he gave me a ball during my first game, also gave me balls from time to time.

⚾ ⚾ ⚾

I had so many baseballs that when I got into high school at Holy Name Institute (which went out of business in 1934 when it merged with Catholic Central), Coach George Schoof made a deal with me. Those were depression days and the school didn't have much money. George was our baseball coach, our football coach, our basketball coach, our chemistry teacher, and he drove his car with a little trailer back and forth to the practice field—all for the magnificent sum of thirty dollars per week. Coach Schoof would buy baseballs from me for twenty-five cents, so I became the baseball supplier for the high school.

The Tigers weren't much in the late Twenties and in the early depression days. If they finished fourth it was a good year, and they didn't finish fourth very often. From 1927 to 1934 they finished fourth under the managership of George Moriarty in 1927. He left the club after the 1928 season and we had five dismal seasons under the managership of Bucky Harris.

In the fall of 1933 Frank Navin, the owner of the Tigers, wanted Babe Ruth, who was near the end of his career, to manage the club. He thought that Ruth would not only make a good manager, but he also would be a good drawing card and bring up the attendance at Navin Field. Navin contacted Ruth and Ruth said he was going to Japan and he would see him when he got back. Navin said, "I can't wait." He talked to H. G. Salsinger, the sports editor for the *Detroit News*, and Salsinger advised Navin to try to get hold of Mickey Cochrane, who was a great catcher for the Philadelphia Athletics. He was also the spark plug.

Connie Mack, who was the manager and owner of the Philadelphia Athletics, needed money badly. Navin didn't have much money but he went to Walter O. Briggs who had bought a half-interest in the Tigers. Briggs put up the $100,000 and Mickey Cochrane came to Detroit as the manager.

Who did Detroit send to Philadelphia for Mickey Cochrane? Of course, it was mainly the cash, but the Tigers also gave up an unknown catcher by the name of Johnny Pasek. John never caught for Philadelphia, but did catch four games for the Chicago White Sox.

In 1934, the Tigers were doomed to defeat in that seventh game, but in 1935 things were changed. Detroit went into the World Series with the Chicago Cubs. After four games the Tigers were ahead 3-1. The Cubs won the fifth game and came back to Detroit for the sixth game.

The ninth inning was one of the most dramatic of all time. Stan Hack, third baseman for the Chicago Cubs, opened the inning with a triple. He was the potential winning run and he stood there on third while Bill Jurges, Larry French and Augie Galan failed to produce the hit to bring him in. The score remained tied.

The Tigers came to bat in the ninth. Mickey Cochrane singled and went to second when Gehringer grounded to Phil Cavarretta at first. Cochrane raced home when Goose Goslin drove the ball over Billy Herman's head at second base. The Tigers were the world champions for the first time.

Catch All The Excitement LAKELAND Has To Offer!

You can be right in the center of everything Florida has to offer–in Lakeland! You'll only be a short drive to Walt Disney World/EPCOT, Sea World, Cypress Gardens, Busch Gardens and the famous Gulf Beaches of Florida. Lakeland is also the winter home of the World Champion Detroit Tigers. You can catch all the Florida excitement you want from Lakeland.

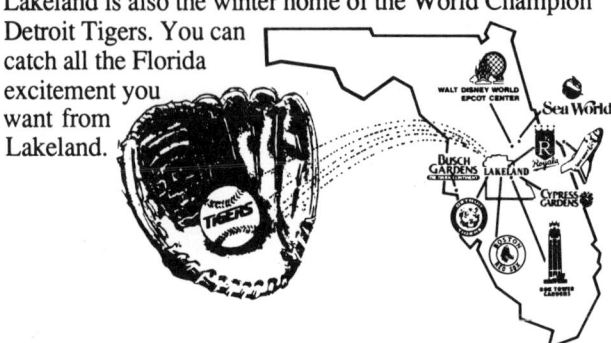

ACKNOWLEDGEMENTS

I am very grateful to those who helped me with this book but particularly to Steve Stein, Jim Evans, Chuck Klonke, Bruce McLeod, Father Frank Canfield S.J., Art Thompson, Vince Desmond, "Trivia Joe" Evans, Judy Nicodemo, Charlie Rutherford, Ernie Harwell, Dan Comer, Jim Northrup and Virginia Smith.

As always, a very special thanks to Susan "Twinkle Fingers" Rothstein for her typing and altruistic friendship.

List of Advertisers

AAA - *Leave your worries at our door step*   70

AAA of Troy - John Duffy - *It pays to call John, Ron and John*   100

Matt Brady's Tavern - *You supply the conversation*   170

Dakota Inn Rathskeller - *You can sing all night*   48

Days Inn - Roseville   194

Days Inn - Downtown - *5 minutes from Tiger Stadium*   32

Designated Hatter, Ltd. - *Everything you ever wanted in souvenirs*   12

A.J. Desmond & Sons - *Utmost in service without extra expense*   116

Detroit Edge Tool Company - *A super place to do business*   152

Detroit Red Wings - *Authentic Red Wings Sports Wear & souvenirs*   158

Al Dittrich Olds-GMC - *New location but the same great service*   Facing Back Cover

Domino's Lodge - *Your place up North*   Inside Back Cover

Dunleavy'z Riverplace - *Friends for nearly 60 years*   26

Dunleavy's Pub & Grub - *Jack and Marty will serve you well*   202

Joe Dwyer Imports - *A great organization*   96

First Edition Lounge - *Where good friends gather*   182

Frank Hall - *Serving contractors and builders since 1939*   108

Frankenmuth Bavarian Inn - *A touch of Bavaria in Michigan*   214

Ginopolis' - *Their meals are delicious*   198

Tom Holzer Ford - *There's a Ford in your future*   88

Honeybaked Hams - *So good it will 'haunt' you 'til its gone*   66

John Laffrey's Steaks on the Hearth - *Choice steaks, chops and catch of the day*   74

Lakeland - *Wonderful, wonderful Lakeland*   314

Gerald H. Lane Schaldenbrand Jewelers, Inc. - *A treasured name in jewelery*   144

Larco's - *A great name in dining*   18

Lebowski & Brodsky, P.C. - *They'll do your taxes right*   92

Lindell AC Lounge - *Jimmy and Johnny and many celebrities*   Inside Front Cover

McVee's Pub & Grub - *Where all good people get together*   186

Mexican Industries in Michigan - *Bill & Hank are still swinging*   190

National Bank of Royal Oak - *Personal Service & 24 Hour silent teller*   148

The Old Ball Park - *Ty Cobb would have loved it*   22

Pass Sports - *Jimmy and Larry bring you all the excitement*   230

Saffron Billiard - *Everything for your game room*   140

Santa Anita - *Win a bundle here*   128

Dr. H.S. Saperstein - *He'll take good care of your feet*   120

Sheraton Oaks Hotel - *Sheraton's got it all*   54

Sibley's Shoes - *There aren't better shoes at any price*   218

Sportland USA - *Pop fly from the ball park*   222

Sports Fantasties, Inc. - *For kids from 8 to 80*   256

The Toledo Mud Hens - *Future stars are there*   226

Troy Stamp & Coin, Inc. - *Complete line of supplies*   38

WJR Radio - *Voice of the Great Lakes*   210

About the Author

Fred T. Smith, a native Detroiter and a graduate of Catholic Central High School, has been a fixture around Tiger baseball since the 1920s. Smith is the author of seven previous baseball books: ***Tiger Trivia*** (with Ernie Harwell); ***Son of Tiger Trivia*** (with Ernie Harwell); ***Brooks Robinson's Quiz*** (with Brooks Robinson); ***The 995 Tigers; 50 Years With the Tigers; Tiger Facts;*** and ***Tiger Tales and Trivia.*** Smith and his wife Virginia live in Lathrop Village, Michigan.